Computational Intelligence in Economics and Finance

Shu-Heng Chen · Paul P. Wang · Tzu-Wen Kuo (Eds.)

Computational Intelligence in Economics and Finance

Volume II

With 64 Figures and 35 Tables

Springer

Editors

Shu-Heng Chen
AI-ECON Research Center
Department of Economics
National Chengchi University
Taipei, Taiwan 11623, R.O.C.
chchen@nccu.edu.tw

Paul P. Wang
Electrical & Computer Engineering
Box 90291, PSE
Duke University
Durham, NC 27708
USA
ppw@ee.duke.edu

Tzu-Wen Kuo
Department of Finance and Banking
Aletheia University
Tamsui, Taipei, Taiwan 25103, R.O.C.
kuo@aiecon.org

ISBN 978-3-642-09193-3   e-ISBN 978-3-540-72821-4
ACM Computing Classification (1998): I.2.1, G.3, J.1

Springer is a part of Springer Science+Business Media

springer.com

© Springer-Verlag Berlin Heidelberg 2010

Cover design: KünkelLopka Werbeagentur, Heidelberg

Printed on acid-free paper   45/3180/YL - 5 4 3 2 1 0

Preface

It was mostly during the last twenty five years of the twentieth century when the business and economics scientific world witnessed the emergence of new computational techniques useful in decision-making. Swiftly advancing computer hardware and software technologies nourished their evolution. It was only during the last decade of the century when disciplines such as *Computational Economics*, *Computational Finance*, and *Computational Statistics* gained attention and earned their place in the scientific arena. These disciplines utilize humanly designed computer techniques such as neural networks, genetic algorithms, genetic programming, evolutionary programming, artificial life, classifier systems, agent based modeling, fuzzy logic, wavelets, molecular computing, and other areas of artificial intelligence to solve complex problems. These techniques utilize optimization and computation algorithms impossible to implement without the existence of computers. The techniques magnificently combine machine- computational capabilities, quantitative methods, and human skills and knowledge to form an emerging new science of *computational intelligence*.

Computational intelligence tackles solving business and economic problems utilizing thoughts that go far beyond traditional statistical and engineering methods that dominated scientific contributions for almost an entire century and continue to dominate early in the twenty-first century. Traditional methods mandate that solutions to problems be based on theoretically defendable foundations. Theoretically founded solutions are governed by impregnable mathematical proofs that are for the most possible only with sets of underlying assumptions and Newtonian mathematics, most of which are linear and frequently unrealistic.

Computational intelligence relies on an exosomatic computational system. An exosomatic computational system is a computerized scheme that operates as an extension to the human mind. It has capabilities that emulate human thinking, biological systems, or other natural systems and conducts complex calculations at a speed that is millions of times faster than that of the human brain. Such capabilities naturally promote *computational intelligence* as the forefront instrument advancing with decision-making.

Chaos theory in the early 1980s brought to our attention limitations of traditional methods when deterministic nonlinear systems were shown to have dynamics that appear random to the untrained eye. The findings rendered linear processes as a unique case in a huge spectrum of possible deterministic systems. Analyzing nonlinear phenomena quickly became particularly important for those of us who have to forecast real world data. One immediately realizes that the underlying data generating process of any observed phenomenon is unknown and that the possibilities are infinite. The oversimplifying assumptions underlying linear models that we build quickly render such models as obsolete. Data generating processes with infinite possibilities may belong to one (or a combination) of five broadly defined groups: linear deterministic, nonlinear deterministic, linear-stochastic, nonlinear-stochastic, or random. Simple linear or linear-stochastic systems are rare in the real world while nonlinear, nonlinear-stochastic, and random systems are ubiquitous.

The existence of infinite possibilities of underlying data generating processes generates much doubt about the ability of the human brain to successfully approximate complex systems using traditional methods. It is only natural then to conclude that those techniques available and being developed under the umbrella of *computational intelligence* must ultimately produce more successful and more reliable systems than those offered by traditional methods. The emerging breed of *computational intelligence* systems may help us understand business and economic dynamics and more importantly help improve our ability in predicting outcomes and optimize decision-making.

Introducing advances in *computational intelligence* thought to practitioners as well as academicians is an important remarkable responsibility. The introduction of such thought in a coherent and consistent manner helps develop new contributions in the field and documents thought evolution chronologically. Those who decide to undertake such responsibility have implicitly accepted to make critical decisions to ascertain that significant research contributions reach their audiences and users in a timely manner and that information included in the presented work is useful, accurate, and have the potential role of helping advance with the science.

This volume is part of a notable and may be considered by many as a world-leading effort to disseminate *computational intelligence* thought. The editors have generously put together this volume to contain a collection of selected papers from a larger group presented during their organized **International Workshop on Computational Intelligence in Economics and Finance** of 2005 (CIEF2005) held as part of the 8th **Joint Conference on Information Sciences** (JCIS2005) V July 21-26, in Salt Lake City, Utah, US. The workshop had plenty of presentations by young minds of scientists embracing the new way of thinking who are eager to link themselves with the future of computational quantitative thought that is destined to dominate the worlds leading paradigm in scientifically reaching optimum decisions. This volume is not the first and hopefully not the last they produce.

Leading among those who generously opted to take such vital notable responsibility are Professor Paul Wang and Professor She-Heng Chen, two of the editors of this volume. They are also managing editors of a relatively new journal New Mathematics and Natural Computation. One of three areas the journal covers is *compu-*

tational intelligence in economics and finance. It is no surprise then that the title of this volume is **Computational Intelligence in Economics and Finance, Vol. 2**. Together, this volume and the journal manifest the role the editors have established as world leaders in the dissemination of *computational intelligence* thought.

Compiling advancements in *computational intelligence* thought is a sensitive matter that demands careful selection of contributions. When compiling this work, the editors paid special attention to addressing the main issue of market efficiency. Investigating the validity of the efficient market hypothesis is a major concerned the finance research community continuously investigates. The editors selection of papers to include in this volume also successfully managed to choose a large number of research efforts that utilizes *computational intelligence* techniques when investigating market efficiency and predicting financial market conditions. Because nonlinear systems characteristically defining the real dynamics of financial markets, use of *computational intelligence* techniques becomes imperative and appropriate.

To maintain an established link as well as consistency and continuation of thoughts, most papers included here comparatively analyze the implementation of traditional methods and implementation of *computational intelligence* techniques. Such comparative analysis is not to establish the superiority of one over the other. It is rather because today's environment for economic and financial decision making is fundamentally different from that of yesterday. Our world is getting more complex and our scientific solutions in decision making problems must advance to accommodate increased complexities and accommodate technological advancements.

This book provides only a sample of papers on *computational intelligence*. The papers present novel thoughts presented in 2005 by thirty scientists from thirteen different countries located in four different continents. This makes the current volume a collection of international research on *computational intelligence*. Techniques used in the papers include fuzzy logic, neural networks, nonlinear principal components analysis, k-mean clustering, instant-based techniques, genetic programming, and hybrid agent-based modeling. This book is therefore useful reading for young scholars learning about *computational intelligence* as well as active researchers and practitioners eager to learn about recent advancements in *computational intelligence*.

Mak Kaboudan, professor of statistics

University of Redlands   May 17, 2007

Contents

List of Contributors

Adenike Y. Bamgbade
Department of Computer Science
University of Manitoba, MB, Canada
adenike@cs.umanitoba.ca

Cesar A. Briano
Informatics, School of Economics
University of Buenos Aires
Cordoba 2122, Buenos Aires, 1120
Argentina
cbriano@econ.uba.ar

Jiah-Shing Chen
Department of Information Management
National Central University
Chungli 320, Taiwan
jschen@mgt.ncu.edu.tw

Jie Chen
CSIRO Mathematical and Information
Sciences, GPO Box 664
Canberra ACT 2601, Australia
Jie.Chen@csiro.au

Shu-Heng Chen
AI-ECON Research Center
Department of Economics
National Chengchi University
Taipei, Taiwan 11623
chchen@nccu.edu.tw

Ernesto Chinkes
Informatics, School of Economics
University of Buenos Aires
Cordoba 2122, Buenos Aires, 1120
Argentina
pchinkes@econ.uba.ar

Raquel Florez-Lopez
Department of Economics and Business
Administration, University of Leon
Campus de Vegazana s/n, Leon, Spain
raquel.florez@unileon.es

Hongxing He
CSIRO Mathematical and Information
Sciences, GPO Box 664
Canberra ACT 2601, Australia
Hongxing.He@csiro.au

Kiyoaki Iimura
Tokyo Metropolitan University
6-6, Asahigaoka, Hino
Tokyo 191-0065, Japan
kiimura@cc.tmit.ac.jp

Huidong Jin
CSIRO Mathematical and Information
Sciences, GPO Box 664
Canberra ACT 2601, Australia
Warren.Jin@csiro.au

Tzu-Wen Kuo
Department of Finance and Banking
Aletheia University
Tamsui, Taipei, Taiwan 25103
kuo@aiecon.org

David B. LeRoux
Open Data Group
Suite 90, 400 Lathrop Ave
River Forest, IL 60305, USA
lerouxdave@gmail.com

Benjamin Penyang Liao
Department of Information Management
Overseas Chinese Institute of Technology, Taichung 407, Taiwan
lpy@ocit.edu.tw

Shi Lihua
Smart Material and Structure Institute
Nanjing University of Aeronautics and
Astronautics, China
shilh@jlonline.com

Ana Marostica
Doctorate Department
School of Economics
University of Buenos Aires
Cordoba 2122, Buenos Aires, 1120
Argentina
mmarost@econ.uba.ar

Raul Yukihiro Matsushita
University of Brasília Department of
Statistics
University of Brasília - UnB
raulmta@unb.br

Aiporê Rodrigues de Moraes
University of Brasília Department of
Statistics
University of Brasília - UnB
aipore@fubra.unb.br

Marco Muselli
Istituto di Elettronica e di
Ingegneria dell'Informazione e delle
Telecomunicazioni
CNR, Genova, Italy
marco.muselli@ieiit.cnr.it

Nicolas Navet
LORIA-INRIA, Campus-Scientifique
BP239, F-54506 Vandoeuvre, France
nnavet@loria.fr

Martin Odening
Humboldt-Universitat zu Berlin
Faculty of Agriculture and Horticulture
Department of Agricultural Economics
and Social Sciences
D-10099 Berlin, Germany
m.odening@agrar.hu-berlin.de

Yukiko Orito
Ashikaga Institute of Technology
268-1, Ohmae-cho, Ashikaga
Tochigi 326-8558, Japan
orito@ashitech.ac.jp

Claudio M. Rocco S
Universidad Central Venezuela
Facultad de Ingeniería
Caracas, Venezuela
crocco@reacciun.ve

Tamer Shahwan
Humboldt-Universitat zu Berlin
School of Business and Economics
Institute of Banking
Stock Exchanges and Insurance
D-10178 Berlin, Germany
Faculty of Agriculture and Horticulture
Department of Agricultural Economics
and Social Sciences
D-10099 Berlin, Germany
shahwan74@hotmail.com

Arnold F. Shapiro
Smeal College of Business
Penn State University
University Park, PA 16802, USA
afs1@psu.edu

Manabu Takeda
Tokyo Metropolitan University
6-6, Asahigaoka, Hino
Tokyo 191-0065, Japan
u05851413@cc.tmit.ac.jp

Ruppa K. Thulasiram
Department of Computer Science
University of Manitoba, MB, Canada
tulsi@cs.umanitoba.ca

Paul Wang
Department of Electrical and
Computer Engineering
P.O. 90291, Duke University
Durham, NC 27708-0291, USA
ppw@ee.duke.edu

Li Weigang
Department of Computer Science
University of Brasília - UnB C.P. 4466
CEP:70919-970, Brasília - DF, Brazil
weigang@cic.unb.br

Genji Yamazaki
Tokyo Metropolitan University
6-6, Asahigaoka, Hino
Tokyo 191-0065, Japan

Omar Zambrano
Inter-American Development Bank
Washington D.C., USA
Omar_Zambrano@ksg05.harvard.edu

Computational Intelligence in Economics and Finance: Shifting the Research Frontier

Shu-Heng Chen[1], Paul P. Wang[2], and Tzu-Wen Kuo[3]

[1] AI-ECON Research Center, Department of Economics, National Chengchi University, Taipei, Taiwan 11623, chchen@nccu.edu.tw
[2] Department of Electrical and Computer Engineering, Duke University, Durham, NC 27708, USA, ppw@ee.duke.edu
[3] Department of Finance and Banking, Aletheia University, Tamsui, Taipei, Taiwan 25103, kuo@aiecon.org

Summary. This chapter provides an overview of the book.

1 About the CIEF Series

This volume is the continuation of the volume with the same title which was published by Springer in 2003 ([18]), and is part of the same series of post-conference publications of the **International Workshop on Computational Intelligence in Economics and Finance** (**CIEF**, hereafter). The previous volume is mainly a collection of selected papers presented in CIEF 2002 (the 2nd CIEF), whereas this one is a collection of selected papers in CIEF 2005 (the 4th CIEF).

The idea of the CIEF was first initiated by Paul P. Wang, one of the editors of this volume. Reference [11] (p. 123) details the historical origin of the CIEF. Intellectually, the CIEF carries on the legacy of Herbert Simon, who broke down the conventional distinctions among economics, computer science and cognitive psychology, and initiated the interdisciplinary research field that we refer to as artificial-intelligence economics. The later development of CIEF, including not only its depth of coverage but also its breadth of coverage, are documented in [12].

The fourth CIEF was held as a part of the 8th Joint Conference on Information Sciences (JCIS 2005) between July 21-26, 2005 in Salt Lake City, Utah. Among the 15 tracks of JCIS 2005, CIEF 2005 is by far the largest one. A total of 18 sessions with 81 presentations were organized. Authors of the 81 papers were encouraged to submit their extended versions of the conference papers to the post conference publications. Twenty-seven submissions were received, and each of them was sent to at least two referees. In the end, only nine out of 27 submissions plus three additional invited papers were accepted. These constitute the contents of this volume.[1]

---

[1] Seven other papers were published in a special issue of *Journal of New Mathematics and Natural Computation*, Vol. 2, No. 3.

2 About this Volume

2.1 Structure of the Volume

To closely connect this volume with the previous one, we structure the book in a similar fashion compared with that of the previous one, i.e., the chapters are grouped and ordered by means of the computational intelligence tools involved. As the organization chart indicated in Fig. 1.1 ([18], p.4), the structure of the book is presented in the order of fuzzy logic, neural networks (including self-organized maps and support vector machines) and evolutionary computation. The same order is applied here. In other words, this volume is also structured by using the same organization chart in Vol. 1.

However, as a continued volume, this volume does not contain a comprehensive overview of the entire economic and financial applications of CI as was the case in the first volume. A number of techniques which can be seen in Vol. 1 are not presented here, including rough sets, wavelets, swarm intelligence (ant algorithms), and agent-based modeling. Nonetheless, there are also "new faces" appearing in this volume, including recursive neural networks, self-associative neural networks, K-means and instance-based learning.

Given the large degree of similarity to Vol. 1, there is no need for a voluminous introductory chapter as we saw in Vol. 1 ([18], Chap. 1). However, for the additional techniques which do not appear in the first volume, a brief introduction is provided. The brief introduction is not meant to be a tutorial, but mainly to show how this specific tool is related to some other tools, which we see in Vol. 1. For example, it shows how the recurrent neural network and the self-associative neural network are related to the feedforward neural network, how K-means is related to self-organizing maps and K-nearest neighbors, and how instance-based learning is related to K-nearest neighbors. In this way, we make an effort to make everything as tight as possible and leave the audience with a comprehensive understanding of the materials.

2.2 Themes

As the second volume, this volume shares a great many similarities, not only in techniques but also in terms of themes, with the previous volume.

Efficient Markets Hypothesis

A large part of this volume can be read as a continuous effort to question and to challenge the efficient markets hypothesis or the random walk hypothesis. Are stock prices predictable? Are trading strategies profitable? While these issues are old, they never die and they are still the central themes of these chapters. Even though financial econometricians nowadays also frequently address these issues, what distinguishes financial econometricians from CI researchers is the way in which they prove the answer.

Financial econometricians test the hypotheses based on *data with probabilistic models*, whereas CI researchers test the hypotheses based on *data with algorithms*. By assuming a probabilistic universe, econometricians like to question the data-generating mechanism and ask whether the data observed are indeed randomly generated. For CI researchers, we treat computational intelligence as an unbounded set of algorithms. These algorithms are intelligent in the sense that each of them articulates well *what the patterns are*, and, by applying these algorithms to data, we inquire of the existence of such kinds of patterns. New algorithms propose new ways of thinking about patterns and of constructing patterns, and hence new tests for the hypotheses. Chapters 3, 7, 8, 9, 11 and 12 are studies of this kind.

Nonlinearity

An issue related to the efficient markets hypothesis is nonlinearity. In fact, one fundamental question regarding the efficient markets hypothesis is whether financial time series are linear or nonlinear. Nonlinearity motivates the use of CI tools in many chapters of this volume. It, in effect, provides the connection between conventional statistics and CI tools. This point has been well illustrated by many chapters. Examples include the artificial neural network, particularly the recurrent neural network, as an extension of linear time series modeling (Chap. 3), the self-associative neural network as an extension of linear principal components analysis (Chap. 4), and the support vector machine as an extension of the linear classification model (Chap. 5). In each of these cases, the central issue is whether one is able to capture the neglected nonlinearity of the linear models from the proposed nonlinear counterparts.

The artificial neural networks and genetic programming are non-parametric and hence are quite flexible to different functional forms. This flexibility can be quite crucial because, as pointed out by [7], "...unlike the theory that is available in many natural sciences, economic theory is not specific about the nonlinear functional forms. Thus economists rarely have theoretic reasons for expecting to find one form of nonlinearity rather than another." (*Ibid*, p.475.)

Statistics and Computational Intelligence

Despite the great flexibility, a repeatedly asked question concerns the superiority of the non-linear models as opposed to linear models in forecasting (Chap. 3) or classification (Chap. 5). The performance of CI tools is therefore frequently compared with conventional statistical models. Chapters 3 and 5 provide two good illustrations.

The remainder of this introductory chapter provides a quick grasp of the 12 chapters included in this volume. As mentioned above, the 12 chapters will be briefly introduced in an order beginning with fuzzy logic (Sect. 3), artificial neural networks (Sect. 4), and then evolutionary computation (Sect. 5).

3 Fuzzy Logic

Fuzzy logic interests us because it enhances our flexibility in modeling the human's inner world. Quite often, we attempt to model human behavior by "fitting" their actual decisions to the observed external environment which is frequently characterized by a large number of features. In this way, a formal decision rule can be explicitly generated.[2] However, humans are not always confident about what they are doing or choosing. They often make decisions based on fears or skepticism. Without knowing this limitation, those decisions rules extracted from the observed data can be misleading.

While neural scientists, over the last decade, have been trying hard to make us know more about this process within the "box", it still largely remains "black" to us. Therefore, a sensible model of decision rules must, to some extent, respond to this "softness." Fuzzy numbers, fuzzy coefficients (in the fuzzy regression models) or fuzzy decision rules may be read as a way of coping with this reality, and there may be a neural foundation for fuzzy logic, which is yet to be established. Alternatively, we may ask: *is the brain fuzzy,* and *in what sense*? Or, we may say: fuzziness is everywhere, because it is in our brain.

For example, in the 1970s, there were some discussions between psycho-linguists and fuzzy theorists on the use of the adverb *very*. For an illustration, two different interpretations of *very large* arise. In one case, the fuzzy set *very large* is included in the fuzzy set *large*. In the other case, it is not; *large* and *very large* denote two different categories.[3] Perhaps by using the scanning technology of neural sciences, we can explore the relationship between *very large* and *large*, and hence provide a neural-scientific foundation for the membership function and its associated mathematical operation.

In Chap. 2, **An Overview of Insurance Use of Fuzzy Logic**, Arnold F. Shapiro provides a comprehensive review of the use of fuzzy logic in insurance, or the field known as *fuzzy insurance*. The unique writing style of the author makes this chapter suitable for readers with various levels of intellectual curiosity.

First, it obviously serves the readers who want to know the relevance of fuzzy logic to insurance. This chapter presents a great number of examples, ranging from risk classification, underwriting, projected liabilities, rate making and pricing, asset allocation and investments. Of course, due to the large number of examples, the authors are unable to give enough discussion to each single case. Therefore, for general audiences, they may experience a little difficulty quickly catching the hard lesson to be learned from each example. Nevertheless, a small taste of each dish in such a rich buffet does, at least, help us get the message that fuzzy logic is indispensable for insurance enterprises.

Secondly, in addition to application *per se*, the author has carefully further categorized the applications into groups from the perspectives of fuzzy logic. Starting

---

[2] This is how software agents are connected to human agents. For more details, see [12].

[3] When a listener hears that x *is large*, he assumes that x *is not* very large, because in the latter case the speaker would have used the more informative utterance x *is very large*. See [29] and [22].

from fuzzy sets and fuzzy numbers, the author concisely goes through fuzzy arithmetic, fuzzy inference systems, fuzzy clustering, fuzzy programming, and fuzzy regression. This, therefore, enables us to ask a more fundamental question: *Why fuzzy? What is the nature and the significance of fuzzy logic?* Certainly, we are not the first to ask and address the question, but the question is so deep and so important that it is worth our asking it and addressing the issue over and over again. This chapter places us in a specific daily life situation, i.e., a risky life, enabling us to revisit the issue. It drives us to think of the value of fuzzy logic while acting as if we are making insurance decisions in dealing with various risky real-life events, such as earthquake damage, health forecasts, etc.

4 Artificial Neural Networks

Among all the economic and financial applications, the artificial neural network (ANN) is probably the most frequently used tool. It has been shown in a great number of studies that artificial neural networks, as representative of a more general class of non-linear models, can outperform many linear models and can sometimes also outperform some other non-linear models. [4]

4.1 Recurrent Neural Networks

Three classes of artificial neural networks have been most frequently used in economics and finance. These are *multilayer perceptron neural networks, radial basis neural networks*, and *recurrent neural networks*. The first two classes were introduced in Vol. 1,[5] whereas the last one is introduced in this volume.

In Vol. 1, we discussed the relationship between time series models and artificial neural networks. Information transmission in the usual multilayer perceptron neural network is *feedforward* in the sense that information is transmitted *forward* from the input layer to the output layer, via all hidden layers in between, as shown in Fig. 1. The reverse direction between any two layers is not allowed.

This specific architecture makes the multilayer perceptron neural network unable to deal with the moving-average series, $MA(q)$, effectively. To see this, consider an $MA(1)$ series as follows.

$$x_t = \epsilon_t - \theta_1 \epsilon_{t-1}. \tag{1}$$

It is well-known that if $| \theta_1 | < 1$, then the above $MA(1)$ series can also be written as an $AR(\infty)$ series.

$$x_t = -\sum_{i=1}^{\infty} \theta^i x_{t-i} + \epsilon_t \tag{2}$$

---

[4] This is not a good place to provide a long list, but interested readers can find some examples from [4], [24], [28], [43], [44], [45], and [47].
[5] See [18], pp. 14–18.

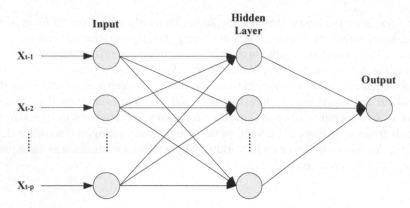

Fig. 1. The multilayer perceptron neural network of a nonlinear AR process

In using the multilayer perceptron neural network to represent (2), one needs to have an input layer with an infinite number of neurons (*infinite memory of the past*), namely, $x_{t-1}, x_{t-2}, ...$, which in practice is impossible. Although, from the viewpoint of approximation, an exact representation is not required and a compromise with a finite number of neurons (*finite memory*) is acceptable, in general quite a few inputs are still required, which inevitably increases the complexity of the network, leads to an unnecessary large number of parameters, and hence slows down the estimation and training process ([38]).

This explains why the multilayer perceptron neural net can only be regarded as the nonlinear extension of autoregressive (AR) time series models

$$x_t = f(x_{t-1}, ..., x_{t-p}) + \epsilon_t, \tag{3}$$

but not the nonlinear extension of the autoregressive moving-average (ARMA) models

$$\begin{aligned} x_t &= f(x_{t-1}, ..., x_{t-p}, \epsilon_{t-1}, ...\epsilon_{t-q}) + \epsilon_t \\ &= f(x_{t-1}, ..., x_{t-p}, x_{t-p-1}, ...) + \epsilon_t \end{aligned} \tag{4}$$

The finite memory problem of the multilayer perceptron neural net is well noticed by ANN researchers. In his celebrated article ([23]), Jeffrey Elman stated

> ...the question of how to represent time in connection models is very important. One approach is to represent time *implicitly* by its effects on processing rather than *explicitly* (as in a spatial representation). (*Ibid*, p.179. Italics added.)

The multilayer perceptron neural net tries to model time by giving it a spatial representation, i.e., an explicit representation. What Elman suggests is to let time have an effect on the network response rather than represent time by an additional input dimension. Using an idea initiated by Michael Jordan ([31]), Elman proposes an internal representation of memory by allowing the hidden unit patterns being to be fed back to themselves. In this way, the network becomes *recurrent*.

The difference between the multilayer perceptron neural network (the feedforward neural network) and the recurrent neural network can be shown as follows. In terms of a multilayer perceptron neural network, (3) can be represented as

$$x_t = h_2(w_0 + \sum_{j=1}^{l} w_j h_1(w_{0j} + \sum_{i=1}^{p} w_{ij} x_{t-i})) + \epsilon_t. \tag{5}$$

Equation (5) is a three-layer neural network (Fig. 1). The input layer has p inputs: $x_{t-1}, ..., x_{t-p}$. The hidden layer has l hidden nodes, and there is a single output for the output layer $\hat{x}_t$. Layers are fully connected by *weights*: w_{ij} is the weight assigned to the ith input for the jth node in the hidden layer, whereas w_j is the weight assigned to the jth node (in the hidden layer) for the output. w_0 and w_{0j} are constants, also called *biases*. h_1 and h_2 are *transfer functions*.

In terms of a recurrent neural network, (4) can then be represented as

$$x_t = h_2(w_0 + \sum_{j=1}^{l} w_j h_1(w_{0j} + \sum_{i=1}^{p} w_{ij} x_{t-i} + \sum_{m=1}^{l} \varpi_{mj} z_{m,t-1})) + \epsilon_t, \tag{6}$$

where

$$z_{m,t} = w_{0m} + \sum_{i=1}^{p} w_{im} x_{t-i} + \sum_{k=1}^{l} \varpi_{kj} z_{k,t-1}, \quad m = 1, ..., l. \tag{7}$$

In the recurrent neural network, positive feedback is used to construct memory in the network as shown in Fig. 2. Special units called *context units* save previous output values of hidden layer neurons (Eq. 7). Context unit values are then fed back fully connected to hidden layer neurons and serve as additional inputs in the network (Eq. 6).

Compared to the multilayer perceptron neural network and the radial basis function neural network, the recurrent neural network is much less explored in the economic and financial domain.[6] This is, indeed, a little surprising, considering the great exposure of its linear counterpart ARMA to economists.

Chapter 3, **Forecasting Agricultural Commodity Prices using Hybrid Neural Networks**, authored by Tamer Shahwan and Martin Odening, uses recurrent neural networks to forecast the prices of hogs and canolas. The performances of recurrent neural networks are compared with those of ARIMA models, which are frequently used as the benchmark for time series prediction competitions. The authors consider two kinds of recurrent neural networks: the one which works alone, and the one which is hybridized with the ARIMA model. Two empirical issues are, therefore, addressed in this chapter: first, whether the recurrent neural network can outperform the ARIMA model; second, whether the hybrid model can make a further improvement.

The idea of hybridizing the two models is very similar to the familiar two-stage least squares method. In the first stage, the ARIMA model serves as a filter to filter out the linear signal. The residuals are then used to feed the recurrent neural network in the second stage.

---

[6] Some early applications can be found in [35] and [9].

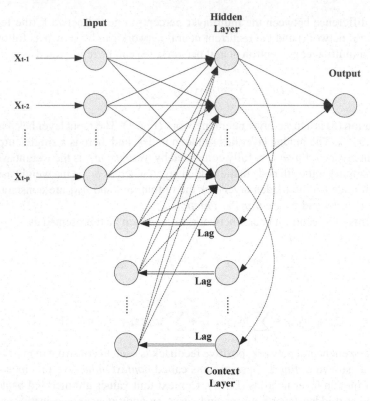

Fig. 2. The recurrent neural network of a nonlinear ARMA process

4.2 Auto-associative Neural Networks

While most economic and financial applications of the neural network consider its capability to develop non-linear forecasting models, as seen in Chap. 3 of the volume, there is one important branch using artificial neural networks to engage in dimension reduction or feature extraction. In this application, ANN can provide a nonlinear generalization of the conventional *principal components analysis* (**PCA**). The specific kind of ANN for this application is referred to as the *auto-associative neural network* (**AANN**).

The fundamental idea of principal components analysis is dimensional reduction, which is a quite general problem when we are presented with a large number of correlated attributes, and hence a large number of redundancies. It is, therefore, a natural attempt to compress or store this original large dataset into a more economical space by getting rid of these redundancies. So, on the one hand, we want to have a reduced space that is as small as possible; on the other hand, we still want to keep the original information. These two objectives are, however, in conflict when attributes with complicated relations are presented. Therefore, techniques to make the least compromise between the two become important.

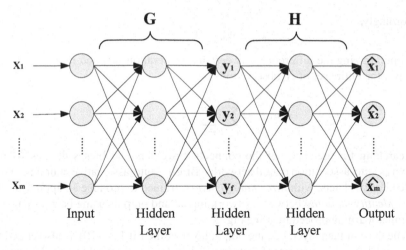

Fig. 3. The Auto-associative Neural Networks

To introduce AANN and its relationship with principal components analysis, let us consider the following two mappings,

$$\mathcal{G} : \mathbf{R}^m \to \mathbf{R}^f \tag{8}$$

and

$$\mathcal{H} : \mathbf{R}^f \to \mathbf{R}^m \tag{9}$$

where $\mathcal{G}$ and $\mathcal{H}$ are, in general, non-linear vector functions with the components indicated as $\mathcal{G} = \{G_1, G_2, ..., G_f\}$ and $\mathcal{H} = \{H_1, H_2, ..., H_m\}$. To represent these functions with multilayer perceptron neural nets, let us rewrite (5) as follows,

$$
\begin{aligned}
y_k &= G_k(x_1, ..., x_m) \\
&= h_2(w_{0k} + \sum_{j=1}^{l_1} w_{jk} h_1(w_{0j}^e + \sum_{i=1}^{m} w_{ij}^e x_i)), \quad k = 1, 2, ..., f,
\end{aligned}
\tag{10}
$$

and

$$
\begin{aligned}
\hat{x}_i &= H_i(y_1, ..., y_f) \\
&= h_4(w_{0i} + \sum_{j=1}^{l_2} w_{ji} h_3(w_{0j}^d + \sum_{k=1}^{f} w_{kj}^d y_k)), \quad i = 1, 2, ..., m.
\end{aligned}
\tag{11}
$$

All the notations used in (10) and (11) share the same interpretation as those in (5), except superscripts e and d standing for the encoding and decoding maps, respectively. By combining the two mappings together, we have a mapping from $\mathbf{X} = \{x_1, ..., x_m\}$ to its own reconstruction $\hat{\mathbf{X}} = \{\hat{x}_1, ..., \hat{x}_m\}$. Let X_n be the nth observation of X, and

$$\mathbf{X}_n = \{x_{n,1}, ..., x_{n,m}\}.$$

Accordingly,

$$\hat{\mathbf{X}}_n = \{\hat{x}_{n,1}, ..., \hat{x}_{n,m}\}.$$

Then minimizing the difference between the observation $\mathbf{X}_n$ and its reconstruction $\hat{\mathbf{X}}_n$ over the entire set of N observations or

$$\min E = \sum_{n=1}^{N} \sum_{i=1}^{m} (x_{n,i} - \hat{x}_{n,i})^2 \tag{12}$$

by searching for the space of the connection weights and biases defines what is known as auto-association neural networks. Briefly, auto-associative neural networks are feedforward nets, with *three hidden layers*, trained to produce an approximation of the *identity mapping* between network inputs and outputs using backpropagation or similar learning procedures(See Fig. 3).

The third hidden layer, i.e., the output layer of the MLPN, (10), is also called the *bottleneck layer*. If the transfer functions h_i $(i = 1, 2, 3, 4)$ are all identical mappings, and we remove all the bias terms, then (10) can be written as

$$y_k = G_k(x_1, ..., x_m)$$

$$= \sum_{j=1}^{l_1} w_{jk} \left(\sum_{i=1}^{m} w_{ij}^e x_i \right) = \sum_{j=1}^{l_1} \sum_{i=1}^{m} w_{jk} w_{ij}^e x_i,$$

$$= \sum_{i=1}^{m} \sum_{j=1}^{l_1} w_{jk} w_{ij}^e x_i, = \sum_{i=1}^{m} \beta_{i,k} x_i \quad k = 1, 2, ..., f, \tag{13}$$

where

$$\beta_{i,k} = \sum_{j=1}^{l_1} w_{jk} w_{ij}^e$$

In the matrix notations, (13) can be written as

$$\begin{bmatrix} x_{11} & x_{12} & \cdots & x_{1m} \\ x_{21} & x_{22} & \cdots & x_{2m} \\ \vdots & \vdots & \ddots & \vdots \\ x_{n1} & x_{n2} & \cdots & x_{nm} \end{bmatrix} \begin{bmatrix} \beta_{11} & \beta_{12} & \cdots & \beta_{1f} \\ \beta_{21} & \beta_{22} & \cdots & \beta_{2f} \\ \vdots & \vdots & \ddots & \vdots \\ \beta_{m1} & \beta_{m2} & \cdots & \beta_{mf} \end{bmatrix} = \begin{bmatrix} y_{11} & y_{12} & \cdots & y_{1f} \\ y_{21} & y_{22} & \cdots & y_{2f} \\ \vdots & \vdots & \ddots & \vdots \\ y_{n1} & y_{n2} & \cdots & y_{nf} \end{bmatrix}, \tag{14}$$

or simply

$$\mathbf{XB} = \mathbf{Y}. \tag{15}$$

$\mathbf{X}$, $\mathbf{B}$ and $\mathbf{Y}$ correspond to the n-by-m, m-by-f, and n-by-f matrices in (14), respectively. Likewise, (11) can be simplified as

$$\mathbf{YB}^* = \hat{\mathbf{X}}. \tag{16}$$

$\mathbf{B}^*$ is the reconstruction mapping and is an f-by-m matrix, and $\hat{\mathbf{X}}$ is the reconstruction of $\mathbf{X}$, and hence is an n-by-m matrix.

Equations (15) and (16) with the objective function (12) define the familiar *linear* principal components analysis. To see this, we can decompose $\mathbf{X}$ as follows:

$$\mathbf{X} = \mathbf{YB}^* + \mathbf{E} = \mathbf{XBB}^* + \mathbf{E} = \mathbf{XP} + \mathbf{E}, \tag{17}$$

where $\mathbf{P} = \mathbf{BB}^*$, and $\mathbf{E}$ is the reconstruction error. Then the PCA frequently presented to us takes the form of the following minimization problem.

$$\min_{\mathbf{P}} \|\mathbf{E}\| \tag{18}$$

It is known that the optimal solution of to problem (18) has the rows of $\mathbf{P}$ being the eigenvectors corresponding to the f largest eigenvalues of the covariance matrix of $\mathbf{X}$. Therefore, we have shown how the self-associative neural network can be a non-linear generalization of the familiar linear PCA and how the linear PCA can be extended to the non-linear PCA through a feedforward neural network with three hidden layers.

The concept of using a neural network with a bottleneck to concentrate information has been previously discussed in the context of *encoder/decoder* problems.[7] Reference [39] indicates some directions of the financial applications of the non-linear PCA. In this volume, Chap. 4, **Nonlinear Principal Components Analysis for the Withdrawal of the Employment Time Guarantee Fund**, by Weigang Li, Aipore Rodrigues de Moraes, Lihua Shi, and Raul Yukihiro Matsushita, applies non-linear principal components analysis to compress a dataset related to employees' withdrawals from a national pension fund in Brazil. It shows how the work on the principal components analysis can be facilitated by the use of artificial neural networks. This chapter provides a good starting point for those who want to see the contribution of artificial neural networks to components analysis. The software mentioned in the paper can be particularly helpful for researchers who want to tackle similar problems of their own.

4.3 Support Vector Machines

The support vector machine (SVM) was introduced in the previous volume ([18], pp. 18–20). Two chapters there provide illustrations on the applications of the support vector machine to classifications ([42]) and time series forecasting ([8]).[8] In this volume, Chap. 5, **Estimating Female Labor Force Participation through Statistical and Machine Learning Methods: A Comparison**, authored by Omar Zambrano, Claudio M. Rocco, and Marco Muselli, the SVM is applied to forecast the participation of the female labor force. In this application, the SVM is formally placed in a competitive environment with the conventional linear classification models, i.e., the logit and probit models. In addition, the authors also include a new classification method, referred to as the Hamming clustering, to the competition. They then address the advantages and disadvantages of each approach.

---

[7] See [34] for a brief review.

[8] Since the publication of the previous volume, the financial applications have kept on expanding, and the interested reader can find some useful references directly from the website of the SVM: http://www.svms.org

4.4 Self-Organizing Maps and K-Means

The genetic programming approach to pattern discovery, as mentioned in Sect. 5.2 below, is a symbolic approach. This approach can also be carried out in different ways by other CI tools, such as decision trees.[9] The symbolic approach makes the patterns or rules discovered explicit in a symbolical way, while, semantically, this is not necessarily so.[10]

However, not all patterns can be expressively demonstrated with symbols. There are other interesting classes of patterns, which can best be visualized as images, trajectories or charts. We see two demonstrations in the first volume. One is [14] which automatically discovers 36 charts by means of the self-organizing map (SOM). In this case, SOM functions as clustering to cluster similar trajectories into the same cluster (cell). The other is [25] which applies K-nearest neighbors (KNN) to choose similar trajectories of time series of exchange rates, and based on those forecasts the future exchange rates. In this volume, we will see the related work of the two. In this section, we introduce the one related to the self-organizing map, i.e., *K-means clustering*, and in the next section, we introduce the one related to K-nearest neighbors, i.e., *instance-based learning*.

K-Means clustering, developed by J.B. MacQueen in 1967 ([37]), is one of the widely used *non-hierarchical clustering algorithms* that groups data with similar characteristics or features together. K-means and SOMs resemble each other. They both involve minimizing some measure of dissimilarity, called the cost function, in the samples within each cluster. The difference between the K-means and the SOM lies in their associated cost function to which we now turn. Consider a series of n observations, each of which has m numeric attributes:

$$\mathbf{X}_1^m, \mathbf{X}_2^m, ..., \mathbf{X}_n^m, \quad \mathbf{X}_i^m \in \mathbf{R}^m, \quad \forall\, i = 1, 2, ..., n \qquad (19)$$

where

$$\mathbf{X}_i^m \equiv \{x_{i,1}, x_{i,2}, ..., x_{i,m}\}. \quad x_{i,l} \in \mathbf{R}, \forall\, l = 1, 2, ..., m. \qquad (20)$$

K-means clustering means to find a series of k clusters, the centroids of which are denoted, respectively, by

$$\mathbf{M}_1, \mathbf{M}_2, ..., \mathbf{M}_k, \quad \mathbf{M}_j \in \mathbf{R}^m, \quad \forall j = 1, 2, ..., k, \qquad (21)$$

such that each of the observations is assigned to one and only one of the clusters with a minimal cost, and the cost function is defined as follows:

$$C_{K-means} = \sum_{i=1}^{n} \sum_{j=1}^{k} d(\mathbf{X}_i^m, \mathbf{M}_j) \cdot \delta_{i,j}, \qquad (22)$$

---

[9] In the first volume, we had a detailed discussion on the use of decision trees in finance. See [18], Sect. 1.3.5 and Chap. 15.

[10] What usually happens is that even experts may sometimes find it difficult to make sense of the discovered patterns, and hence it is not certain whether these discovered patterns are spurious. See [19] for a through discussion of the rules discovered by genetic programming. Also see [33] for some related discussion on this issue.

where $d(\mathbf{X}_i^m, \mathbf{M}_j)$ is the standard Euclidean distance between $\mathbf{X}_i^m$ and $\mathbf{M}_j$[11], and $\delta_{i,j}$ is the delta function:

$$\delta_{i,j} = \begin{cases} 1, & if \ \mathbf{X}_i^m \in \mathbf{Cluster}_j, \\ 0, & if \ \mathbf{X}_i^m \notin \mathbf{Cluster}_j. \end{cases} \tag{23}$$

To minimize the cost function (22), one can begin by initializing a set of k cluster centroids. The positions of these centroids are then adjusted iteratively by first assigning the data samples to the nearest clusters and then recomputing the centroids. The details can be found in Chap. 7, **Trading Strategies Based on K-means Clustering and Regression Models**, written by Hongxing He, Jie Chen, Huidong Jin, and Shu-Heng Chen.

Corresponding to (22), the cost function associated with SOM can be roughly treated as follows[12]

$$C_{SOM} = \sum_{i=1}^{n} \sum_{j=1}^{k} d(\mathbf{X}_i^m, \mathbf{M}_j) \cdot h_{w(\mathbf{X}_i^m),j}, \tag{24}$$

where $h_{w(\mathbf{X}_i^m),j}$ is the neighborhood function or the neighborhood kernel, and $w_{\mathbf{X}_i^m}$, the winner function, outputs the cluster whose centroid is nearest to input $\mathbf{X}_i^m$. In practice, the neighborhood kernel is chosen to be wide at the beginning of the learning process to guarantee the global ordering of the map, and both its width and height decrease slowly during learning. For example, the Gaussian kernel whose variance monotonically decreases with iteration times t is frequently used.[13] By comparing Eq. (22) with (24), one can see in SOM the distance of each input from all of the centroids weighted by the neighborhood kernel h, instead of just the closest one being taken into account.

In this volume, Chap. 6 and Chap. 7 are devoted to SOM and KNN, respectively. Chapter 6, **An Application of Kohonen's SOFM to the Management of Benchmarking Policies** authored by Raquel Florez-Lopez, can be read as a continuation of Chap. 9 ([26]) of the first volume. In terms of the research question, it is even closely related to [27]. The core of economic theory of firms is to identify the features of the productivity, efficiency, competitiveness or survivability of firms, or more generally, to answer what makes some firms thrive and others decline. Using observations of firms, economic theory provides different approaches to the answer. Some are more theoretical and require rigid assumptions, while others do not. Data envelopment analysis ([20]) and stochastic frontier analysis ([36]) belong to the former, whereas self-organizing maps belong to the latter. However, what Florez-Lopez does in this chapter is to combine the two: DEA and SOM.

---

[11] Standard Euclidean distance assumes that the attributes are normalized and are of equal importance. However, this assumption may not hold in many application domains. In fact, one of the main problems in learning is to determine which are the important features.

[12] The rigorous mathematical treatment of the SOM algorithm is extremely difficult in general. See [32].

[13] For details, see the first volume ([18]), Chap. 8, p. 205.

Using DEA, one can distinguish those firms that are on the efficient frontier from those that are not. Nonetheless, without a visualization tool, it is hard to see how similar or different these firms are, be they efficient or inefficient. For example, it is almost impossible by using the conventional DEA to see whether efficient firms are uniformly distributed on the efficient frontier, or whether they are grouped into a few clusters. Hence, it is hard to answer how many viable strategies are available in the market. Using SOM, not only can one see the feature distribution of the efficient firms, but one can also notice how distant, and in what direction, those inefficient firms are from them.

Despite its greater simplicity, the economic and financial applications of K-means are surprisingly much less available than those of SOM and KNN. K-means have occasionally been applied to classify hedge funds ([21]), listed companies ([41]), and houses ([30]), and in this volume, He et al., in Chap. 7, apply them to the classification of trajectories of financial time series. To see this, we rewrite (19) and (20) to fit the notations used in the context of time series:

$$\mathbf{X}_1^m, \mathbf{X}_2^m, ..., \mathbf{X}_T^m, \quad \mathbf{X}_t^m \in \mathbf{R}^m, \quad \forall \, t = 1, 2, ..., T \tag{25}$$

$$\mathbf{X}_t^m \equiv \{x_t, x_{t-1}, ..., x_{t-m}\}, \quad x_{t-l} \in \mathbf{R}, \forall \, l = 0, 1, ..., m - 1. \tag{26}$$

$\mathbf{X}_t^m$ is a windowed series with an immediate past of m observations, also called the m-history. Equation (25), therefore, represents a sequence of T m-histories which are derived from the original time series, $\{x_t\}_{t=-m+1}^T$, by moving the m-long window consecutively, each with one step. Accordingly, the end-product of applying K-means or SOMs to these windowed series is a number of centroids $\mathbf{M}_j$, which represents a specific shape of an m-long trajectory, also known as charts for technical analysts.[14]

Then the essential question pursued by Chap. 7, as a continuation of Chap. 8 ([14]) in the first volume, is whether we can meaningfully cluster the windowed financial time series $\mathbf{X}_t^m$ by the k associated geometrical trajectories, $\mathbf{M}_1, \mathbf{M}_2, ..., \mathbf{M}_k$. The clustering work can be meaningful if it can help us predict the future. In other words, conditional on a specific trajectory, we can predict the future better than without being provided this information, e.g.,

$$Prob(|\, \xi_{t+1} \,|>|\, \epsilon_{t+1} \,|) > 0.5$$

where

$$\xi_{t+1} = x_{t+1} - E(x_{t+1}), \tag{27}$$

and

$$\epsilon_{t+1} = x_{t+1} - E(x_{t+1}|\mathbf{X}_t^m \in \mathbf{Cluster_j}), \quad t > T. \tag{28}$$

The conditional expectations above are made with the information of the trajectory (the cluster). Reference [14], in the first volume, is the first one to give this idea a test. They used self-organizing maps to first cluster the windowed time series of the stock index into different clusters, by using the historical data to learn whether these clusters reveal any information, in particular, the future trend of the price. In Chap. 7, the same attempt is carried out again, but now by using K-means clustering.

---

[14] For example, see the charts presented in [14], pp. 206-207.

4.5 K Nearest Neighbors and Instance-Based Learning

In the first volume, we introduce the financial applications of K-nearest neighbors (KNN) [25]. KNN can be regarded as a special case of a broader class of algorithms, known as *instance-based learning* (IBL). To see this, let us use the notations introduced in Sect. 4.4, and use the time series prediction problem as an illustration.

Consider (28). We have been given information regarding a time series up to time t, and we wish to forecast the next by using the current m-history, $\mathbf{X}_t^m$. In SOM or KNN, we will first decide to which cluster $\mathbf{X}_t^m$ belongs by checking $d(\mathbf{X}_t^m, \mathbf{M}_j)$ for all j ($j = 1, 2, ..., k$), and use the forecast model associated with that cluster to forecast x_{t+1}. In other words, forecasting models are tailored to each cluster, say, $\hat{f}_j$ ($j = 1, 2, ..., k$).[15] Then

$$\hat{x}_{t+1} = \hat{f}_{j^*}(\mathbf{X}_t^m), \ \ if \ \ j^* = \arg\min_j d(\mathbf{X}_t^m, \mathbf{M}_j), \ \ j = 1, 2, ..., k. \quad (29)$$

KNN, however, does not have such established clusters $\mathbf{M}_j$. Instead, it forms a cluster based on each $\mathbf{X}_t^m$, $\mathcal{N}(\mathbf{X}_t^m)$, as follows:

$$\mathcal{N}(\mathbf{X}_t^m) = \{s \mid Rank(d(\mathbf{X}_t^m, \mathbf{X}_s^m)) \leq k, \forall s < t\}, \quad (30)$$

In other words, $\mathbf{X}_t^m$ itself serves as the centroid of a cluster, called the *neighborhood* of $\mathbf{X}_t^m$, $\mathcal{N}(\mathbf{X}_t^m)$. It then invites its k *nearest neighbors* to be the members of $\mathcal{N}(\mathbf{X}_t^m)$ by ranking the distance $d(\mathbf{X}_t^m, \mathbf{X}_s^m)$ over the entire community

$$\{\mathbf{X}_s^m \mid s < t\} \quad (31)$$

from the closest to the farthest. Then, by assuming a functional relation, f, between x_{s+1} and $\mathbf{X}_s^m$ and using only the observations associated with $\mathcal{N}(\mathbf{X}_t^m)$ to estimate this function f_t,[16] one can construct the tailor-made forecast for each x_t,

$$\hat{x}_{t+1} = \hat{f}_t(\mathbf{X}_t^m). \quad (32)$$

In practice, the function f used in (32) can be very simple, either taking the *unconditional mean* or the *conditional mean*. In the case of the latter, the mean is usually assumed to be linear. In the case of the unconditional mean, one can simply use the simple average in the forecast,

$$\hat{x}_{t+1} = \frac{\sum_{s \in \mathcal{N}(\mathbf{X}_t^m)} x_{s+1}}{k}, \quad (33)$$

---

[15] The notation $\hat{f}$ is used, instead of f, to reserve f for the true relation, if it exists, and in that case, $\hat{f}$ is the estimation of f. In addition, there are variations when constructing (29). See [14] and Chap. 15 in this volume.

[16] Even though the functional form is the same, the coefficients can vary depending on $\mathbf{X}_t^m$ and its resultant $\mathcal{N}(\mathbf{X}_t^m)$. So, we add a subscript t as f_t to make this time-variant property clear.

but one can also take the weighted average based on the distance of each member. The same idea can be applied to deal with the linear conditional mean (linear regression model): we can either take the ordinal least squares or the weighted least squares.[17]

From the above description, we can find that KNN is different from K-means and SOM in the sense that, not just the forecasting function, but also the cluster for KNN is tailor-made. This style of tailor-made learning is known as *lazy learning* in the literature ([2]). It is called *lazy* because learning takes place when the time comes to classify a new instance, say $\mathbf{X}^m_{T+t}$, rather than when the *training set*, (25), *is processed*, say T.[18]

To make this clear, consider two types of agents: the K-means agent and the KNN agent. The K-means agent learns from the history before new instances come, and the resultant knowledge from learning is represented by a set of clusters, which is *extracted* from a set of historical instances. Based on these clusters, some *generalization pictures* are already produced before the advent of new instances, say $\mathbf{X}^m_{T+t}$.[19] The KNN agent, however, is not eager to learn. While he does store every instance observed, he never tries to extract knowledge (general rules) from them. In other words, he has the simplest form of "learning," i.e., rote learning (plain memorization). When the time $T + t$ comes and a new instance $\mathbf{X}^m_{T+t}$ is encountered, his memory is then searched for the historical instances that most strongly resemble $\mathbf{X}^m_{T+t}$.

As said, KNN, as a style of rote learning, stores all the historical instances, as shown in (31). Therefore, amounts of storage increase with time. This may make the nearest-neighbor calculation unbearably slow. In addition, some instances may be regarded as redundant with regard to the information gained. This can be particularly the case when KNN is applied to *classification* rather than regression or time series forecasting. For example, if we are interested in not x_{t+1} itself, but in whether x_{t+1} will be greater than x_t, i.e., whether x_t will go up or go down, then some regions of the instance space may be very stable with regard to class, e.g., up (1) or down (0), and just a few exemplars are needed inside stable regions. In other words, we do not have to keep all historical instances or training instances. The *storage-reduction algorithm* is then used to decide which instances in (31) to save and which to discard. This KNN with the storage-reduction algorithm is called *instance-based learning* (IBL) and is initiated by [3].[20]

---

[17] All details can be found in [25].

[18] Note that a fixed T in (25) implies a fixed training set without increments. A non-incremental training set can be typical for using K-means or SOM. However, KNN learning, also known as *rote learning*, memorizes everything that happens up to the present; therefore, the "training set" (memory) for KNN grows with time.

[19] For example, see Chap. 7 of this volume.

[20] As a matter of fact, the storage-reduction algorithms are not just to deal with the *redundancy* issue, but also the *noise-tolerance* issue. Reference [3] distinguishes the two by calling the former *memory updating functions*, and the latter *noise-tolerant algorithms*. The details can also be found in Chap. 9 of this volume.

The addition of a storage-reduction algorithm to KNN is also interesting from the perspectives of both neural sciences and economics. Considering the brain with its limited capacity for memory, we find that an essential question to ask is how the brain deals with increasing information by not memorizing all of it or by forgetting some of it. How does it do pruning? This is still a non-trivial issue pursued by neural scientists today. The same issue can interest economists as well, because it concerns the efficient use of limited space. A recent study on reward-motivated memory formation by neural scientists may provide an economic foundation for the memory formation ([1]).[21]

In this vein, the *marginal productivity* of the new instance in IBL can be considered as the reward. The marginal productivity of an instance can be defined by its contribution to enhance the capability to perform a correct classification. For those instances which have low marginal productivity, it will be discarded (not be remembered), and for those already stored instances, if their classification performances are poor, they will be discarded, too (be forgotten). In this way, one can interpret the mechanism of the pruning algorithms or the storage-reduction algorithms used in computational intelligence in the fashion of neural economics.

There are two chapters devoted to the financial applications of KNN and IBL. Chapter 8, **Comparison of Instance-Based Techniques for Learning to Predict Changes in Stock Prices**, authored by David LeRoux, uses publicly available monthly economic index data from the Federal Reserve to forecast changes in the S&P 500 stock index. This chapter effectively summarizes a number of technical issues arising from using KNN, including similarity metrics, feature selection, data normalization, choice of the number of neighbors, distance-based weights assigned to the neighbors, and cross validation. The author addresses well the consequence of choosing too many or too few neighbors and involving too many features by demonstrating empirically the impact of different choices of these parameters on accuracy performance.

In addition, the paper serves as a tutorial on a "how-to" guide on using the data mining software known as **WEKA** ([46]).[22] WEKA, along with the book ([46]) actually provides the beginning readers of CIEF with a good starting point to try something on their own.

Chapter 9, **Application of an Instance Based Learning Algorithm for Predicting the Stock Market Index**, authored by Ruppa K. Thulasiram and Adenike Y. Bamgbade, is very similar to Chap. 8 except that it uses IBL, instead of KNN, for predicting the price changes in the S&P 500 daily stock index.

---

[21] Reference [1] reports brain-scanning studies in humans that reveal how specific *reward-related brain regions* trigger the brain's learning and memory regions to promote memory formation.

[22] WEKA is a collection of machine learning algorithms for solving real-world data mining problems. It is written in Java and runs on almost any platform. The algorithms can either be applied directly to a dataset or called from the users' own Java code.

5 Evolutionary Computation

5.1 Genetic Algorithms

A general introduction to evolutionary computation is given in the previous volume ([18], pp. 33-39). Four branches of evolutionary computation are discussed there. They are genetic algorithms, genetic programming, evolutionary strategies, and evolutionary programming. Reference [15] provides a bibliography of the uses of evolutionary computation in economics and finance. Among the four, the genetic algorithm is the most popular one used in economics and finance.

Chapter 10, **Evaluating the Efficiency of Index Fund Selections over the Fund's Future Period**, authored by Yukiko Orito, Manabu Takeda, Kiyoaki Iimura, and Genji Yamazaki, applies genetic algorithms to the composition of an index fund. The index fund describes a type of mutual fund whose investment objective typically is to achieve the same return as a particular market index, such as Nikkei 255. An index fund will attempt to achieve its investment objective primarily by investing in the securities (stocks or bonds) of companies that are included in a selected index. Some index funds invest in all of the companies included in an index; other index funds invest in a representative sample of the companies included in an index. This paper adopts the second approach, and applies the genetic algorithm to optimize the sample structure, i.e., the portfolio of the representative sample.

5.2 Genetic Programming

Among all kinds of "intelligence" applied to finance, genetic programming is probably the one which requires the most intensive efforts on programming, and its execution is very time-consuming. Therefore, the applications of GP to finance are relatively sparse.[23] In the first volume, [16] provides a review on the financial applications of GP, and, in this volume, two more chapters are added to move the research frontier forward.

In Chap. 11, **The Failure of Computational-Intelligence Induced Trading Strategies: Distinguishing between Efficient Markets and Inefficient Algorithms**, Shu-Heng Chen and Nicolas Navet consider a very fundamental issue: when GP fails to discover profitable trading strategies, how should we react? In the literature, generally, there are two responses: the market is efficient or GP is inefficient. However, there is little clue about which case may be more likely. The two responses can lead to quite different decisions: one is to give up any further attempts on GP, and the other is to propose modified, or even more advanced, versions of GP.

In this chapter, the authors propose a test (a pretest) to help decide which case may be more likely. The test is based upon a very simple idea, namely, comparing the performance of GP with a good choice of benchmark. The authors argued clearly that a good benchmark is not "Buy and Hold", but either random trading strategies or random trading behavior. It involves using these random benchmarks to decide how much we have advanced, and then deciding which case we should refer to.

---

[23] Up to the present, [10] is the only edited volume devoted to this subject.

The idea of using random benchmarks is not new, and it has been used in developing econometric tests of the predictability of financial time series, which is also well explained in their chapter. Nonetheless, how to define random trading strategies (or trading behavior) is less evident than random time series. Therefore, the two contributions of this chapter are to build these random benchmarks upon a technically acceptable ground, and, as the second part of this chapter, to propose pretests associated with these random benchmarks.

The performance of these pretests is evaluated in light of the earlier results obtained in [19].[24] It is found that when the pretest shows that there is something to learn, GP always performs well; whereas when there is little to learn, GP, as anticipated, accordingly performs rather poorly. Therefore, there is no strong evidence to show that the simple GP is ineffective. It is market efficiency which fails GP. However, the pretests also show that the market is not always efficient; this property changes over time. Therefore, it should not discourage the further use of GP in the financial domain. Basically, when it should work, it works as expected.

As to the flavor which we get from the previous chapter, the earlier applications of financial GP mostly focus on *returns*. While there are some applications which also address risk or volatility, GP has been rarely applied to design a trading strategy which can protect investors against falling stock prices, the so-called *downside risk*.

In Chap. 12, **Nonlinear Goal-Directed CPPI Strategy**, Jiah-Shing Chen and Benjamin Penyang Liao, take up a new challenge of the financial application of GP. CPPI, which stands for *constant proportion portfolio insurance*, is a strategy that allows an investor to limit downside risk while retaining some upside potential by maintaining an exposure to risky assets. It has recently become one of the most popular types of cautious investment instruments ([40]).

However, when investors have a targeted return to pursue, the CPPI strategy may adversely reduce their chances of achieving the goal. To handle this problem, one needs to simultaneously take care of two constraints: the floor (downside risk) constraint and the goal constraint. However, the exact mathematical problem corresponding to solving the two constraint issues may be analytically difficult. Therefore, the authors propose a goal-directed CPPI strategy based on the heuristic motivated by mathematical finance ([6]).

The proposed strategy has a nice property: it is piecewise linear, and hence is simple to operate. The property of linearity is actually based on the assumption of Brownian motion, the cornerstone of modern mathematical finance. It is, however, no longer valid when this assumption is violated. The authors consider two possible cases. In the first case, linearity remains, but the slope coefficient (investment in risky assets) becomes unknown. In the second case, even worse, the linear property is destroyed, and investment in risk assets becomes a non-linear function of wealth. The authors propose a solution for each case separately. A genetic algorithm is used to determine the coefficient of the risky portfolio, and genetic programming is used to determine the nonlinearity relation between the risky portfolio and wealth.

---

[24] In fact, this chapter can be read as a continuation of the systematic study of the trading application of genetic programming conducted in [19].

The investment strategies developed by GA and GP are further tested by using five stocks selected from the Dow Jones Industrial group. It is found that the piece-wise non-linear investment strategy developed by GP performs the best, followed by the piecewise linear investment strategy developed by GA. The piecewise linear investment strategy based on the assumption of Brownian motion performs the worst.

6 Agents

As in the previous volume, the book ends with a chapter on agents. Computational intelligence serves as a foundation for algorithmic agents. By using CI tools, one can then endow agents with capability to learn and to adapt. As to how learning actually takes place, it is detailed by the respective CI tool in an algorithmic manner. These algorithmic agents are then placed in a social (interacting) environment, and the aggregate phenomena are then generated by the collective behavior of these algorithmic agents. It then becomes an experimental study to see how the choice of these algorithms may impact the observed aggregate dynamics ([17]). Based on the sensitivity outcome, one can explore the potential richness of a model, and hence gauge the degree of the inherent uncertainty in the model.

Based on what we have discussed in the previous sections, there are many ways of comparing different learning algorithms when applied to building algorithmic agents. Reference [5], for example, from a viewpoint of cognitive psychology provides a way of comparing some frequently used learning algorithms in economics. [25] Cognitive loading is certainly an important concern when one wants to choose an appropriate learning algorithm to model boundedly rational agents. A highly relevant question to ask is how demanding these algorithms are in terms of cognitive loading, and whether there is a threshold beyond which the agents' "humble mind" can simply not afford those demanding tasks. Answers to these questions are more subtle than one may think at first sight.

Reference [17] addresses the problem of how to relate and compare agent behavior based on computational intelligence models to human behavior, and proposes the condition of computational equivalence to deal with this difficult issue. The paper describes the design of a computational equivalence lab where both humans and software agents have the same computational intelligence methods at their disposal. In a similar vein, Chap. 13, **Hybrid-Agent Organization Modeling: A Logic-Heuristic Approach**, authored by Ana Marostica, Cesar A. Briano and Ernesto Chinkes, proposes a hybrid-agent organization model by using some ideas from scientific semiotics. This chapter illustrates the idea of integrating human agents (decision makers) with software agents (heuristic decision support system) and the connection between the two.

---

[25] In addition, these learning algorithms are not just confined to individual agents, i.e., agents only learn from their own experience. In fact, a class of learning algorithms, called *social learning*, explicitly or implicitly assumes the existence of a social network and indicates how agents learn from others' experiences as well. For example, see [13].

7 Concluding Remarks

While this second volume provides us with a good opportunity to include some interesting subjects which are missing in the first volume, these two volumes together are still not large enough to accommodate all state-of-the-art CI techniques with their economic and financial applications. To name a few, reinforcement learning, independent component analysis, and artificial immune systems are techniques that we hope to include in the next volume. In addition, some popular hybrid systems, such as fuzzy C-means, neuro-fuzzy systems, fuzzy-neural networks, genetic fuzzy systems, fuzzy evolutionary algorithms and genetic Bayesian networks are other techniques that will be included in the future as well.

Acknowledgements

The editors would like to acknowledge the efforts made by all referees, including Chao-Hsien Chu, Wei Gao, Steven C. Gustafson, Chao-Fu Hong, Carson Kai-Sang Leung, Tong Li, Jie-Shin Lin, Ping-Chen Lin, Martin Odening, Yukiko Orit, Claudio M. Rocco, Giulia Rotundo, Jishou Ruan, Arnold F. Shapiro, Theodore Theodosopoulos, Ruppa K. Thulasiram, Chueh-Yung Tsao, Chung-Tsen Tsao, Chiu-Che Tseng, Tzai-Der Wang, Weigang Li, Ana Marostica, Fernando Tohme and Raquel Florez-Lopez. To enhance the quality of the volume, all chapters, apart from those that are authored by native speakers, have been sent to an English editor for reviewing. In this regard, we are particularly grateful to Bruce Stewart for his excellent editing service.

References

1. Adcock A, Thangavel A, Whitfield-Gabrieli S, Knutson B, Gabrieli J (2006) Reward-motivated learning: mesolimbic activation precedes memory formation. Neuron 50(3):507–517
2. Aha D (1997) Lazy learning. Kluwer
3. Aha D, Kibler D, Marc K (1991) Instance-based learning algorithms. Machine Learning 6(1):37–66
4. Alvarez-Diaz M, Alvarez A (2005) Genetic multi-model composite forecast for nonlinear prediction of exchange rates. Empirical Economics 30:643–663
5. Brenner T (2006) Agent learning representation: Advice on modelling economic learning. In: Tesfatsion L, Judd K (eds) Handbook of computational economics, volume 2: agent-based computational economics. North-Holland, Amsterdam:895–947
6. Browne S (1997) Survival and growth with a liability: optimal portfolio strategies in continuous time. Mathematics of Operations Research 22(2):468–493
7. Campbell J, Lo A, MacKinlay C (1997) The econometrics of financial markets. Princeton University Press, NJ
8. Cao L, Tay F (2003) Saliency analysis of support vector machines for feature selection in financial time series forecasting. In: Chen SH, Wang P (eds) Computational intelligence in economics and finance. Springer-Verlag:182–199

9. Chen J, Xu D (1998) An economic forecasting system based on recurrent neural networks. In: Proceedings of IEEE international conference on systems, man, and cybernetics:1762–1767
10. Chen SH (ed) (2002) Genetic algorithms and genetic programming in computational finance. Kluwer.
11. Chen SH (2005) Computational intelligence in economics and finance: carrying on the legacy of Herbert Simon. Information Sciences 170:121–131
12. Chen SH (2007a) Computationally intelligent agents in economics and finance. Information Sciences 177(5):1153-1168
13. Chen SH (2007b) Graphs, networks and ACE. New Mathematics and Natural Computation 2(3):299–314
14. Chen SH, He H (2003) Searching financial patterns with self-organizing maps. In Chen SH, Wang P (eds) Computational intelligence in economics and finance. Springer-Verlag:203–216
15. Chen SH, Kuo TW (2002) Evolutionary computation in economics and finance: A bibliography. In: Chen SH (eds) Computational intelligence in economics and finance. Springer-Verlag:419–455
16. Chen SH, Kuo TW (2003) Discovering hidden patterns with genetic programming. In Chen SH, Wang P (eds) Computational intelligence in economics and finance. Springer-Verlag:329-347
17. Chen SH, Tai CC (2007) On the selection of adaptive algorithms in ABM: a computational-equivalence approach. Computational Economics 28:313–331
18. Chen SH, Wang P (eds) (2003) Computational intelligence in economics and finance. Springer-Verlag.
19. Chen SH, Kuo TW, Hoi KM (2007) Genetic programming and financial trading: how much about "What we Know"? In: Zopounidis C, Doumpos M, Pardalos PM (eds) Handbook of financial engineering. Springer. Forthcoming.
20. Cooper W, Seiford L, Tone K (2005) Introduction to data envelopment analysis and its uses: with DEA-Solver software and references. Springer.
21. Das N (2003) Hedge fund classification using K-means method. EconPapers, No. 204
22. De Cock M (1999) Representing the adverb very in fuzzy set theory. ESSLLI Student Papers 1999:223–232
23. Elamn J (1990) Finding structure in time. Cognitive Science 14:179–211
24. Episcopos A, Davis J (1996) Predicting returns on Canadian exchange rates with artificial neural networks and EGARCHM-M models. Neural Computing and Application 4:168–174
25. Fernández-Rodríguez F, Sosvilla-Rivero S., Andrada-Félix J (2003) Nearest-neighbour predictions in foreign exchange markets. In Chen SH, Wang P (eds) Computational intelligence in economics and finance. Springer-Verlag:297–325
26. Florez-Lopez R (2003) Effective position of European firms in the face of monetary integration using Kohonen's SOFM. In Chen SH, Wang P (eds) Computational intelligence in economics and finance. Springer-Verlag:217–233
27. Florez-Lopez R (2007) Strategic supplier selection in the added-value perspective: a CI approach. Information Science 177(5):1169–1179
28. Hann T, Steurer E (1996) Much ado about nothing? Exchange rate forecasting: neural networks vs. linear models using monthly and weekly data. Neurocomputing 10:323–339
29. Hersh H, Caramazza A (1976) A fuzzy set approach to modifiers and vagueness in natural language. Journal of Experimental Psychology–General 105 (3):254–276

30. Hollans H, Munneke HJ (2003) Housing markets and house price appreciation: an Intercity Analysis. Working paper. Univeristy of Georgia.
31. Jordan M (1986) Serial order: a parallel distributed processing approach. Technical Report, No. 8604. Institute for Cognitive Science, UC San Diego
32. Kohonen T (1995) Self-organizing Maps. Springer.
33. Kovalerchuk B, Vityaev E (2000) Data mining in finance: advances in relational and hybrid methods. Kluwer.
34. Kramer M (1990) Nonlinear principal analysis using autoassociative neural networks. AIChE Journal 37(2):233–243
35. Kuan CM, Liu T (1995) Forecasting exchange rates using feedforward and recurrent neural networks. Journal of Applied Econometrics 10:347–364
36. Kumbhakar S, Knox Lovell C (2003) Stochastic frontier analysis. Cambridge.
37. MacQueen JB (1967) Some methods for classification and analysis of multivariate observations. Proceedings of 5th Berkeley Symposium on Mathematical Statistics and Probability. University of California Press 1:281–297
38. Mandic D, Chambers J (2001) Recurrent neural networks for prediction: learning Algorithms, architectures, and stability. John Wiley and Sons, New York
39. McNelis P (2005) Neural networks in finance: gaining predictive edge in the market. Elsvier.
40. Overhaus M, Bermudez A, Buehler H, Ferraris A, Jordinson C, Lamnouar A (2007) Equity hybrid derivatives. Wiley Finance
41. Qian Y (2006) K-means algorithm and its application for clustering companies listed in Zhejiang province. WIT Transaction on Information and Communication Technologies 37:35–44
42. Rocco C, Moreno J (2003) A support vector machine model for currency crises discrimination. In: Chen SH, Wang P (eds) Computational intelligence in economics and finance. Springer-Verlag:171–181
43. Shi S, Xu L, Liu B (1999) Improving the acuracy of nonlinear combined forecasting using neural networks. Expert Systems with Applications 16:49–54
44. Wei WX, Jiang ZH (1995) Artificial neural network forecasting model for exchange rate and empirical analysis. Forecasting 2:67-V69
45. Weigend A, Huberman B, Rumelhart D (1992) Predicting sunspots and exchange rates with connectionist networks. In: Casdagli M, Eubank S (eds) Nonlinear modeling and forecasting. Addison-Wesley:395V-432
46. Witten I, Frank E (2005) Data mining: practical machine learning tools and techniques (2nd Edition). Morgan Kaufmann
47. Wu B (1995) Model-free forecasting for nonlinear time series (with application to exchange rates). Computational Statistics and Data Analysis 19:433–459

An Overview of Insurance Uses of Fuzzy Logic

Arnold F. Shapiro

Smeal College of Business, Penn State University, University Park, PA 16802
afs1@psu.edu

It has been twenty-five years since DeWit(1982) first applied fuzzy logic (FL) to insurance. That article sought to quantify the fuzziness in underwriting. Since then, the universe of discourse has expanded considerably and now also includes FL applications involving classification, projected liabilities, future and present values, pricing, asset allocations and cash flows, and investments. This article presents an overview of these studies. The two specific purposes of the article are to document the FL technologies have been employed in insurance-related areas and to review the FL applications so as to document the unique characteristics of insurance as an application area.

Key words: Actuarial, Fuzzy Logic, Fuzzy Sets, Fuzzy Arithmetic, Fuzzy Inference Systems, Fuzzy Clustering, Insurance

1 Introduction

The first article to use fuzzy logic (FL) in insurance was [29][1], which sought to quantify the fuzziness in underwriting. Since then, the universe of discourse has expanded considerably and now includes FL applications involving classification, underwriting, projected liabilities, future and present values, pricing, asset allocations and cash flows, and investments.

This article presents an overview of these FL applications in insurance. The specific purposes of the article are twofold: first, to document the FL technologies have been employed in insurance-related areas; and, second, to review the FL applications so as to document the unique characteristics of insurance as an application area.

---

[1] While DeWit was the first to write an article that gave an explicit example of the use of FL in insurance, FL, as it related to insurance, was a topic of discussion at the time. Reference [43], for example, remarked that "... not all expert knowledge is a set of "black and white" logic facts - much expert knowledge is codifiable only as alternatives, possibles, guesses and opinions (i.e., as fuzzy heuristics)."

Before continuing, the term FL needs to be clarified. In this article, we generally follow the lead of Zadeh and use the term FL in its wide sense. According to [85],

> Fuzzy logic (FL), in its wide sense, has four principal facets. First, the logical facet, FL/L, [fuzzy logic in its narrow sense], is a logical system which underlies approximate reasoning and inference from imprecisely defined premises. Second, the set-theoretic facet, FL/S, is focused on the theory of sets which have unsharp boundaries, rather than on issues which relate to logical inference, [examples of which are fuzzy sets and fuzzy mathematics]. Third is the relational facet, FL/R, which is concerned in the main with representation and analysis of imprecise dependencies. Of central importance in FL/R are the concepts of a linguistic variable and the calculus of fuzzy if-then rules. Most of the applications of fuzzy logic in control and systems analysis relate to this facet of fuzzy logic. Fourth is the epistemic facet of fuzzy logic, FL/E, which is focused on knowledge, meaning and imprecise information. Possibility theory is a part of this facet.

The methodologies of the studies reviewed in this article cover all of these FL facets. The term "fuzzy systems" also is used to denote these concepts, as indicated by some of the titles in the reference section of this paper, and will be used interchangeably with the term FL.

The next section of this article contains a brief overview of insurance application areas. Thereafter, the article is subdivided by the fuzzy techniques [2] shown in Fig. 1.

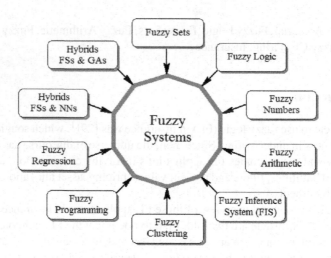

Fig. 1. Fuzzy Logic

---

[2] This article could have been structured by fuzzy technique, as was done by [75] or by insurance topic, as was done by [28] and [66]. Given the anticipated audience, the former structure was adopted.

As indicated, the topics covered include fuzzy set theory, fuzzy numbers, fuzzy arithmetic, fuzzy inference systems, fuzzy clustering, fuzzy programming, fuzzy regression, and soft computing. Each section begins with a brief description of the technique[3] and is followed by a chronological review of the insurance applications of that technique. When an application involves more than one technique, it is only discussed in one section. The article ends with a comment regarding future insurance applications of FL.

2 Insurance Application Areas

The major application areas of insurance include classification, underwriting, projected liabilities, ratemaking and pricing, and asset allocations and investments. In this section, we briefly describe each of these areas so that readers who are unfamiliar with the insurance field will have a context for the rest of the paper.

2.1 Classification

Classification is fundamental to insurance. On the one hand, classification is the prelude to the underwriting of potential coverage, while on the other hand, risks need to be properly classified and segregated for pricing purposes. Operationally, risk may be viewed from the perspective of the four classes of assets (physical, financial, human, intangible) and their size, type, and location.

2.2 Underwriting

Underwriting is the process of selection through which an insurer determines which of the risks offered to it should be accepted, and the conditions and amounts of the accepted risks. The goal of underwriting is to obtain a safe, yet profitable, distribution of risks. Operationally, underwriting determines the risk associated with an applicant and either assigns the appropriate rating class for an insurance policy or declines to offer a policy.

2.3 Projected Liabilities

In the context of this article, projected liabilities are future financial obligations that arise either because of a claim against and insurance company or a contractual benefit agreement between employers and their employees. The evaluation of projected liabilities is fundamental to the insurance and employee benefit industry, so it is not surprising that we are beginning to see SC technologies applied in this area.

---

[3] Only a cursory review of the FL methodologies is discussed in this paper. Readers who prefer a more extensive introduction to the topic, with an insurance perspective, are referred to [56]. Those who are interested in a comprehensive introduction to the topic are referred to [90] and [32]. Readers interested in a grand tour of the first 30 years of fuzzy logic are urged to read the collection of Zadeh's papers contained in [74] and [45].

2.4 Ratemaking and Pricing

Ratemaking and pricing refer to the process of establishing rates used in insurance or other risk transfer mechanisms. This process involves a number of considerations including marketing goals, competition and legal restrictions to the extent they affect the estimation of future costs associated with the transfer of risk. Such future costs include claims, claim settlement expenses, operational and administrative expenses, and the cost of capital.

2.5 Asset Allocation and Investments

The analysis of assets and investments is a major component in the management of an insurance enterprise. Of course, this is true of any financial intermediary, and many of the functions performed are uniform across financial companies. Thus, insurers are involved with market and individual stock price forecasting, the forecasting of currency futures, credit decision-making, forecasting direction and magnitude of changes in stock indexes, and so on.

3 Linguistic Variables and Fuzzy Set Theory

Linguistic variables are the building blocks of FL. They may be defined ([82], [83]) as variables whose values are expressed as words or sentences. Risk capacity, for example, a common concern in insurance, may be viewed both as a numerical value ranging over the interval [0,100%], and a linguistic variable that can take on values like high, not very high, and so on. Each of these linguistic values may be interpreted as a label of a fuzzy subset of the universe of discourse X = [0,100%], whose base variable, x, is the generic numerical value risk capacity. Such a set, an example of which is shown in Fig. 2, is characterized by a membership function (MF), $\mu_{high}(x)$ here, which assigns to each object a grade of membership ranging between zero and one.

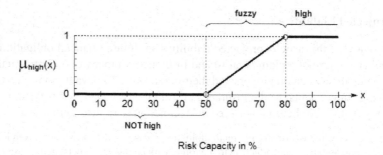

Fig. 2. (Fuzzy) Set of Clients with High Risk Capacity

In this case, which represents the set of clients with a high risk capacity, individuals with a risk capacity of 50 percent, or less, are assigned a membership grade of zero and those with a risk capacity of 80 percent, or more, are assigned a grade of one. Between those risk capacities, (50%, 80%), the grade of membership is fuzzy.

In addition to the S-shaped MF depicted in Fig. 2, insurance applications also employ the triangular, trapezoidal, Gaussian, and generalized bell classes of MFs. As with other areas of application, fuzzy sets are implemented by extending many of the basic identities that hold for ordinary sets.

3.1 Applications

This subsection presents an overview of some insurance applications of linguistic variables and fuzzy set theory. The topics addressed include: earthquake insurance, optimal excess of loss retention in a reinsurance program, the selection of a "good" forecast, where goodness is defined using multiple criteria that may be vague or fuzzy, resolve statistical problems involving sparse, high dimensional data with categorical responses, the definition and measurement of risk from the perspective of a risk manager, and deriving an overall disability Index.

An early study was by [7], who used pattern recognition and FL in the evaluation of seismic intensity and damage forecasting, and for the development of models to estimate earthquake insurance premium rates and insurance strategies. The influences on the performance of structures include quantifiable factors, which can be captured by probability models, and nonquantifiable factors, such as construction quality and architectural details, which are best formulated using fuzzy set models. For example, he defined the percentage of a building damaged by an earthquake by fuzzy terms such as medium, severe and total, and represented the membership functions of these terms as shown in Fig. 3.[4]

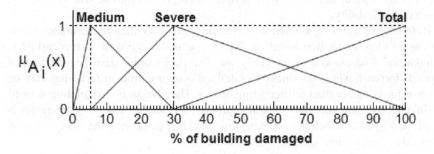

Fig. 3. MFs of Building Damage

Two methods of identifying earthquake intensity were presented and compared. The first method was based on the theory of pattern recognition where a discrimina-

---

[4] Adapted from [7, Figure 6.3].

tive function was developed using Bayes' criterion and the second method applied FL.

Reference [49] envisioned the decision-making procedure in the selection of an optimal excess of loss retention in a reinsurance program as essentially a maximin technique, similar to the selection of an optimum strategy in noncooperative game theory. As an example, he considered four decision variables (two goals and two constraints) and their membership functions: probability of ruin, coefficient of variation, reinsurance premium as a percentage of cedent's premium income (Rel. Reins. Prem.) and deductible (retention) as a percentage of cedent's premium income (Rel. Deductible). The grades of membership for the decision variables (where the vertical lines cut the MFs) and their degree of applicability (DOA), or rule strength, may be represented as shown Fig. 4.[5]

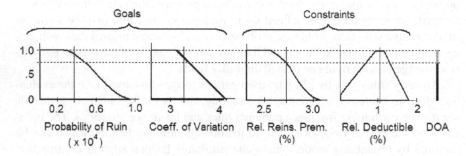

Fig. 4. Retention Given Fuzzy Goals and Constraints

In the choice represented in the figure, the relative reinsurance premium has the minimum membership value and defines the degree of applicability for this particular excess of loss reinsurance program. The optimal program is the one with the highest degree of applicability.

Reference [22, p. 434] studied fuzzy trends in property-liability insurance claim costs as a follow-up to their assertion that "the actuarial approach to forecasting is rudimentary." The essence of the study was that they emphasized the selection of a "good" forecast, where goodness was defined using multiple criteria that may be vague or fuzzy, rather than a forecasting model. They began by calculating several possible trends using accepted statistical procedures[6] and for each trend they determined the degree to which the estimate was good by intersecting the fuzzy goals of historical accuracy, unbiasedness and reasonableness.

---

[5] Adapted from [49, Figure 2].

[6] Each forecast method was characterized by an estimation period, an estimation technique, and a frequency model. These were combined with severity estimates to obtain pure premium trend factors. ([22, Table 1])

The flavor of the article can be obtained by comparing the graphs in Fig. 5, which show the fuzzy membership values for 30 forecasts[7] according to historical accuracy (goal 1), ordered from best to worst, and unbiasedness (goal 2), before intersection, graph (a) and after intersection, graph (b).

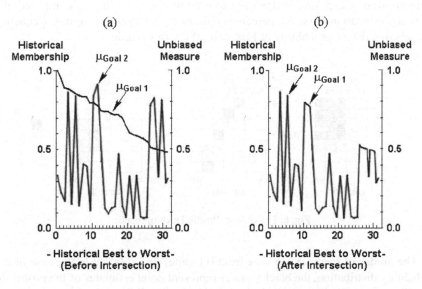

Fig. 5. The Intersection of Historical Accuracy and Unbiasedness

They suggested that one may choose the trend that has the highest degree of goodness and proposed that a trend that accounts for all the trends can be calculated by forming a weighted average using the membership degrees as weights. They concluded that FL provides an effective method for combining statistical and judgmental criteria in insurance decision-making.

Another interesting aspect of the [22] study was their α-cut for trend factors, which they conceptualized in terms of a multiple of the standard deviation of the trend factors beyond their grand mean. In their analysis, an α-cut corresponded to only including those trend factors within $2(1 - \alpha)$ standard deviations.

A novel classification issue was addressed by [51], who used FST to resolve statistical problems involving sparse, high dimensional data with categorical responses. They began with a concept of extreme profile, which, for the health of the elderly, two examples might be "active, age 50" and "frail, age 100."" From there, their focus was on g_{ik}, a grade of membership (GoM) score that represents the degree to which the i-th individual belongs to the k-th extreme profile in a fuzzy partition, and they presented statistical procedures that directly reflect fuzzy set principles in the estimation of the parameters. In addition to describing how the parameters estimated from

---

[7] Adapted from [22, Figures 2 and 3], which compared the membership values for 72 forecasts.

the model may be used to make various types of health forecasts, they discussed how GoM may be used to combine data from multiple sources and they analyzed multiple versions of fuzzy set models under a wide range of empirical conditions.

Reference [41] investigated the use of FST to represent uncertainty in both the definition and measurement of risk, from the perspective of a risk manager. His conceptualization of exposure analysis is captured in Fig. 6[8], which is composed of a fuzzy representation of (a) the perceived risk, as a contoured function of frequency and severity, (b) the probability of loss, and (c) the risk profile.

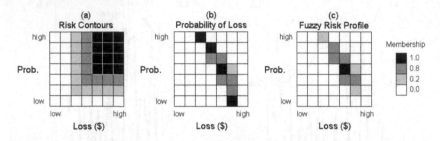

Fig. 6. Fuzzy Risk Profile Development

The grades of membership vary from 0 (white) to 1 (black); in the case of the probability distribution, the black squares represent point estimates of the probabilities. The risk profile is the intersection of the first two, using only the min operator. He concluded that FST provides a realistic approach to the formal analysis of risk.

Reference [42] examined the problems for risk managers associated with knowledge imperfections, under which model parameters and measurements can only be specified as a range of possibilities, and described how FL can be used to deal with such situations. However, unlike [41], not much detail was provided.

The last example of this section is from the life and health area. Reference [19] presented a methodology for deriving an Overall Disability Index (ODI) for measuring an individual's disability. Their approach involved the transformation of the ODI derivation problem into a multiple-criteria decision-making problem. Essentially, they used the analytic hierarchy process, a multicriteria decision making technique that uses pairwise comparisons to estimate the relative importance of each risk factor ([60]), along with entropy theory and FST, to elicit the weights among the attributes and to aggregate the multiple attributes into a single ODI measurement.

4 Fuzzy Numbers and Fuzzy Arithmetic

Fuzzy numbers are numbers that have fuzzy properties, examples of which are the notions of "around six percent" and "relatively high". The general characteristic of a

---

[8] Adapted from [41, Figures 7, 8 and 9]

fuzzy number ([82] and [31]) often is represented as shown in Fig. 7, although any of the MF classes, such as Gaussian and generalized bell, can serve as a fuzzy number, depending on the situation.

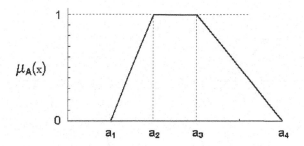

Fig. 7. Flat Fuzzy Number

This shape of a fuzzy number is referred to as trapezoidal or "flat" and its MF often is denoted as (a_1,a_2,a_3,a_4) or $(a_1/a_2, a_3/a_4)$; when a_2 is equal to a_3, we get the triangular fuzzy number. A fuzzy number is positive if $a_1 \geq 0$ and negative if $a_4 \leq 0$, and, as indicated, it is taken to be a convex fuzzy subset of the real line.

4.1 Fuzzy Arithmetic

As one would anticipate, fuzzy arithmetic can be applied to the fuzzy numbers. Using the extension principle ([82]), the nonfuzzy arithmetic operations can be extended to incorporate fuzzy sets and fuzzy numbers[9]. Briefly, if $*$ is a binary operation such as addition (+), min (∧), or max (∨), the fuzzy number z, defined by $z = x * y$, is given as a fuzzy set by

$$\mu_z(w) = \vee_{u,v} \, \mu_x(u) \wedge \mu_y(v), \ u,v,w \in \Re \tag{1}$$

subject to the constraint that $w = u*v$, where μ_x, μ_y, and μ_z denote the membership functions of x, y, and z, respectively, and $\vee_{u,v}$ denotes the supremum over u, v.[10]

A simple application of the extension principle is the sum of the fuzzy numbers A and B, denoted by $A \oplus B = C$, which has the membership function:

---

[9] Fuzzy arithmetic is related to interval arithmetic or categorical calculus, where the operations use intervals, consisting of the range of numbers bounded by the interval endpoints, as the basic data objects. The primary difference between the two is that interval arithmetic involves crisp (rather than overlapping) boundaries at the extremes of each interval and it provides no intrinsic measure (like membership functions) of the degree to which a value belongs to a given interval. Reference [2] discussed the use interval arithmetic in an insurance context.

[10] See [90, Chap. 5], for a discussion of the extension principle.

$$\mu_c(z) = \max\{\min[\mu_A(x), \mu_B(y)] : x + y = z\} \qquad (2)$$

The general nature of the fuzzy arithmetic operations is depicted in Fig. 8 for $A = (-1, 1, 3)$ and $B = (1, 3, 5)^{11}$.

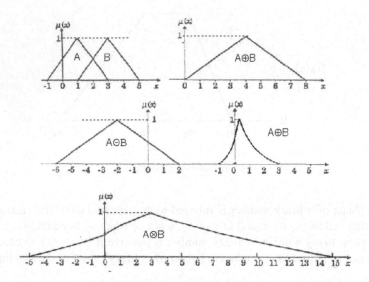

Fig. 8. Fuzzy Arithmetic Operations

The first row shows the two membership functions A and B and their sum; the second row shows their difference and their ratio; and the third row shows their product.

4.2 Applications

This subsection presents an overview of insurance applications involving fuzzy arithmetic. The topics addressed include: the fuzzy future and present values of fuzzy cash amounts, using fuzzy interest rates, and both crisp and fuzzy periods; the computation of the fuzzy premium for a pure endowment policy; fuzzy interest rate whose fuzziness was a function of duration; net single premium for a term insurance; the effective tax rate and after-tax rate of return on the asset and liability portfolio of a property-liability insurance company; cash-flow matching when the occurrence dates are uncertain; and the financial pricing of property-liability insurance contracts.

Reference [10] appears to have been the first author to address the fuzzy time-value-of-money aspects of actuarial pricing, when he investigated the fuzzy future and present values of fuzzy cash amounts, using fuzzy interest rates, and both crisp

---

[11] This figure is similar to [55, Figure 18, p. 157], after correcting for an apparent discrepancy in their multiplication and division representations.

and fuzzy periods. His approach, generally speaking, was based on the premise that "the arithmetic of fuzzy numbers is easily handled when x is a function of y." ([10, p. 258]) For a flat fuzzy number and straight line segments for $\mu_{A(x)}$ on $[a_1, a_2]$ and $[a_3, a_4]$, this can be conceptualized as shown in Fig. 9

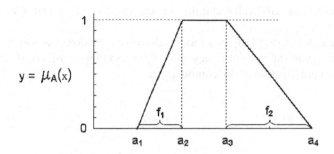

Fig. 9. MF and Inverse MF

where $f_1(y|A) = a_1 + y(a_2 - a_1)$ and $f_2(y|A) = a_4 - y(a_4 - a_3)$. The points a_j, $j = 1, 2, 3, 4$, and the functions $f_j(y|A), j = 1, 2$, "A" a fuzzy number, which are inverse functions mapping the membership function onto the real line, characterize the fuzzy number.

If the investment is A and the interest rate per period is i, where both values are fuzzy numbers, he showed that the accumulated value (S_n), a fuzzy number, after n periods, a crisp number, is

$$S_n = A \otimes (1 \oplus i)^n \qquad (3)$$

because, for positive fuzzy numbers, multiplication distributes over addition and is associative. It follows that the membership function for S_n takes the form

$$\mu(x|S_n) = (s_{n1}, f_{n1}(y|S_n)/s_{n2}, s_{n3}/f_{n2}(y|S_n), s_{n4}) \qquad (4)$$

where, for $j = 1, 2$,

$$f_{nj}(y|S_n) = f_j(y|A) \cdot (1 + f_j(y|i))^n \qquad (5)$$

and can be represented in a manner similar to Fig. 9, except that a_j is replaced with S_{nj}.

Then, using the extension principle ([31]), he showed how to extend the analysis to include a fuzzy duration.

Buckley then went on to extend the literature to fuzzy discounted values and fuzzy annuities. In the case of positive discounted values, he showed ([10, pp. 263-4]) that:

$$\text{If } S > 0 \text{ then } PV_2(S, n) \text{ exists; otherwise it may not, where :}$$
$$PV_2(S, n) = A \text{ iif } A \text{ is a fuzzy number and } A = S \otimes (1 \oplus i)^{-n} \qquad (6)$$

The essence of his argument was that this function does not exist when using it leads to contradictions such as $a_2 < a_1$ or $a_4 < a_3$.

The inverse membership function of $PV_2(S, n)$ is:

$$f_j(y|A) = f_j(y|S) \cdot (1 + f_{3-j}(y|i))^{-n}, j = 1, 2 \qquad (7)$$

Both the accumulated value and the present value of fuzzy annuities were discussed.[12]

Reference [49], using [10] as a model, discussed the computation of the fuzzy premium for a pure endowment policy using fuzzy arithmetic. Figure 10 is an adaptation of his representation of the computation.

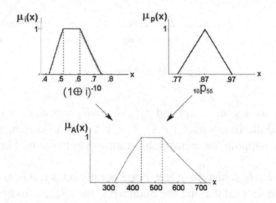

Fig. 10. Fuzzy Present Value of a Pure Endowment

As indicated, the top left figure represents the MF of the discounted value after ten years at the fuzzy effective interest rate per annum of (.03, .05, .07, .09), while the top right figure represents the MF of $_{10}p_{55}$, the probability that a life aged 55 will survive to age 65. The figure on the bottom represents the MF for the present value of the pure endowment.

Reference [56, pp. 29-38] extended the pure endowment analysis of [49]. First, he incorporated a fuzzy interest rate whose fuzziness was a function of duration. This involved a current crisp rate of 6 percent, a 10-year Treasury Note yield of 8 percent, and a linearly increasing fuzzy rate between the two. Figure 11 shows a conceptualization of his idea.

Then he investigated the more challenging situation of a net single premium for a term insurance, where the progressive fuzzification of rates plays a major role.

Along the same lines, [72] explored the membership functions associated with the net single premium of some basic life insurance products assuming a crisp morality rate and a fuzzy interest rate. Their focus was on α-cuts, and, starting with a

---

[12] While not pursued here, the use of fuzzy arithmetic in more general finance applications can be found in [12] and [68].

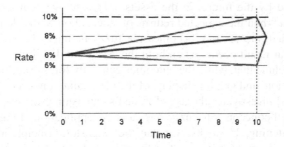

Fig. 11. Fuzzy Interest Rate

fuzzy interest rate, they gave fuzzy numbers for such products as term insurance and deferred annuities, and used the extension principle to develop the associated membership functions.

Reference [26] and [27] illustrated how FL can be used to estimate the effective tax rate and after-tax rate of return on the asset and liability portfolio of a property-liability insurance company. They began with the observation that the effective tax rate and the risk-free rate fully determine the present value of the expected investment tax liability. This leads to differential tax treatment for stocks and bonds, which, together with the tax shield of underwriting losses, determine the overall effective tax rate for the firm. They then argued that the estimation of the effective tax rate is an important tool of asset-liability management and that FL is the appropriate technology for this estimation.

The essence of their paper is illustrated in Fig. 12[13], which shows the membership functions for the fuzzy investment tax rates of a beta one company[14], with assumed investments, liabilities and underwriting profit, before and after the effect of the liability tax shield.

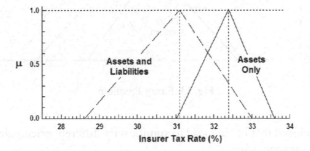

Fig. 12. Fuzzy Interest Rate

---

[13] Adapted from [27, Figure 1]

[14] A beta one company has a completely diversified stock holding, and thus has the same amount of risk ($\beta = 1$) as the entire market.

As suggested by the figure, in the assets-only case, the non-fuzzy tax rate is 32.4 percent, but when the expected returns of stocks, bonds, dividends and capital gains are fuzzified, the tax rate becomes the fuzzy number (31%, 32.4%, 32.4%, 33.6%). A similar result occurs when both the assets and liabilities are considered. The authors conclude that, while the outcomes generally follow intuition, the benefit is the quantification, and graphic display, of the uncertainty involved.

Reference [8] investigates the use of Zadeh's extension principle for transforming crisp financial concepts into fuzzy ones and the application of the methodology to cash-flow matching. They observer that the extension principle allows them to rigorously define the fuzzy equivalent of financial and economical concepts such as duration and utility, and to interpret them. A primary contribution of their study was the investigation of the matching of cash flows whose occurrence dates are uncertain.

The final study of this section is [23], who used FL to address the financial pricing of property-liability insurance contracts. Observing that much of the information about cash flows, future economic conditions, risk premiums, and other factors affecting the pricing decision is subjective and thus difficult to quantify using conventional methods, they incorporated both probabilistic and nonprobabilistic types of uncertainty in their model. The authors focused primarily on the FL aspects needed to solve the insurance-pricing problem, and in the process "fuzzified" a well-known insurance financial pricing model, provided numerical examples of fuzzy pricing, and proposed fuzzy rules for project decision-making. Their methodology was based on Buckley's inverse membership function (See Fig. 9 and related discussion).

Figure 13 shows their conceptualization of a fuzzy loss, the fuzzy present value of that loss, and the fuzzy premium, net of fuzzy taxes, using a one-period model. [15]

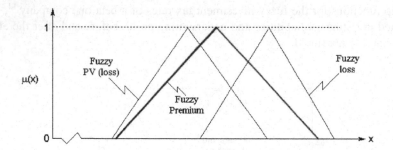

Fig. 13. Fuzzy Premium

They concluded that FL can lead to significantly different pricing decisions than the conventional approach.

---

[15] Adapted from [23], Fig. 5.

5 Fuzzy Inference Systems

The fuzzy inference system (FIS) is a popular methodology for implementing FL. FISs are also known as fuzzy rule based systems, fuzzy expert systems (FES), fuzzy models, fuzzy associative memories (FAM), or fuzzy logic controllers when used as controllers ([40, p. 73]), although not everyone agrees that all these terms are synonymous. Reference [5, p.77], for example, observes that a FIS based on IF-THEN rules is practically an expert system if the rules are developed from expert knowledge, but if the rules are based on common sense reasoning then the term expert system does not apply. The essence of a FIS can be represented as shown in Fig. 14.[16]

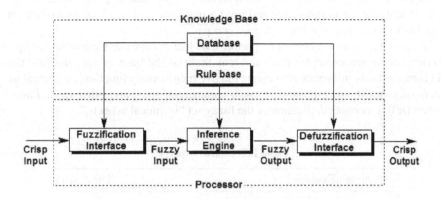

Fig. 14. Fuzzy Inference System (FIS)

As indicated in the figure, the FIS can be envisioned as involving a knowledge base and a processing stage. The knowledge base provides MFs and fuzzy rules needed for the process. In the processing stage, numerical crisp variables are the input of the system.[17] These variables are passed through a fuzzification stage where they are transformed to linguistic variables, which become the fuzzy input for the inference engine. This fuzzy input is transformed by the rules of the inference engine to fuzzy output. These linguistic results are then changed by a defuzzification stage into numerical values that become the output of the system.

The Mamdani FIS has been the most commonly mentioned FIS in the insurance literature, and most often the t-norm and the t-conorm are the min-operator and max-

---

[16] Adapted from [58], Fig. 2.

[17] In practice, input and output scaling factors are often used to normalize the crisp inputs and outputs. Also, the numerical input can be crisp or fuzzy. In this latter event, the input does not have to be fuzzified.

operator, respectively.[18] Commonly, the centre of gravity (COG) approach is used for defuzzification.

5.1 Applications

This subsection presents an overview of insurance applications of FISs. In most instances, as indicated, an FES was used. The application areas include: life and health underwriting; classification; modeling the selection process in group health insurance; evaluating risks, including occupational injury risk; pricing group health insurance using fuzzy ancillary data; adjusting workers compensation insurance rates; financial forecasting; and budgeting for national health care.

As mentioned above, the first recognition that fuzzy systems could be applied to the problem of individual insurance underwriting was due to [29]. He recognized that underwriting was subjective and used a basic form of the FES to analyze the underwriting practice of a life insurance company.

Using what is now a common approach, he had underwriters evaluate 30 hypothetical life insurance applications and rank them on the basis of various attributes. He then used this information to create the five membership functions: technical aspects (μ_t), health (μ_h), profession (μ_p), commercial (μ_c), and other (μ_o). Table 1 shows DeWit's conceptualization of the fuzzy set "technical aspects."

Table 1. Technical Aspects

Description	Example	Fuzzy value
good	remunerative, good policy	1.0
moderate	unattractive policy provisions	0.5
bad	sum insured does not match wealth of insured	0.2
impossible	child inappropriately insured for large amount	0.0

Next, by way of example, he combined these membership functions and an array of fuzzy set operations into a fuzzy expert underwriting system, using the formula:

$$W = \left(I(\mu_t)\mu_h \sqrt{\mu_p}\mu_o^2 \sqrt{2\min(0.5,\mu_c)} \right)^{[1-\max(0,\mu_c-0.5)]} \tag{8}$$

where intensification ($I(\mu_t)$) increases the grade of membership for membership functions above some value (often 0.5) and decreases it otherwise, concentration (μ_o^2) reduces the grade of membership, and dilation ($\sqrt{\mu_p}$) increases the grade of membership. He then suggested hypothetical underwriting decision rules related to the values of W.[19]

---

[18] Reference [35] shows that many copulas can serve as t-norms.

[19] The hypothetical decision rules took the form:

   $0.0 \leq W < 0.1$ refuse

   $0.1 \leq W < 0.3$ try to improve the condition, if not possible: refuse

Reference [49] used a FES to provide a flexible definition of a preferred policyholder in life insurance. As a part of this effort, he extended the insurance underwriting literature in three ways: he used continuous membership functions; he extended the definition of intersection to include the bounded difference, Hamacher and Yager operators; and he showed how α-cuts could be implemented to refine the decision rule for the minimum operator, where the α-cuts is applied to each membership function, and the algebraic product, where the minimum acceptable product is equal to the α-cut. Whereas [29] focused on technical and behavioral features, Lemaire focused on the preferred policyholder underwriting features of cholesterol, blood pressure, weight and smoker status, and their intersection.

An early classification study was [33], which discussed how measures of fuzziness can be used to classify life insurance risks. They envisioned a two-stage process. In the first stage, a risk was assigned a vector, whose cell values represented the degree to which the risk satisfies the preferred risk requirement associated with that cell. In the second stage, the overall degree of membership in the preferred risk category was computed. This could be done using the fuzzy intersection operator of [49] (see Fig. 4) or a fuzzy inference system. Measures of fuzziness were compared and discussed within the context of risk classification, both with respect to a fuzzy preferred risk whose fuzziness is minimized and the evaluation of a fuzzy set of preferred risks.

Following Lemaire's lead ([49]), [39] and [78] used FES to model the selection process in group health insurance. First single-plan underwriting was considered and then the study was extended to multiple-option plans. In the single-plan situation, Young focused on such fuzzy input features as change in the age/sex factor in the previous two years, change in the group size, proportion of employees selecting group coverage, proportion of premium for the employee and the dependent paid by the employer, claims as a proportion of total expected claims, the loss ratio, adjusted for employer size, and turnover rate. She completed the section with a discussion of a matrix of the interaction between the features (criteria) and their interpretation in the context of fuzzy intersection operators.

In the multiple-option case, the additional fuzzy features include single and family age factors, desired participation in each plan, age/sex factors, the difference in the cost of each plan, and the relative richness of each plan. The age factors depended on the possibility of participation, given access cost, the richness of the benefits, employee cost, marital status, and age. The underwriting decision in this case included the single-plan decision as a criterion.

Reference [13] developed a knowledge based system (KBS) that combines fuzzy processing with a rule-based expert system in order to provide an improved decision aid for evaluating life insurance risks. Their system used two types of inputs: the base inputs age, weight and height; and incremental inputs, which deal with particular habits and characteristics of prospective clients. The output of their system was a risk factor used to develop the premium surcharge.

$0.3 \leq W < 0.7$ try to improve the condition, if not possible: accept

$0.7 \leq W < 1.0$ accept

One of the advantages that Carreno and Jani identify is the ability of FL to smooth out functions that have jump discontinuities and are broadly defined under traditional methods. By way of example, they investigated risk as a function of age, other characteristics held constant, and replaced a risk function that had jumps at ages 30, 60 and 90, with a FL function where the risk increased smoothly along the entire support.

Another expert opinion-based study was [37], which used a FES to identify Finnish municipalities that were of average size and well managed, but whose insurance coverage was inadequate. The study was prompted by a request from the marketing department of her insurance company.

The steps taken included: identify and classify the economic and insurance factors, have an expert subjectively evaluate each factor, preprocessing the conclusions of the expert, and incorporate this knowledge base into an expert system. The economic factors included population size, gross margin rating (based on funds available for capital expenditures), solidity rating, potential for growth, and whether the municipality was in a crisis situation. The insurance factors were non-life insurance premium written with the company and the claims ratio for three years. Figure 15 shows an example of how Hellman pre-processed the expert's opinion regarding his amount of interest in the non-life insurance premiums written, to construct the associated membership function.

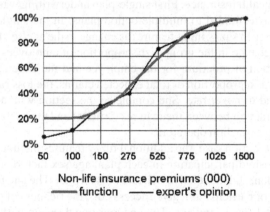

Fig. 15. Preprocessing Expert Opinion

In this instance, two modifications were imposed: first, the piece-wise linear interest function of the expert was replaced with a smooth interest function (equation); and second, a minimum of 20 percent was imposed on the function, in recognition of the advantage gained because the municipality was already a customer. Finally, convex combinations of the interest membership functions became the knowledge base of the FES.

Hellman concluded that the important features of the FESs included that they were easily modified, the smooth functions give continuity to the values, and adding new fuzzy features is easy. Other applications she envisioned included customer evaluation and ratings for bonus-malus tariff premium decisions.

Reference [52] and [53] discussed a two-phase research project to develop a fuzzy-linguistic expert system for quantifying and predicting the risk of occupational injury of the forearm and hand. The first phase of the research focused on the development and representation of linguistic variables to qualify risk levels. These variables were then quantified using FST. The second phase used analytic hierarchy processing (AHP) to assign relative weights to the identified risk factors. Using the linguistic variables obtained in the first part of the research, a fuzzy rule base was constructed with all of the potential combinations for the given factors.

The study was particularly interesting because, unlike studies such as [24] and [25], which rely on unprocessed expert opinion, McCauley-Bell and Badiru use processed expert opinion. The essential difference is that they use concept mapping to capture a detailed representation of the expert's knowledge relative to the problem space as well as an understanding of the relationships between concepts.

Reference [79] described how FL can be used to make pricing decisions in group health insurance that consistently consider supplementary data, including vague or linguistic objectives of the insurer, which are ancillary to statistical experience data. She conceptualized the building of a fuzzy inference rate-making model as involving: a prescriptive phase based on expert opinion, which verbalizes the linguistic rules, creates the fuzzy sets corresponding to the hypotheses, and determines the output values for the conclusions; and a descriptive phase based on past actions of the company, which involves fine-tuning the fuzzy rules, if applicable. By way of a benchmark, she compared the resulting fuzzy models with linear regressions to judge their performance.

Using group health insurance data from an insurance company, an illustrative competitive rate-changing model was built that employed only linguistic constraints to adjust insurance rates. The essence of the type of fuzzy rules considered by Young is depicted in Table 2

Table 2. Fuzzy Rate Change Rules

		Amount of Business		
		Small	Mod	Large
Underwriting	Small	-	NA	NA
Ratio (%)	Mod	NA	0	NA
	Large	NA	NA	+

"NA" implies not applicable for this illustration.

Thus, for example, if the amount of business was small and the underwriting ratio was small (profit was large), the rates were reduced, while the rate was increased if the amount of business was large and the underwriting ratio was large (profit was small). A useful conceptualization of the intersection of these rules, based on the min operator, was provided by Young using contour curves, a simplified representation of which is shown in Fig. 16.

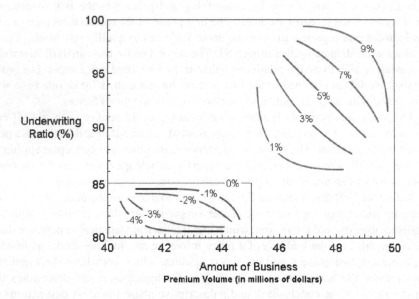

Fig. 16. Contours of Rate Change

In this example, the contours are of rate changes, whose space is [-5%, 10%], which are based on the space of the amount of business, as measured by premium volume, [40M,50M], and the space of the underwriting ratio, [80%, 100%]. The rate changes associated with underwriting ratios and amount of business values outside these limits are bounded by the rate changes at these limits.

Young did not necessarily advocate using such a model without considering experience studies but presented the simplified model to demonstrate more clearly how to represent linguistic rules.

Reference [79] was extended to include claim experience data in [80]. In this later article, Young described step-by-step how an actuary/decision maker could use FL to adjust workers compensation insurance rates. Expanding on her previous article, she walked through the prescriptive and descriptive phases with a focus on targeted adjustments to filed rates and rate departures. In this case, the fuzzy models were fine-tuned by minimizing a weighted sum of squared errors, where the weights reflected the relative amount of business in each state. Young concludes that even though a given FL model may fit only slightly better than a standard linear regression model, the main advantage of FL is that an actuary can begin with verbal rules and create a mathematical model that follows those rules.

A practical application was reported by [38], who applied a FES to the issue of diabetes mellitus in the medical underwriting of life insurance applicants. This was an interesting application because it involved a complex system of mutually interacting factors where neither the prognosticating factors themselves nor their impact on the mortality risk was clear cut. Moreover, it was good example of medical situations where it was easy to reach a consensus among physicians that a disease or a symptom is mild, moderate, or severe, but where a method of quantifying that assessment normally is not available.

In a step-by-step fashion, the authors show how expert knowledge about underwriting diabetes mellitus in life insurance can be processed. Briefly, focusing on the therapy factor, there were three inputs to the system: the blood sugar level, which was represented as very low, low, normal, high, and very high; the blood sugar level over a period of around 90 days, with the same categories; and the insulin injections per week, which had the categories low, medium, high, and very high. The center of gravity (COG) method was used for defussification.

Given the success of the application, the authors concluded that techniques of fuzzy underwriting will become standard tools for underwriters in the future.

Reference [59] developed an evolving rule based expert system for financial forecasting. Their approach was to merge FL and rule induction so as to develop a system with generalization capability and high comprehensibility. In this way the changing market dynamics are continuously taken into account as time progresses and the rulebase does not become outdated. They concluded that their methodology showed promise.

The final review of this section is of a study by [54], which discussed the development of methodological tools for investigating the Belgium health care budget using both global and detailed data. Their model involved four steps: preprocessing the data, segregating the health care channels, validating the channels and data analysis, and calculating the assignment of various categories of the insured to these channels using a multicriteria sorting procedure that was based on t-norms weighted through fuzzy implication operators. The authors concluded that their fuzzy multicriteria sorting procedure could be applied in a more general context and could open new application fields.

6 Fuzzy Clustering

The foregoing fuzzy system allows us to convert and embed empirical qualitative knowledge into reasoning systems capable of performing approximate pattern matching and interpolation. However, these systems cannot adapt or learn because they are unable to extract knowledge from existing data. One approach for overcoming this limitation is to use fuzzy clustering. The essence of fuzzy clustering is that it produces reasonable centers for clusters of data, in the sense that the centers capture the essential feature of the cluster, and then groups data vectors around cluster centers that are reasonably close to them.

The fuzzy c-means algorithm ([6]) is a fuzzy clustering method referred to by a number of studies mentioned in this review.[20] A flowchart of the algorithm is depicted in Fig. 17:

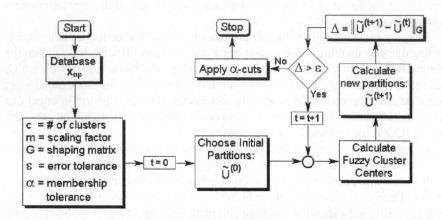

Fig. 17. Flowchart of c-Means Algorithm

As indicated, the database consists of the $n \times p$ matrix, x_{np}, where n indicates the number of patterns and p denotes the number of features. The algorithm seeks to segregate these n patterns into c, $2 \le c \le n - 1$, clusters, where the within clusters variances are minimized and the between clusters variances are maximized. To this end, the algorithm is initialized by resetting the counter, t, to zero, and choosing: c, the number of clusters; m, the exponential weight, which acts to reduce the influence of noise in the data because it limits the influence of small values of membership functions; G, a symmetric, positive-definite (all its principal minors have strictly positive determinants), $p \times p$ shaping matrix, which represents the relative importance of the elements of the data set and the correlation between them, examples of which are the identity and covariance matrixes; ϵ, the tolerance, which controls the stopping rule; and α, the membership tolerance, which defines the relevant portion of the membership functions.

Given the database and the initialized values, the counter, t, is set to zero. The next step is to choose the initial partition (membership matrix), $\tilde{U}^{(0)}$, which may be based on a best guess or experience. Next, the fuzzy cluster centers are computed, which, in effect, are elements that capture the essential feature of the cluster. Using these fuzzy cluster centers, a new (updated) partition, $\tilde{U}^{(t+1)}$, is calculated. The partitions are compared using the matrix norm $\left\| \tilde{U}^{(t+1)} - \tilde{U}^{(t)} \right\|_G$ and if the difference exceeds ϵ, the counter, t, is increased and the process continues. If the difference

---

[20] Although the c-means algorithm was implemented by a number of studies mentioned in this review, not all authors advocate the method. Reference [76], for example, found that the c-means clustering model produced inferior results.

does not exceed ϵ, the process stops. As part of this final step, α-cuts are applied to clarify the results and make interpretation easier, that is, all membership function values less than α are set to zero and the function is renormalized.

6.1 Applications

This subsection presents an overview of insurance applications of the c-means algorithm. The application areas include: an alternate tool for estimating credibility; risk classification in both life and non-life insurance; and age groupings in general insurance.

Reference [57] explored the use of fuzzy clustering methods as an alternate tool for estimating credibility. Given $\{x_{ij}, i = 1, \ldots, n, j = 1, \ldots, p\}$, a data set representing historical loss experience, and $\underline{y} = \{y_j, j = 1, \ldots, p\}$, a data set representing the recent experience (risk characteristics and loss features), the essential idea is that one can use a clustering algorithm to assign the recent experience to fuzzy clusters in the data. Thus, if μ is the maximum membership degree of $\underline{y}$ in a cluster, $Z = 1 - \mu$ could be used as the credibility measure of the experience provided by $\underline{y}$, while μ gives the membership degree for the historical experience indicated by the cluster.

As an example they consider an insurer with historical experience in three large geographical areas extending its business to a fourth large area. The insurer can cluster new data from this fourth area into patterns from the other areas, and thereby derive a credibility rating for its loss experience in the new market. Using the c-means algorithm, the means and standard deviations as features, and two partitions ($c = 2$), they arrived at the credibility factor for the data of the fourth area.

Reference [56, Chap. 6] observed that lack of actuarially fair classification is economically equivalent to price discrimination in favor of high risk individuals and suggested "... a possible precaution against [discrimination] is to create classification methods with no assumptions, but rather methods which discover patterns used in classification." To his end, he was among the first to suggest the use of the c-means algorithm for classification in an insurance context.

By way of introducing the topic to actuaries, he discussed an insightful example involving the classification of four prospective insureds, two males and two females, into two clusters, based on the features height, gender, weight, and resting pulse. [21] The two initial clusters were on the basis of gender. In a step-by-step fashion through three iterations, Ostaszewski developed a more efficient classification based on all the features.

Reference [24] and [25] extended the work of [56, Chap. 6] by showing how the c-means clustering algorithm could provide an alternative way to view risk and claims classification. Their focus was on applying fuzzy clustering to the two problems of grouping towns into auto rating territories and the classification of insurance claims according to their suspected level of fraud. Both studies were based on Massachusetts automobile insurance data.

---

[21] Age also was a factor, but it was irrelevant to the analysis since the applicants were all the same age. Moreover, the other feature values were intentionally exaggerated for illustrative purposes.

The auto rating territories portion of the study involved 350 towns and the 10 Boston rated subdivisions, with the features bodily injury (BI) liability, personal injury protection (PIP), property damage liability (PDL), collision, comprehensive, and a sixth category comprising the five individual coverages combined. The parameters of the c-means algorithm were five coverage partitions ($c = 5$), which was the number of categories in a previous territory assignment grouping, a scaling factor of 2 ($m = 2$), a tolerance of 5 percent ($\epsilon = 0.05$), and an α-cut of 20 percent.

Figure 18[22] shows a representation of the impact of the clustering algorithm when applied to the auto rating territories of a subset of 12 towns ($x - axis$) and five clusters ($y - axis$). The subscripts "I" and "F" denote the initial and final clusters, respectively.

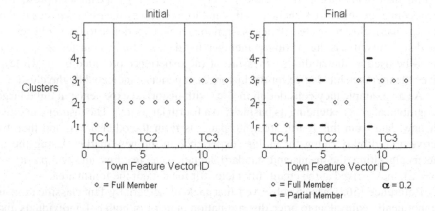

Fig. 18. Town Clustering Using c-Means Algorithm

As indicated, in the left figure, the initial groups are crisp in the sense that the memberships of the territories are unique. In contrast, as a consequence of applying the c-means algorithm, the optimum classification resulted in some towns belonging to more than one cluster (risk class). Similar results were found for the entire database.

Their second study was based on an interesting use of information derived from experts. Beginning with 387 claims and two independent coders, 62 claims that were deemed fraudulent by either coder were identified. Then, starting with 127 claims (the 62 deemed fraudulent plus 65 from remaining 325), experienced claim managers and experienced investigators were each asked to rank each claim on a scale of 0 to 10. Their responses were grouped into the five initial clusters ($c = 5$): none (0), slight (1-3), moderate (4-6), strong (7-9), and certain (10). [23] In this instance, the three features were the adjuster suspicion value, the investigator suspicion value, and a third category labeled the "fraud vote," which was equal to the number of reviewers

---

[22] Adapted from [25, Figures 1 and 2]

[23] This data has been used for a number of studies.

who designated the claim as fraudulent. The results of their analysis supported the hypothesis that adjuster suspicion levels can serve well to screen suspicious claims. The authors concluded that fuzzy clustering is a valuable addition to the methods of risk and claim classification, but they did not conclude that it was the best way.

The last study of this section is by [73], who showed how the fuzzy c-means algorithm could be used to specify a data-based procedure for investigating age groupings in general insurance. Their database included the total cost of claims associated with more than 50,000 motor policies. Starting with the assumption that distortion effects have already been removed and policyholder age was the only significant factor, they focused on the coverages of automobile material damage and bodily injury.

The heuristic nature of their approach was interesting. They pre-processed the data by grouping the low ages and high ages where data was sparse and categorized it by adjusted frequency, computed as the product of the frequency at each age and the average severity. Then, using an ad hoc approach, they settled on six clusters ($c = 6$) and an α-cut of 20 percent, from which the c-means algorithm results led them to the conclude that a first approximation of the appropriate age grouping were those shown in row three of Table 3.

Table 3. Policyholder Age Groupings

	Age Groupings						
Group	1	2	3	4	5	6	7
Risk Cluster	1	2	3	4	3	5	6
Age	-25	26-27	28-31	32-47	48-51	52-68	69-
Relative Risk	406	136	115	90	100	72	61

The relative risk of each group (the last row of the table), coupled with the requirement that sequential ages have similar membership, let them to conclude that group 5 was an anomaly, and groups 4 and 5 likely should be amalgamated.

They concluded that, while other methods can be used, the flexibility of the fuzzy approach makes it most suitable for grouping policyholder age. They noted also that the algorithm could be applied to other explanatory variables and in other types of insurance, such as the classification of vehicles into vehicle rating groups, the grouping of car engine sizes, and the classification of excess mortality risk in life insurance according to blood pressure.

7 Fuzzy Programming

Many of the fuzzy logic studies in insurance involve decision making, and most of these studies rely on the framework established by [3]. The essential notion is that, given a non-fuzzy space of options, X, a fuzzy goal, G, and a fuzzy constraint, C, then G and C combine to form a decision, D, which is a fuzzy set resulting from the intersection of G and C. Assuming the goals and constraints enter into the expression for D in exactly the same way, a simple representation of the relationship between G, C and D is given in Fig. 19.

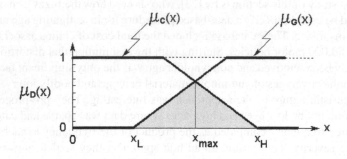

Fig. 19. Decision Making

As indicated, the decision involves the fuzzy intersection of the goal and constraint MFs, and the set of possible options in the interval x_L to x_H. If the optimal decision is the option with the highest degree of membership in the decision set, the crisp solution to this problem would be

$$x^* = \arg[\max_x \min\{\mu_G(x), \mu_C(x)\}]$$

In this section, we focus on the role of fuzzy linear programming (LP) in decision making. Like its crisp counterpart, fuzzy LP might involve finding an x such that ([90]: 289)

$$C = \sum_{ij} c_{ij} x_{ij} \overset{\sim}{\leq} C_0$$

$$z_i = \sum_j a_{ij} x_{ij} \overset{\sim}{\geq} b_i$$

$$x_{ij} \geq 0$$

where C_0 is the aspiration level for the objective function, "~" over a symbol denotes the fuzzy version of that symbol, and the coefficients a_{ij}, b_i, and c_{ij} are not necessarily crisp numbers.

This fuzzy LP problem can be resolved by reformulating it as a crisp LP problem. The essence of one approach[24] to doing this is depicted in Fig. 20.

As indicated, z_i is a fuzzy number, whose membership function is zero for $z_i \leq b_i - \lambda_i$, one for $z_i \geq bi$, and linearly increasing in the interval. Zimmermann refers to λ as a tolerance interval. Using an α-cut to provide a minimum acceptable satisfaction level, that is, $\mu(z_i) \geq \alpha$ is an acceptable constraint, we see from the diagram that an equivalent constraint is $z_i \geq b_i - \lambda_i + \lambda_i \alpha$. Similarly, $C \leq C_0 + \lambda - \lambda \alpha$.

---

[24] Adapted from [9, pp. 34-38]

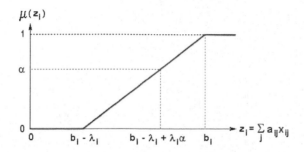

Fig. 20. Equivalent Crisp Constraint

Thus, given the values of λ, the equivalent crisp programming problem becomes one of maximizing α subject to the equivalent constraints, that is:

$$Maximize: \alpha$$
$$Subject\,to: z_i - \lambda_i\alpha \geq b_i - \lambda_i;$$
$$C + \lambda\alpha \leq C_o + \lambda; and$$
$$0 \leq \alpha \leq 1$$

7.1 Applications

A number of the foregoing articles used decision making, but, since they have already been reviewed, they will not be revisited here. Instead, we focus on three articles that explicitly incorporate linear programming. The topics addressed include optimal asset allocation, insurance pricing, and immunization theory and the matching of assets and liabilities.

Reference [36] used a possibilistic linear programming method for optimal asset allocation based on simultaneously maximizing the portfolio return, minimizing the portfolio risk and maximizing the possibility of reaching higher returns. This was analogous to maximizing mean return, minimizing variance and maximizing skewness for a random rate of return.

The authors conceptualize the possibility distribution $(\pi_{\tilde{r}_i})$ of the imprecise rate of return of the $i - th$ asset of the portfolio as shown in Fig. 21(a), where $\tilde{r}_i = (r_i^p, r_i^m, r_i^o)$ and r_i^p, r_i^m, r_i^o are the most pessimistic value, the most possible value, and the most optimistic value for the rate of return, respectively.

Then, as depicted in Fig. 21(b), taking the weighted averages of these values, they defined the imprecise rate of return for the entire portfolio as $\tilde{r} = (r^P, r^m, r^o)$, the portfolio risk as $(r^m - r^P)$, and the portfolio skewness as $(r^o - r^m)$. The authors then showed in a step-by-step fashion how the portfolio could be optimized using [86] fuzzy programming method. They concluded that their algorithm provides maximal flexibility for decision makers to effectively balance the portfolio's return and risk.

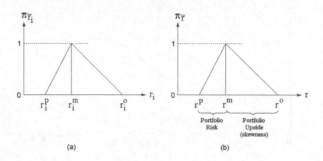

Fig. 21. Possibility Distribution of Portfolio Return

Reference [16] investigated the use of fuzzy mathematical programming for insurance pricing decisions with respect to a bonus-malus rating system[25] in automobile insurance. They used the max-min operator and followed Zimmermann's approach ([87], [88]), which led to an optimal solution of the form:

$$\mu_D(x^*) = \max_x \{m\underset{x}{in}\{\mu_O(x), \mu_{R_i}(x)\}\}, i = 1, ..., k \qquad (9)$$

where μ_D, μ_O, and μ_R denote the membership function for the fuzzy set "decision D," the fuzzy objective function, and the fuzzy constraints, respectively. Their assumed objective was "attractive income from premiums" while the constraints involved the spread of policies among the risk classes, the weighted sum of the absolute variation of the insured's premium, and the deviation from perfect elasticity of the policyholder's payments with respect to their claim frequency. The system was tested on a large database of third-party personal liability claims of a Spanish insurer and they concluded that their fuzzy linear programming approach avoids unrealistic modeling and may reduce information costs. Reference [15] provides further commentary on the approach.

Finally, [17] developed fuzzy mathematical analogues of the classical immunization theory and the matching of assets and liabilities. Essentially, he reformulated concepts about immunization and the matching of assets and liabilities into fuzzy mathematics, and then expressed the objective in terms of a fuzzy linear programming problem. He concluded that his approach offers the advantages of flexibility, improved conformity with situations encountered in practice and the extension of solutions.

8 Fuzzy Regression

Two general approaches have been used to develop fuzzy regression models. The earlier approach, the possibilistic model of [71], took the general form

---

[25] A bonus-malus rating system rewards claim-free policyholders by awarding them bonuses or discounts and penalizes policyholders responsible for accidents by assessing them maluses or premium surcharges.

$$\tilde{Y} = \tilde{A}_0 + \tilde{A}_1 x_1 + \cdots + \tilde{A}_n x_n \tag{10}$$

where $\tilde{Y}$ is the fuzzy output, $\tilde{A}_j$, $j = 1, 2, ..., n$, is a fuzzy coefficient, and $\mathbf{x} = (x_1, ..., x_n)$ is an n-dimensional non-fuzzy input vector. The fuzzy components were assumed to be triangular fuzzy numbers (TFNs). The methodology was to minimize the fuzziness of the model by minimizing the total spreads of its fuzzy coefficients, subject to including the data points of each sample within a specified feasible data interval.

The second approach, the least-squares model of [30], used distance measures to minimize the distance between the output of the model and the observed output. Essentially, he defined an L^2-metric $d(.,.)^2$ between two TFNs by [30, p. 143, Eq. (2)].

$$d\left(\langle m_1, l_1, r_1 \rangle, \langle m_2, l_2, r_2 \rangle\right)^2 = $$
$$(m_1 - m_2)^2 + \left((m_1 - l_1) - (m_2 - l_2)\right)^2 + \left((m_1 + r_1) - (m_2 + r_2)\right)^2 \tag{11}$$

As indicated, it measures the distance between two fuzzy numbers based on their modes, left spreads and right spreads.

8.1 Applications

This subsection presents an overview of some insurance applications involving fuzzy regression. The applications include life insurance sales as a function of price changes, the modeling of the term structure of interest rates, and a fuzzy formulation of a mortality forcasting model.

Reference [47], in a study of life insurance sales as a response to price changes, sketched out the essence of a fuzzy regression model applied to the S-shaped response curve

$$S_i = \sigma_i P_i^{e_i} \prod_{j=1}^{n} P_j^{e_{ij}} f(i) \tag{12}$$

where S_i is the sales response, P_i is the price of the i-th product, σ_i is a scaling coefficient, e_i and e_{ij} are direct and cross elasticities, respectively, and $f(i)$ accounts for factors such as advertising expenses and number of insurance agents. Their model incorporated the possibility measure and its counterpart, the necessity measure, and they focused on the case where no sample data is available, such as the new market economies of the former socialist countries. Unfortunately, the authors gave no detail about the application.

Reference [53] developed a fuzzy linear regression model to predict the relationship of known risk factors to the onset of occupational injury. Following [71], their model was constructed using four fuzzy sub-modules to represent the risk associated with task, anthropometrics, joint deviation, and personal factors. These modules were combined to produce an overall risk level and a final risk prediction model. The results indicate that fuzzy linear regression is a useful technique for addressing the uncertainty associated with the definition and modeling of occupational injury risk factors.

Reference [61] used possibilistic regression to analyze the Term Structure of Interest Rates (TSIR). Key components of their methodology included constructing a discount function from a linear combination of quadratic splines, the coefficients of which were assumed to be STFNs, and using the minimum and maximum negotiated price of fixed income assets to obtain the spreads of the dependent variable observations. Given the fuzzy discount functions, the authors provide TFN approximations for the spot rates and forward rates,[26] and then go on to show how to use the discount functions to obtain the net single premiums for some basic life insurance contracts.

Reference [61] also used possibilistic regression to estimate incurred claims that have not yet been reported to the insurer, IBNR claims. Their used a common claims run-off model, but instead of OLS, they used the fuzzy linear relation

$$\tilde{Z}_{i+1,j} = \tilde{b}_i + \tilde{c}_i Z_{i,j} \tag{13}$$

where $Z_{i,j}$ is the accumulated incurred losses of accident year j at the end of development year i and $\tilde{b}_i$ and $\tilde{c}_i$ are STFNs. $\tilde{Z}_{n,j}$ is not a STFN because it is obtained by iteration, but the authors give a reasonable STFN approximation of it. The final phase of their model provides a FN for the IBNR reserve for the $j - th$ year of occurrence, which is summed to produce the whole IBNR reserve.

The last study in this subsection is from [46], who used fuzzy regression to formulate the Lee-Carter (LC) model for mortality forecasting. The LC fuzzy-equation is interpreted as

$$\tilde{Y}_{x,t} = \ln(m_{x,t}) = \tilde{A}_x + \tilde{B}_x \tilde{K}_t + \tilde{\varepsilon}_{x,t} \tag{14}$$

where $x = x_1, ..., x_p$, $t = t_1, t_1 + 1, ..., t_1 + T - 1$, $\tilde{Y}_{x,t}$ is the known (fuzzy or non-fuzzy) log-central death rates and $\tilde{A}$, $\tilde{B}$, $\tilde{K}$ and $\tilde{\varepsilon}$ are unknown fuzzy parameters. The Tanaka et al. ([71]) approach is used to develop the spreads, the weakest (drastic) t-norm is used for shape-preserving under multiplication, and Diamond's least-squares model was used to optimize the regression. An advantage of the fuzzy approach is that the errors are viewed as fuzziness of the model structure, so that homoscedasticity is not an issue. The authors reported that this fuzzy formulation of the LC model leads to good fits of death rates and life expectancies at birth.

9 Soft Computing

Most of the previously discussed studies focused on FL to the exclusion of other technologies. While their approach has been productive, it may have been sub-optimal,

---

[26] Since the spot rates and forward rates are nonlinear functions of the discount function, they are not TFNs even though the discount function is a TFN.

in the sense that studies may have been constrained by the limitations of FL, and opportunities may have been missed to take advantage of potential synergies afforded by other technologies.

This notion was embodied in the concept of soft computing (SC), which was introduced by [84].[27] He envisioned SC as being "concerned with modes of computing in which precision is traded for tractability, robustness and ease of implementation." For the most part, SC encompasses the technologies of fuzzy logic, genetic algorithms (GAs), and neural networks (NNs), and it has emerged as an effective tool for dealing with control, modelling, and decision problems in complex systems.[28] In this context, FL is used to deal with imprecision and uncertainty, GAs are used for search and optimization, and NNs are used for learning and curve fitting. In spite of these dichotomies, there are natural synergies between these technologies, the technical aspects of which are discussed in [64].

9.1 Applications

This section provides a brief overview of a few representative insurance-related articles that have merged FL with either GAs or NNs. The application area considered is classification and involves four representative SC articles in insurance, two on the property-casualty side and two on the life-health side.[29]

Our first example of a SC approach is the study of [77], which proposed it as an auto insurance claim processing system for Korea. In Korea, given personal and/or property damage in a car accident, the compensation rate depends on comparative negligence, which is assigned using responsibility rates. The authors first describe the expert knowledge structure and the claims processing system. They then explain in general terms how they determined the responsibility rate, and hence the compensation rate, using a fuzzy database, a rule based system, and a feed-forward NN learning mechanism, and the problems associated with implementing their system.

Reference [21] reported on a SC-based fraud and abuse detection system for managed healthcare. The essence of the system was that it detected "anomalous"

---

[27] There are a number of ways that hybrid models could be defined. One approach would be to focus on all adaptive techniques, including such things as chaos theory and fractal analysis. Another approach could be that taken by [75, pp. 75-81], who defined hybrid models as fuzzy techniques in combination with other deterministic and statistical methods. In this article we concentrate on the SC technologies.

[28] While FL, NNs, and GAs are only a subset of the soft computing technologies, they are regarded as the three principal components ([67, p. 406]).

[29] By far, the greatest number of SC articles involving fuzzy systems in insurance-related areas is associated with investment models. See [65] for a review of capital market applications of SC. However, while these studies have implications in the insurance area, they generally are directed at other financial intermediaries, so they have not been included in the text of this article. A flavor for the types of analysis that have been done are found in [1], who investigated hybridized SC techniques for automated stock market forecasting and trend analysis, and [48], who developed a GA-based fuzzy NN (GFNN) to formulate the knowledge base of fuzzy inference rules, which can measure the qualitative effect (such as the political effect) in the stock market.

behavior by comparing an individual medical provider to a peer group. The preparation of the system involved three steps: identify the proper peer population, identify behavior patterns, and analyze behavior pattern properties. The peer population was envisioned as a three-dimensional space composed of organization type, geographic region, and organization size.

The behavior patterns were developed using the experience of a fraud-detection department, an unsupervised NN that learnt the relationships inherent in the claim data, and a supervised approach that automatically generate a fuzzy model from a knowledge of the decision variables. Finally, the behavior pattern properties were analyzed using the statistical measures mean, variance, standard deviation, mean absolute deviation, Kolmogorov-Smirnov (KS) test, skewness, and kurtosis.

The discovery properties of the fuzzy model were based on three static and one time varying criteria metrics. The static metrics were the insurer's exposure to fraudulent behavior, as measured by total claim dollars, the degree of variance from the center of the peer population for each behavior pattern, which was referred to as the population compatibility number, and the number of behaviors that are significantly at variance. The time varying metric was the change in the behavior population dynamics over time. Given the prepared system and the discovery properties, the distribution of data points for the behavior patterns of any individual provider within this population could be computed and compared with all the providers of a similar type, a similar organization size, and within the same geographic area. Thus, the fuzzy system-based fraud and abuse detection system identifies a provider that has significant variance from the peer population.

Cox concluded that the system was capable of detecting anomalous behaviors equal to or better than the best fraud-detection departments.

Reference [58] used GA-constructed FISs to automatically produce diagnostic systems for breast cancer diagnosis. The Pittsburgh-style[30] of GAs was used to generate the database and rulebase for the FISs, based on a data furnished by specialists, which contained 444 benign cases and 239 malignant cases, which had been evaluated based on 9 features. They claimed to have obtained the best classification performance to date for breast cancer diagnosis and, because their final systems involve just a few simple rules, high human-interpretability.

Reference [4] used an evolutionary-fuzzy approach to investigate suspicious home insurance claims, where genetic programming was employed to evolve FL rules that classified claims into "suspicious" and "non-suspicious" classes. Notable features of his methodology were that it used clustering to develop membership functions and committee decisions to identify the best-evolved rules. With respect to the former, the features of the claims were clustered into low, medium, and high groups, and the minimum and maximum value in each cluster was used to define the domains of the membership functions. The committee decisions were based on different versions of the system that were run in parallel on the same data set and weighted for intelligibility, which was defined as inversely proportional to the number of rules,

---

[30] Every individual in the GA is encoded as a string with variable length.

and accuracy. Bentley reported that the results of his model when applied to actual data agreed with the results of previous analysis.

10 Conclusions

The purpose of this article has been to provide an overview of insurance applications of FL. As we have seen, many of the FL techniques have been applied in the insurance area, including fuzzy set theory, fuzzy arithmetic, fuzzy inference systems, fuzzy clustering, fuzzy programming, and fuzzy regression. By the same token, FL has been applied in many insurance areas including classification, underwriting, projected liabilities, fuzzy future and present values, pricing, asset allocation, cash flows, and investments.

The overviews verify that FL has been successfully implemented in insurance. Given this success, and the fact that there are many more insurance problems that could be resolved using fuzzy systems, we are likely to see a number of new applications emerge. There are at least two catalysts for this. One is that the industry should now have a greater appreciation of potential areas of application, specifically those areas that are characterized by qualitative conditions for which a mathematical model is needed that reflects those conditions. The second is that, while fuzzy systems have made inroads into many facets of the business, in most instances the applications did not capitalized on the synergies between the SC technologies and, as a consequence, there are opportunities to extend the studies. These things considered, FL applications in insurance and related areas should be a fruitful area for exploration for the foreseeable future.

Acknowledgements

This work was supported in part by the Robert G. Schwartz Faculty Fellowship and the Smeal Research Grants Program at the Penn State University. The assistance of Asheesh Choudhary, Bharath Nemali, Laura E. Campbell and Michelle L. Fultz is gratefully acknowledged.

References

1. Abraham A, Nath B , Mahanti PK (2001) Hybrid intelligent systems for stock market analysis. In: Alexandrov VN, Dongarra JJ, Juliano BA, Renner RS (eds) Computational science. Springer-Verlag Germany, San Francisco, USA:337–345
2. Babad YM, Berliner B (1995) Reduction of uncertainty through actualization of intervals of possibilities and its applications to reinsurance. 25th TICA 2:23–35
3. Bellman R, Zadeh LA (1970) Decision-making in a fuzzy environment. Management Science 17:141–164

4. Bentley PJ (2000) "Evolutionary, my dear Watson" Investigating committee-based evolution of fuzzy rules for the detection of suspicious insurance claims. In: Whitley D, Goldberg D, Cantu-Paz E, Spector L, Parmee I, Beyer HG (eds) Proceedings of the second genetic and evolutionary computation conference:702–709
5. Berkan RC, Trubatch SL (1997) Fuzzy systems design principles: building fuzzy if-then rule bases. Wiley-IEEE Press.
6. Bezdek JC (1981) Pattern recognition with fuzzy objective function algorithms. New York, Plenum Press.
7. Boissonnade AC (1984) Earthquake damage and insurance risk. Ph.D. Dissertation, Stanford University.
8. Bouet G, Dalaud R (1996) Extension de Concepts Financiers en Calcul Flou et Application à l' Adossement de Flux. 6th AFIR, Vol. 2:827–843
9. Brockett PL, Xia X (1995) Operations research in insurance: a review. Transactions of Society of Actuaries 47:7–87
10. Buckley JJ (1987) The fuzzy mathematics of finance. Fuzzy Sets and Systems 21:257–273
11. Buehlmann N, Berliner B (1992) Fuzzy zooming of cash flows. 24th TICA 6:437–453
12. Calzi ML (1990) Towards a general setting for the fuzzy mathematics of finance. Fuzzy Sets and Systems 35:265–280
13. Carreno LA, Jani Y (1993) A fuzzy expert system approach to insurance risk assessment using FuzzyCLIPS. WESCON Conference Record:536-541
14. Carretero RC (2000) New approaches for designing a Bonus-Malus system. 2000 IME Congress, Barcelona, Spain
15. Carretero RC (2003) Fuzzy logic techniques in the non-life insurance industry. In: Shapiro AF, Jain LC (eds) Intelligent and other computational techniques in insurance: theory and applications. World Scientific Publishing Company:229–257
16. Carretero RC, Viejo AS (2000) A Bonus-Malus system in the fuzzy set theory [insurance pricing decisions]. IEEE international conference on fuzzy systems 2:1033–1036
17. Chang C (2003) A fuzzy set theoretical approach to asset and liability management and decision making. In: Shapiro AF, Jain LC (eds) Intelligent and other computational techniques in insurance: theory and applications. World Scientific Publishing Company:301–333
18. Chang C, Wang P (1995) The matching of assets and liabilities with fuzzy mathematics. 25th International Congress of Actuaries, 123
19. Chen JJG, He Z (1997) Using analytic hierarchy process and fuzzy set theory to rate and rank the disability. Fuzzy Sets and Systems 88:1–22
20. Chorafas DN (1994) Chaos theory in the financial markets: applying fractals, fuzzy logic, genetic algorithms. Probus Publishing Company, Chicago
21. Cox E (1995) A fuzzy system for detecting anomalous behaviors in healthcare provider claims. In: Goonatilake S, Treleven P (eds) Intelligent systems for finance and business. John Wiley & Sons:111–135
22. Cummins JD, Derrig RA (1993) Fuzzy trends in property-liability insurance claim costs. Journal of Risk and Insurance 60:429–465
23. Cummins JD, Derrig RA (1997) Fuzzy financial pricing of property-liability insurance. North American Actuarial Journal 1(4):21
24. Derrig RA, Ostaszewski KM (1994) Fuzzy techniques of pattern recognition in risk and claim classification. 4th AFIR International Colloquium 1:141–171
25. Derrig RA, Ostaszewski KM (1995a) Fuzzy techniques of pattern recognition in risk and claim classification. Journal of Risk and Insurance 62:447–482

26. Derrig RA, Ostaszewski KM (1995b) The fuzzy problem of hedging the tax liability of a property - liability insurance company. 5th AFIR International Colloquium 1:17–42
27. Derrig RA, Ostaszewski KM (1997) Managing the tax liability of a property-liability insurance company. Journal of Risk and Insurance 64:694
28. Derrig RA, Ostaszewski KM (1999) Fuzzy sets methodologies in actuarial science. In: Zimmerman HJ (ed) Practical applications of fuzzy technologies. Kluwer Academic Publishers, Boston
29. DeWit GW (1982) Underwriting and Uncertainty. Insurance: Mathematics and Economics 1:277–285
30. Diamond P (1988) Fuzzy least squares. Information Sciences 46(3):141–157
31. Dubois DJ (1980) Fuzzy sets and systems: theory and applications. Academic Press, San Diego, CA
32. DuBois D, Prade H (1997) Fuzzy sets and systems: theory and applications. Academic Press, San Diego, CA
33. Ebanks B, Kanvowski W, Ostaszewski KM (1992) Application of measures of fuzziness to risk classification in insurance. In: Proceedings of the fourth international conference on computing and information: computing and information. IEEE Computer Society Press, Los Alamitos, California:290–291
34. Erbach DW, Seah E (1993) Discussion of "The Application of Fuzzy Sets to Group Health Underwriting" by Young VR. Transactions of the Society of Actuaries 45:585
35. Frees EW, Valdez EA (1998) Understanding relationships using copulas. NAAJ 2(1):1–25
36. Guo L, Huang Z (1996) A possibilistic linear programming method for asset allocation. Journal of Actuarial Practice 2:67–90
37. Hellman A (1995) A fuzzy expert system for evaluation of municipalities - an application. 25h TICA 1:159–187
38. Horgby P, Lohse R, Sittaro N (1997) Fuzzy underwriting: an application of fuzzy logic to medical underwriting. Journal of Actuarial Practice 5(1):79
39. Hosler VR (1992) The application of fuzzy sets to group health underwriting. ARCH 2:1–63
40. Jang JSR, Sun CT, Mizutani E (1997) Neuro-fuzzy and soft computing: a computational approach to learning and machine intelligence. Prentice Hall, Upper Saddle River, NJ.
41. Jablonowski M (1996) A new perspective on risk. Chartered Property and Casualty Underwriters Journal 49(4):225–236
42. Jablonowski M (1997) Modeling imperfect knowledge in risk management and insurance. Risk Management and Insurance Review 1(1):98
43. Joseph EC (1982) Future expert computer systems for actuarial professionals. ARCH 1982.1:1-9
44. Kieselbach R (1997) Systematic failure analysis using fault tree and fuzzy logic. Technology, Law and Insurance 2:13–20
45. Klir GJ, Yuan B (1996) Fuzzy sets, fuzzy logic, and fuzzy systems: selected papers by Lotfi A. Zadeh. World Scientific, New Jersey.
46. Koissi MC, Shapiro AF (2006) Fuzzy formulation of the Lee-Carter model for mortality forecasting. Insurance Mathematics and Economics 39(3):287–309
47. Krasteva EB, Singh MG, Sotirov GR, Bennavail JC, Mincoff NC (1994) Model building for pricing decision making in an uncertain environment. Systems, Man, and Cybernetics, 1994. Humans, Information and Technology, 1994 IEEE International Conference on Volume 1:194–199

48. Kuo RJ, Chen CH, Hwang YC (2001) An intelligent stock trading decision support system through integration of genetic algorithm based fuzzy neural network and artificial neural network. Fuzzy Sets and Systems 118(1):21–45
49. Lemaire J (1990) Fuzzy insurance. ASTIN Bulletin 20(1):33–55
50. Lu Y, Zhang L, Guan Z, Shang H (2001) Fuzzy mathematics applied to insurance game. IFSA World Congress and 20th NAFIPS International Conference, Vol.2:941–945
51. Manton KG, Woodbury MA, Tolley HD (1994) Statistical applications using fuzzy sets. Joh. Wiley & sons, Inc.
52. McCauley-Bell PR, Badiru A (1996) Fuzzy modelling and analytic hierarchy processing to quantify risk levels associated with occupational injuries. Part I and II. IEEE Transactions on Fuzzy Systems 4:124–138
53. McCauley-Bell PR, Crumpton LL, Wang H (1999) Measurement of cumulative trauma disorder risk in clerical tasks using fuzzy linear regression. IEEE Transactions on Systems, Man, and Cybernetics-Part C: Applications and Reviews 29(1):1–14
54. Mosmans A, Praet JC, Dumont C (2002) A decision support system for the budgeting of the Belgian health care system. European Journal of Operational Research 139(2):449–460
55. Musilek P, Gupta MM(2000) Neural networks and fuzzy systems. In: Sinha NK, Gupta MM (eds) Soft computing and intelligent systems. Academic Press
56. Ostaszewski K (1993) Fuzzy set methods in actuarial science. Society of Actuaries, Schaumburg, IL
57. Ostaszewski K, Karwowski W (1992) An analysis of possible applications of fuzzy set theory to the actuarial credibility theory. In: Proceeding of the annual meeting of the North American fuzzy information processing society, Puerto Vallaria
58. Peña-Reyes CA, Sipper M (1999) A fuzzy-genetic approach to breast cancer diagnosis. Artificial Intelligence in Medicine 17:131–155
59. Romahi Y, Shen Q (2000) Dynamic financial forecasting with automatically induced fuzzy associations. IEEE:493–498
60. Saaty T (1980) The analytic hierarchy process. McGraw-Hill, New York
61. Sánchez J de A, Gómez AT (2003) Applications of fuzzy regression in actuarial analysis. Journal of Risk and Insurance 70(4):665–699
62. Siegel PH, Korvin A de, Omer K (1995) Applications of fuzzy sets and the theory of evidence to accounting. JAI Press, Greenwich, Conn
63. Shapiro AF (2000) A hitchhiker's guide to the techniques of adaptive nonlinear models. Insurance: Mathematics and Economics 26:119–132
64. Shapiro AF (2002) The merging of neural networks, fuzzy logic, and genetic algorithms. Insurance: Mathematics and Economics 31:115–131
65. Shapiro AF (2003) Capital market applications of neural networks, fuzzy logic and genetic algorithms. Proceedings of the 13th international AFIR colloquium, Vol 1:493–514
66. Shapiro AF (2004) Fuzzy logic in insurance. Insurance: Mathematics and Economics 35:399–424
67. Shukla KK (2000) Soft computing paradigms for artificial vision. In: Sinha NK, Gupta MM (eds) Soft computing and intelligent systems: theory and applications. Academic Press, San Diego:405–417
68. Simonelli MR (2001) Fuzziness in valuing financial instruments by certainty equivalents. European Journal of Operational Research 135:296–302
69. Sinha NK, Gupta MM (2000) Soft computing and intelligent systems: theory and applications. Academic Press, San Diego, Cal
70. Smith E, Eloff J (2000) Cognitive fuzzy modeling for enhanced risk assessment in a health care institution. IEEE Intelligent Systems 15(2):69–75

71. Tanaka H, Uejima S, Asai K (1982) Linear regression analysis with fuzzy model. IEEE Transactions on Systems, Man and Cybernetics 12(6):903–907
72. Terceno A, De Andres J, Belvis C, Barbera G (1996) Fuzzy methods incorporated to the study of personal insurances. Neuro-Fuzzy Systems, 1996. AT'96., International Symposium on:187–202
73. Verrall RJ, Yakoubov YH (1999) A fuzzy approach to grouping by policyholder age in general insurance. Journal of Actuarial Practice 7:181–203
74. Yager RR, Ovchinnikov S, Tong RM, Ngugen HT (1987) Fuzzy sets and applications: collected papers of Lotfi A. Zadeh. John Wiley & Sons, New York
75. Yakoubov YH, Haberman S (1998) Review of actuarial applications of fuzzy set theory. Actuarial Research Paper No. 105, Department of Actuarial Science and Statistics, City University, London.
76. Yeo AC, Smith KA, Willis RJ, Brooks M (2001) Clustering technique for risk classification and prediction of claim cost in the automobile insurance industry. International Journal of Intelligent Systems in Accounting, Finance and Management 10:39–50
77. Yoo JH, Kang BH, Choi JU (1994) A hybrid approach to auto-insurance claim processing system. IEEE International Conference on Systems, Man, and Cybernetics 1:537–542
78. Young VR (1993) The application of fuzzy sets to group health underwriting. Transactions of the Society of Actuaries 45:551–590
79. Young VR (1996) Insurance rate changing: a fuzzy logic approach. Journal of Risk and Insurance 63:461–483
80. Young VR (1997) Adjusting indicated insurance rates: fuzzy rules that consider both experience and auxiliary data. Proceedings of the casualty actuarial society 84:734
81. Zadeh LA (1965) Fuzzy sets. Information and Control 8:338–353
82. Zadeh LA (1975, 1976) The concept of linguistic variable and its application to approximate reasoning (Parts 1-3). Information Sciences 8:199–249, 301–357, and 9:43–80
83. Zadeh LA (1981) Fuzzy systems theory: a framework for the analysis of humanistic systems. In: Cavallo RE (ed) Recent developments in systems methodology in social science research. Kluwer, Boston:25–41
84. Zadeh LA (1992) Foreword of the proceedings of the second international conference on fuzzy logic and neural networks:xiii-xiv
85. Zadeh LA (2000) Foreword. Dubois D, Prade H (eds) Fundamentals of fuzzy sets, volume 1. Kluwer Academic Publishers
86. Zimmermann HJ (1978) Fuzzy programming and linear programming with several objective functions. Fuzzy Sets and Systems:281–298
87. Zimmermann HJ (1983) Fuzzy mathematical programming. Computers and Operations Research:281–298
88. Zimmermann HJ (1985) Applications of fuzzy set theory to mathematical programming. Information Sciences 36:29–58
89. Zimmermann HJ (1987) Fuzzy sets, decision making and expert systems. Kluwer Academic Publishers, Boston, Massachusetts
90. Zimmermann HJ (1996) Fuzzy set theory and its applications. Kluwer Academic Publishers, Boston, Massachusetts

Forecasting Agricultural Commodity Prices using Hybrid Neural Networks

Tamer Shahwan[1] and Martin Odening[2]

[1] Humboldt-Universitat zu Berlin, School of Business and Economics
Institute of Banking, Stock Exchanges and Insurance, D-10178 Berlin, Germany
and Faculty of Agriculture and Horticulture, Department of Agricultural Economics and
Social Sciences, D-10099 Berlin, Germany
shahwan74@hotmail.com
[2] Humboldt-Universitat zu Berlin, Faculty of Agriculture and Horticulture
Department of Agricultural Economics and Social Sciences, D-10099 Berlin, Germany
m.odening@agrar.hu-berlin.de

Traditionally, autoregressive integrated moving average (ARIMA) models have been one of the most widely used linear models in time series forecasting. However, ARIMA models can not easily capture nonlinear patterns. In the last two decades artificial neural networks (ANNs) have been proposed as an alternative to traditional linear models, particularly in the presence of nonlinear data patterns. Recent research suggests that a hybrid approach combining both ARIMA models and ANNs can lead to further improvements in the forecasting accuracy compared with pure models. In this paper, a hybrid model that combines a seasonal ARIMA model and an Elman neural network (ENN) is used to forecast agricultural commodity prices. Different approaches for specifying the ANNs are investigated among others, and a genetic algorithm (GA) is employed to determine the optimal architecture of the ANNs. It turns out that the out-of-sample prediction can be improved slightly with the hybrid model.

Key words: Time Series Forecasting, ARIMA, Elman Neural Network, Genetic Algorithms, Hybrid System, Commodity Prices

1 Introduction

Time series analysis is an important approach to forecasting in which past observations of the same variable are collected and analyzed to develop a model describing the underlying data generating process. Much effort has been devoted over the past decades to the development of time series forecasting models. One of the most important and widely used time series models is the autoregressive integrated moving average (ARIMA) model, which serves as a benchmark model for creating linear models because of its theoretical elaborateness and accuracy in short term forecasting ([7]).

Recently, artificial neural networks (ANNs) have been proposed as an alternative forecasting technique. Reference [23] summarizes the different applications of neural networks for forecasting. There are a number of studies in which neural networks are used to address financial economic problems. For instance, [8] provides a general introduction as to how to model financial and economic time series using ANNs. Reference [19] uses backpropagation neural networks for forecasting the option prices of Nikkei 225 index futures. For predicting agricultural commodity prices, there are also a few articles using artificial neural networks. For instance, [10] uses backpropagation networks to model monthly live cattle and wheat prices and compare the results with those obtained by ARIMA models. They conclude that neural networks perform better in terms of mean absolute error (MAE). Moreover, neural networks are also better at capturing turning points. Reference [16] compares two methods for estimating a reduced form model of fresh tomato marketing margins: an econometric and an artificial neural network approach. The neural network is able to forecast with approximately half the mean square error of the econometric model, but both are equally adept at predicting turning points in the time series.

In this paper, we will investigate the ability of a hybrid approach combining ARIMA and evolutionary Elman neural network models to time series forecasting against each stand-alone model. The motivation behind this approach is largely due to the fact that a real-world problem is often complex in nature and any individual model may not be able to capture different patterns equally well ([22]).

The use of different hybrid models could be complementary in capturing patterns of data sets and could improve the forecasting accuracy. The literature on hybrid models has expanded rapidly since the early work of [2]. Reference [4] provides a comprehensive review and annotated bibliography in this area. Reference [17] describes a combining methodology using radial basis function networks and Box-Jenkins models. Reference [12] offers a good guideline for combined forecasting. Reference [15] proposes a hybrid evolutionary neural approach for binary classification. Reference [22] combines the ARIMA and feedforward neural networks models in forecasting. Reference [14] combines ARIMA and support vector machines models in stock price forecasting. The current study will examine the forecasting accuracy of a hybrid model of both ARIMA and ENN to forecast agricultural commodity prices.

2 A Hybrid Forecast Model and Its Components

2.1 Box-Jenkins Model

The familiar Box-Jenkins approach combines two types of processes: autoregressive (AR) and moving average (MA) processes. Furthermore, the regular and seasonal components of a time series can be captured by a general multiplicative ARIMA model. This model has the following form ([13]):

$$\phi_p(B)\Phi_P(B^s)(1-B)^d(1-B^s)^D y_t = \theta_q(B)\Theta_Q(B^S)a_t \qquad (1)$$

where a_t is a white noise series, p and q are non negative integers, and B is the back shift operator with $B(y_t) = y_{t-1}$ where y_t denotes the monthly prices. B^s is the seasonal back shift operator, and $\Phi_P(B^s) = (1 - \phi_{1s}B^s - \phi_{2s}B^{2s} - ... - \phi_{ps}B^{ps})$ is the seasonal auto-regressive process. $\Theta_Q(B^s) = (1 - \Theta_s B^s - \Theta 2s B^{2s} - ... - \Theta_{Qs}B^{Qs})$ is the seasonal moving average process. In general, s equals 4 or 12. P, D, Q have values of 0, 1 or 2. A useful notation to describe the order of the various components in this multiplicative model is given by $(p, d, q) \times (P, D, Q)^s$ where P is the seasonal level of the auto-regressions, D is the seasonal level of differences and Q is the seasonal level of moving averages.

Basically, the application of ARIMA models consists of three phases: model identification, parameter estimation and diagnostic checking. The identification step requires an intensive data analysis where expert judgment must be exercised to interpret the behavior of the autocorrelation function (ACF) and the partial autocorrelation function (PACF). However, any significant nonlinearity limits the application of the ARIMA models. Therefore, a hybrid model that also uses an Elman neural network is proposed to deal with a nonlinear pattern possibly present in the data.

2.2 Elman Neural Networks

The Elman neural network (ENN) is one kind of global feedforward locally recurrent network model proposed by [5]. An ENN can be considered to be an extension of multilayer perceptron (MLP) with an additional input layer (state layer) that receives a feedback copy of the activations from the hidden layer at the previous time step. These context units in the state layer of the Elman network make it sensitive to the history of input data, which is essentially useful in dynamical system modeling ([18]). Fig. 1 depicts the idea of the ENN where the activations in the hidden layer at time $t - 1$ are copied into the context vector as an input in the network at time t ([3]).

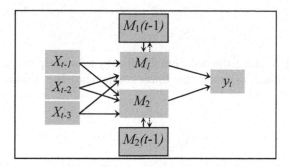

Fig. 1. Elman Neural Network from [11]

An ENN with a "tanh sigmoidal activation function" has the following structure ([11]):

$$n_{k,t} = w_{k,o} + \sum_{i=1}^{i^*} w_{k,i} x_{i,t} + \sum_{k=1}^{k*} \phi_k M_{k,t-1} \tag{2}$$

$$M_{k,t} = \frac{e^{n_{k,t}} - e^{-n_{k,t}}}{e^{n_{k,t}} + e^{-n_{k,t}}} \tag{3}$$

$$y_t = \gamma_0 + \sum_{k=1}^{k^*} \gamma_k M_{k,t} \tag{4}$$

Where the x_i are input variables $(1, 2, ..., i^*)$. k^* is the number of neurons, $w_{k,0}$ is a constant term, the $w_{k,i}$ are the synaptic weights of the input variables, $n_{k,t}$ is a linear combination of these input variables observed at time t, γ_0 is a constant term, γ_k is a coefficient scalar between the hidden and the output layer and the ϕ_k are weights between the context units and hidden units. Hence, the output (y_t) depends not only on the new inputs but also on the preceding context units.

2.3 Hybrid Models

The behavior of commodity prices may not easily be captured by stand-alone models because a time series could include a variety of characteristics such as seasonality, heteroskedasticity or a non-Gaussian error. It is also difficult for a forecaster to determine whether the time series under study is generated from a linear or a nonlinear underlying process ([22]). Therefore, a hybrid model having both linear and nonlinear modeling abilities could be a good alternative for forecasting commodity prices. Following [22] and [21], we assume that S_t is a time series that is composed of a linear part L_t and a nonlinear part N_t:

$$S_t = L_t + N_t \tag{5}$$

Both L_t and N_t are estimated from the data by a two-step procedure. First, we use an ARIMA model to capture the linear component. The residuals e_t from this linear model defined by

$$e_t = S_t - \hat{L}_t \tag{6}$$

can be considered to be an approximation of the nonlinear part N_t, where $\hat{L}_t$ is the estimated value of the ARIMA model at time t. In a second step, the residuals are modeled by an evolutionary Elman neural network, in which the nonlinear pattern in the residuals can be discovered. With m input nodes, these residuals are modeled as follows

$$e_t = f(e_{t-1}, e_{t-2}, e_{t-3}, \cdots, e_{t-m}) + \epsilon_t \qquad (7)$$

where f is a nonlinear function determined by the neural network and ϵ_t is the random error. Finally, the combined forecast is

$$\hat{S}_t = \hat{L}_t + \hat{e}_t \qquad (8)$$

with $\hat{e}_t$ being the forecast of the residual using the ENN.

3 Empirical Analysis

3.1 Data

Two data sets, namely, those of monthly hog prices and canola prices from Germany, are now used to investigate the effectiveness of the proposed hybrid model compared to an ARIMA model and an ENN.[1] We assess the forecasting performance by means of an out-of-sample technique. Each time series is divided into a training set and testing set. The training set is used for model specification and then the testing set is used to evaluate the established model. In order to achieve a good generalization of the ENN, a cross-validation approach is adopted. This means that the training set is further partitioned into two subsets: 80 percent of the training set is assigned to the estimation and the remaining 20 percent is assigned to the validation subset ([6]). Before estimating, the data are normalized to the range between [-1,1]. The decomposition of the two data sets is given in Table 1 below:[2]

Table 1. Sample decomposition

Series	Total sample	Training set	Crossvalidation set	Test set
Hog prices	1972-2003	1972-1999	20% of training set	2000-2003
	(384)	(336)	(67)	(48)
Canola prices	1992-July 2004	1992-2001	20% of training set	2002-July 2004
	(151)	(120)	(24)	(31)

---

[1] The data are obtained from the "Zentrale Markt-und Preisberichtstelle GmbH-Marktberichtstelle" (ZMP), Berlin.

[2] Monthly canola prices include missing data in the following months: July 92, June 93, April 94, May 94, June 94, July 94, July 95, July 96, July 97, July 98, July 2000, July 2002 and July 2003. The interpolation method is used to replace the missing observations.

The prediction performance measurement of the three models is based on one-step-ahead forecasts over the testing set. The mean absolute percentage error (MAPE) and Theils U statistics are employed to measure the forecasting errors:

$$MAPE = \frac{100}{T} \sum |\frac{\hat{y}_t - y_t}{y_t}| \tag{9}$$

$$Theil'sU = \frac{\sqrt{\frac{1}{T} \sum_{t=1}^{T} (\hat{y}_t - y_t)^2}}{\sqrt{\frac{1}{T} \sum_{t=1}^{T} (\hat{y}_t)^2} + \sqrt{\frac{1}{T} \sum_{t=1}^{T} (y_t)^2}} \tag{10}$$

where y_t and $\hat{y}_t$ are the actual and the predicted price, respectively, at time t and T is the number of observations in the testing set. In addition to these measures, we conduct a turning point analysis of the price forecasts. A turning point forecast is predicted correctly if

$$sign(\hat{y}_t - y_{t-1}) = sign(y_t - y_{t-1}) \tag{11}$$

3.2 Specification of the Forecasting Models

The estimated ARIMA model for the hog data has the structure $(2, 0, 0) \times (1, 0, 1)_{12}$. The canola data is fitted best with an autoregressive model (AR) of order 3. Next, we test for the presence of nonlinearities in the data. If the nonlinearities are statistically significant, then choosing a class of nonlinear models such as ANNs might improve the predictive power. In this context, we apply the Ljung-Box Q-statistic to the squared residuals of the two ARIMA models.

Table 2. The Ljung-Box statistics for the squared residuals of an ARMA model

Time series	Q (5)	Q (10)	Q (15)	Q (20)	Q (24)
Hog Prices	36.27	43.97*	51.30*	81.18*	89.53*
Canola Prices	6.10	6.11	6.12	6.12	6.13

∗ denotes statistical significance at the 5 % level

The results in Table 2 show that there is evidence of the presence of GARCH effects (i.e., conditional heteroskedasticity) in the hog prices. No such effect occurs in the canola data. Conditional heteroskedasticity implies that the underlying time series is nonlinear in terms of variance. Reference [1] shows that conditional heteroskedasticity changes the mean square error (MSE) of the predictor. Reference [20] successfully applies multilayer perceptrons (MLPs) to data that reveal conditional heteroskedasticity. In his study, MLPs are proved to be superior to ARIMA-GARCH models. Due to this finding, we conjecture that the ENN will outperform the traditional ARIMA models particularly for the hog price data.

The implementation of the ENNs requires specifying a large number of parameters. In order to specify the ENNs, we apply a mixture of different methods. The selection of the input variables is carried out using two different approaches. First, the inputs are determined heuristically by choosing the autoregressive terms of the ARIMA models that have been specified before. Alternatively, the input nodes are determined by means of a genetic algorithm (GA). The mean square error of the cross-validation set constitutes the fitness function of the GA. Table 3 depicts the optimal input nodes selected by the two approaches. The weight decay method is then used as a pruning technique to reduce the weights and to find a parsimonious structure for the ENN. The number of hidden nodes, the value of the learning rate, the momentum term and the weight decay constant are also genetically optimized. The hyperbolic tangent function is chosen as a transfer function between the input and the hidden layer. The identity transfer function connects the hidden with the output layer. The ENN is trained by backpropagation. Batch updating is chosen as the sequence in which the patterns are presented to the network. As mentioned above, the cross-validation approach is used to determine the optimal number of training epochs. That means the training procedure is terminated as soon as the mean square error of the cross-validation set increases, since this indicates that the network has begun to overtrain. This prevents the ENNs from memorizing unnecessary noise in time series.

To set up the hybrid models, the linear part of the price data is filtered by the afore-mentioned ARIMA models. The residuals of the ARIMA models are then fed into an ENN as explained in Sect. 2.3. The specification of the ENNs in the hybrid models follows the same principles described above.

Theoretical economists might be skeptical regarding our attempt to identify patterns in past price data and to use this structure for forecasting. According to the efficient markets hypothesis, price changes are purely random and cannot be predicted. Based on such a view, futures prices constitute the best forecast for commodity prices in the future. Clearly, the assumptions underlying the efficient markets hypothesis are not completely fulfilled in real world markets. Nevertheless, futures prices (if available) are frequently used by practitioners as cheap forecasts. Hence we resort to futures prices as a further benchmark for our statistical models. The commodities under investigation are traded on the Hanover Commodity Exchange (WTB).[3] In order to obtain one-month-ahead forecasts, we follow [9] and choose the contract with the expiration date nearest to the target month. The price quotation 28 days before expiration is then used as the predictor.

3.3 Results

ARIMA models are estimated using Statgraphics Plus software. The software package NeuroSolutions V4.32 was employed for the estimation of the ENNs. NeuroSolutions also includes a GA to optimize the structure of the ANN. The out-of-sample

---

[3] Unfortunately only the contracts for hogs show a sufficiently large number of expiration dates.

Table 3. Input variables of the ANN according to different specification procedures

	ENN		Hybrid model	
	Hogs	Canola	Hogs	Canola
Input determined by ARIMA	Y_{t-1}	Y_{t-1}	Y_{t-1}	Y_{t-1}
	Y_{t-2}	Y_{t-2}	Y_{t-2}	Y_{t-2}
	Y_{t-12}	Y_{t-3}	Y_{t-12}	Y_{t-3}
	Y_{t-13}		Y_{t-13}	
	Y_{t-14}		Y_{t-14}	
Input determined by Genetic Algorithm	Y_{t-1}	Y_{t-1}	Y_{t-1}	Y_{t-1}
	Y_{t-2}	Y_{t-2}	Y_{t-2}	Y_{t-2}
	Y_{t-4}	Y_{t-3}	Y_{t-3}	Y_{t-3}
	Y_{t-5}	Y_{t-4}	Y_{t-5}	Y_{t-10}
	Y_{t-6}	Y_{t-5}	Y_{t-8}	Y_{t-14}
	Y_{t-10}	Y_{t-6}	Y_{t-10}	
	Y_{t-12}	Y_{t-8}	Y_{t-13}	
	Y_{t-14}	Y_{t-11}	Y_{t-15}	
	Y_{t-15}	Y_{t-13}	Y_{t-16}	
	Y_{t-18}	Y_{t-17}	Y_{t-18}	
		Y_{t-19}	Y_{t-19}	
		Y_{t-20}		

forecast performances of the ARIMA model, the ENN and the hybrid model for both hog and canola price data are reported in Tables 4 and 5, respectively (see also Figs. 2 and 3 in the Appendix, where both of them depict the best forecasts between different approaches).

The figures in Table 4 indicate that only slight differences in the predictive power of the various methods exist. With regard to the canola price data, no improvement in the forecast accuracy can be achieved by using a (pure) ENN instead of a traditional ARIMA model. The latter is even better than the former. This raises some doubt if the optimal specification of the ENN has been identified for this time series. Surprisingly, the heuristic specification (ENN1) leads to better results than the optimization procedure (ENN2). The joint use of both methods in the hybrid model leads to a minor increase in the accuracy compared with the single ARIMA model. In accordance with our initial guess, the ENN outperforms the ARIMA model in regard to the hog prices, which follow a more complex and nonlinear pattern. The benefits from merging the two methods are not clear. While the MAPE of the hybrid model is smaller than that for the ENN, the opposite is true for Theils U. Note that the futures prices represent worse forecasts than the linear time series model. It should be mentioned that the differences in the prediction errors are not statistically significant at the 5 % level based on a t-test.

Table 5 reveals that all methods under consideration have difficulties in correctly predicting turning points in the price series. It is not possible to constitute a clear ranking. While the nonlinear models seem to be superior in the case of hog prices, this is not true for the canola prices.

Table 4. Comparison of forecast errors for hogs and canola prices

Models	MAPE	Theils U
a) hog prices		
ARIMA	4.5463	0.0304
Futures Prices	5.8073	0.0347
ENN 1	4.4741	**0.0297**
ENN 2	5.7029	0.0353
Hybrid Model 1	**4.4674**	0.0300
Hybrid Model 2	4.4916	0.0298
b) canola prices		
ARIMA	3.0841	0.0223
ENN 1	3.2333	0.0225
ENN 2	4.1882	0.0277
Hybrid Model 1	**3.0531**	**0.0219**
Hybrid Model 2	3.0725	0.0219

Bold letters indicate minimal errors

4 Conclusions

In this study we explore the usefulness of ANNs for the short-term forecasting of agricultural commodity prices. Traditional ARIMA models and futures prices serve as a benchmark for their evaluation. Moreover, we investigate whether a hybrid model is beneficial compared to the application of single forecast methods as the recent literature suggests. Our results are not unambiguous. Obviously, the potential gain from the ANN and hybrid models seems to depend on the characteristics of the time series under consideration. A more complex time series justifies the use of an ANN. However, the greater flexibility of this model class and its ability to handle nonlinear data patterns comes at the cost of a more demanding specification procedure. While the Box-Jenkins approach is straightforward, there is no simple clear-cut method to determine the optimal structure of the ANN. Reference [23] concedes that the design of an ANN is more of an art than a science. This means that the danger of missspecifying an ANN is higher than in the case of an ARIMA model. This may erode the potential superiority of the ANN and it also hampers the ability to generalize during comparisons between the ANN and other forecasting methods.

Furthermore, our calculations confirm that a hybrid model may reduce the prediction errors of single forecasting methods. However, the question remains as to when it is actually worthwhile to apply such a complex model, for which the setup costs are relatively high. In order to identify situations more clearly where the use of hybrid models is recommended, comprehensive and systematic experiments with simulated data are necessary. We recommend that such simulation experiments be performed in future research.

Table 5. Turning point analysis

a) Hog Prices		Actual		
Predicted		TP (17)	NTP (29)	% Correct
ARIMA	TP 7	10	41	
	NTP 10	19	66	
Futures	TP 9	9	53	
Prices	NTP 8	20	69	
ENN 1	TP 11	6	65	
	NTP 6	23	79	
ENN 2	TP 9	16	65	
	NTP 8	13	79	
Hybrid	TP 11	10	65	
Model 1	NTP 6	19	66	
Hybrid	TP 11	9	65	
Model 2	NTP 6	20	69	

b) Canola Prices		Actual		
Predicted		TP (8)	NTP (21)	% Correct
ARIMA	TP 3	4	38	
	NTP 5	17	81	
ENN 1	TP 2	5	25	
	NTP 6	16	76	
ENN 2	TP 4	14	50	
	NTP 4	7	33	
Hybrid	TP 2	2	**25**	
Model 1	NTP 6	19	**90**	
Hybrid	TP 3	4	38	
Model 2	NTP 5	17	81	

TP: Turning point, NTP: No Turning Point

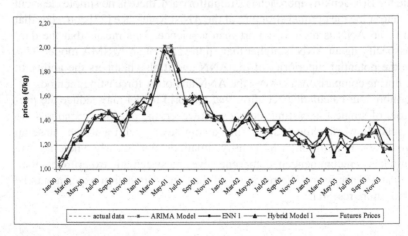

Fig. 2. One-step-ahead forecasts of hog prices (Germany, January 2000 to December 2003)

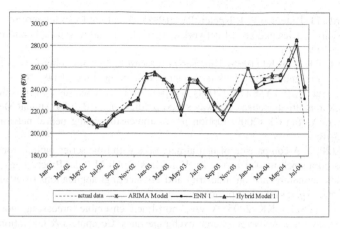

Fig. 3. One-step-ahead forecasts of canola prices (Germany, January 2002 to July 2004)

References

1. Baillie RT, Bollerslev T (1992) Prediction in dynamic models with time-dependent conditional variance. Journal of Econometrics 52:91–113
2. Bates JM, Granger CWJ (1969) The combination of forecasts. Operations Research 20:451–468
3. Cho V (2003) A comparison of three different approaches to tourist arrival forecasting. Tourism Management 24:323–330
4. Clemen R (1989) Combining forecasts: a review and annotated bibliography with discussion. International Journal of Forecasting 5:559–608
5. Elman JL (1990) Finding structure in time. Cognitive Science 14:179–211
6. Haykin S (1999) Neural networks: a comprehensive foundation. Second Edition, Prentice-Hall, New Jersey
7. Jhee WC, Shaw MJ (1996) Time series prediction using minimally structured neural networks: an empirical test. In: Trippi RR, Turban E (eds) Neural networks in finance and investing. Revised Edition, Irwin, Chicago
8. Kaastra I, Boyd M (1996) Designing a neural network for forecasting financial economic time series. Neurocomputing 10:215–236
9. Kellard N, Newbold P, Rayner T, Ennew C (1999) The relative efficiency of commodity futures markets. The Journal of Futures Markets 19:413–432
10. Kohzadi NM, Boyd S, Kermanshahi B (1996) A comparison of artificial neural network and time series models for forecasting commodity prices. Neurocomputing 10:169–181
11. McNelis PD (2005) Neural networks in finance: gaining predictive edge in the market. Elsevier Academic press
12. Menezes LM, Bunn DW, Taylor JW (2000) Review of guidelines for the use of combined forecasts. European Journal of Operational Research 120:190–204
13. Nelson CR (1973) Applied time series analysis for managerial forecasting. Holland-Day, San Francisco
14. Pai PF, Lin CS (2005) A hybrid ARIMA and support vector machines model in stock price forecasting. Omega 33:497–505
15. Pendharkar PC (2001) An empirical study of designing and testing of hybrid evolutionary-neural approach for classification. Omega 29:361–374

16. Richards TJ, Patterson PM, Ispelen PV (1998) Modelling fresh tomato marketing margins: econometrics and neural networks. Agricultural and Resource Economics Review 27:186–199
17. Wedding DK, Cios KJ (1996) Time series forecasting by combining RBF networks, certainty factors, and the Box-Jenkins models. Neurocomputing 10:149–168
18. Yang F, Sun H, Tao Y, Ran B (2004) Temporal difference learning with recurrent neural network in multi-step ahead freeway speed prediction. TRB 2004 Annual Meeting
19. Yao J, Li Y, Tan CL (2000) Option prices forecasting using neural networks. Omega 28:455–466
20. Yim J (2002) A comparison of neural networks with time series models for forecasting returns on a stock market index. In: Hendtlass T, Ali M (eds) Proceedings of the 15th international conference on industrial and engineering, applications of artificial intelligence and expert systems. Springer
21. Yu L, Wang S, Lai KK (2005) A novel non-linear ensemble forecasting model incorporating GLAR and ANN for foreign exchange rates. Computers & Operations Research 32:2523–2541
22. Zhang GP (2003) Time series forecasting using a hybrid ARIMA and neural network model. Neurocomputing 50:159–175
23. Zhang G, Patuwo BE, Hu MY (1998) Forecasting with artificial neural networks: the state of the art. International Journal of Forecasting 14:35–62

Nonlinear Principal Component Analysis for Withdrawal from the Employment Time Guarantee Fund

Li Weigang[1], Aiporê Rodrigues de Moraes[2], Shi Lihua[3], and Raul Yukihiro Matsushita[2]

[1] Department of Computer Science, University of Brasília - UnB C.P. 4466, CEP:70919-970, Brasília - DF, Brazil. weigang@cic.unb.br
[2] University of Brasília Department of Statistics, University of Brasília - UnB
[3] Smart Material and Structure Institute, Nanjing University of Aeronautics and Astronautics, China

To improve the management of the Employment Time Guarantee Fund (Fundo de Garantia do Tempo de Serviço - FGTS), a study in Brazil is conducted to analyze past data and anticipate the future trends of this fund. In this paper, Nonlinear Principal Component Analysis (NLPCA) - with the Artificial Neural Network architecture and Back-Propagation algorithm - is used to reduce the data dimension in describing various causes of withdrawals from the FGTS. With the analysis of the properties of these withdrawals, the paper discusses the correlation between the policy of free treatment of AIDS patients and their withdrawal from the plan. Nonlinear time series corresponding to each cause of withdrawal over 75 months - from 1994 to 2000 - are collected from the administrator of the FGTS. Using NLPCA, 17 small quantity time series (Group 1) are combined into one variable and then combined with other 7 middle quantity series (Group 2) to form another variable. Finally, four combined time series (Group 3) are formed which can well represent features of the total of 27 kinds of withdrawals with respect to their different causes. As a criterion for dimension reducing, the coefficient of correlation between the output of Group 1 and the sum of 17 is 0.8486 and that between Group 2 and sum of 8 is 0.9765.

Key words: Data Mining, FGTS, Neural Networks, NLPCA, PCA

1 Introduction

The Employment Time Guarantee Fund (Fundo de Garantia do Tempo de Serviço - FGTS) is a kind of severance pay fund administered by the Brazilian Federal Government. Under the FGTS, employers deposit 1/12 of a worker's salary into a restricted bank account, the balance of which is released to the worker if and when a worker is fired without a suitable reason. In February 2001, there were almost 63 million accounts amounting to US$ 40 billion in the FGTS ([2, 4]).

Under the FGTS system, a worker can use the fund for a limited number of reasons (27 at this moment). It is of no consequence to a company whether it fires an employee or not because severance pay has already been deposited every month. To counteract this undesirable trend, employers are now required to make an additional payment equivalent to 40% of all previous payments to the employee's account every time they wish to fire someone. Among the various other reasons enabling employees to withdraw their funds are financing a home under a government-sponsored housing program or being an AIDS patient.

To improve the administration of the FGTS, an Actuarial System for the FGTS has been proposed with the general objective being to establish a technical base for the actuarial evaluation of the FGTS. According to the procedures for actuarial evaluation, the development of a system starts with an analysis of the data and all other available information. The results of the actuarial evaluation, the technical description and the detailed diagnosis of the data can then be used to evaluate the stability of the balance between incomes (employers' deposits, interest on financial applications and others) and expenses (employees' withdrawals, administration fees, 3% annual interest on every account and others.), i.e. the future behavior of the fund.

As an important factor which affects the balance of the FGTS, an employees' withdrawal should be well represented in the Actuarial System of the FGTS. However, for various reasons and based on long time records, there is a large amount of data that needs to be taken into account in the system. The basic idea of this research is thus to combine the series with small values into one, and make it comparable with large groups while also capable of reproducing the original small value time series. To reduce the required data dimension, we have analyzed the part of the employees' withdrawal based on the reason for dismissal: termination, retirement and others. Four time series have been extracted to represent the 27 series of monthly withdrawals - with respect to various reasons - from 1994 to 2001.

In general, a dimension reduction can be performed either linearly or nonlinearly. The most well-known method is principal component analysis (PCA) or the Karhunen-Loeve expansion, which effectively approximates the data by a linear subspace using the mean squared error criterion ([9, 15]). Another linear method, independent component analysis (ICA), is also proposed to extract linear feature combinations that define independent sources ([6]). Because representing data sets just by linear combinations implies a potential oversimplification of the original data, with the advent of the Artificial Neural Network (ANN) model, nonlinear mapping was introduced to the PCA problem and led to the occurrence of Nonlinear Principal Component Analysis (NLPCA) [10]. The advent of ANN models, a class of powerful nonlinear empirical modeling methods, originated from the field of Artificial Intelligence and Electronic Engineering. With ANN's architecture and learning algorithms, the nonlinear signal processing problem is generally well treated. Various ANN methods have been developed for performing PCA ([14, 11]). Nonlinear principal component analysis using ANN was first introduced by [10] in the chemical engineering literature. These dimension reduction methods have been widely used in multivariate time series analysis, such as signals processing, climate forecasting, financial analysis and other areas ([10, 14, 12, 13, 7, 5, 11]).

In this paper, we use PCA and NLPCA to perform the dimension reduction of the time series for the withdrawal from the FGTS. The remainder of the text is organized as follows: Section 2 describes the 27 reasons for withdrawal from the FGTS. Section 3 gives a brief description of the methods used in this paper. The analytical results using PCA and NLPCA for the combination of multivariate time series for the FGTS are shown in Sect. 4. Finally, the conclusions are described in Sect. 5.

2 Withdrawal from the FGTS

Based on the Brazilian labor law, called the Consolidation of Labor (CLT), there are 27 reasons for an employee to make use of the FGTS fund ([2]). These reasons can be classified into the following categories:

- Dismissal payment (for the codes of 01, 01S and 02);
- Bankruptcy of Company (03);
- End of contract (04, 04S);
- Retirement (05, 05A);
- Death (23, 23A);
- Diseases (AIDS, cancer and others). (80 and 81);
- Judicial determination (88, 88P and 88R);
- Home financing (91, 92, 93, 95);
- Other reasons (06, 07, 10, 26, 27, 86, 87 and 87N);

We analyzed 27 time series which were collected over the period from July 1994 to September 2000 ([4]). Some of the statistical results for these withdrawals are reported in Table 1. The variances of some of the time series are reported in Figs. 1, 2 and 3. In the following subsections, we describe four main properties of the time series for the withdrawal from the FGTS plan.

2.1 Variance of the Time Series

The scale of the 27 time series varies greatly. We can see in Table 1, that the largest value of all withdrawals is Code 01 (Withdrawal for dismissal without cause), 60.21%, but the smallest value is only less than 0.01% (Withdrawal for dismissal for an unexpected reason (Code 02)). Five main withdrawals (60.21% for code 01, 15.83% for code 05 and 13.15% for codes 91, 92 and 93) make up nearly 90% of all withdrawal values while the remaining 22 reasons only account for 10.81%. The unit for the Code 01 variable is in millions of Reals (BRL$, Brazilian currency), but for some other variables (such as Codes 02, 27 and others.) the unit is the Real. This constitutes a challenge while trying to scale the input variance of the system. We have therefore divided the 27 series into 3 Groups: a) Group 1 (small quantity) includes 17 series (Codes 01S, 02, 03, 04S, 05A, 06, 07, 10, 23A, 26, 27, 80, 81, 87, 88P, 88R, 95), in which, the average yearly number of operations or value is less than

Code	Reason	Average use per operation (BRL$)	Average percent (%) In number of operations*	In value**
01	Dismissal without cause	864	65.22	60.21
01S	Dismissal without cause - special	1602	0.02	0.02
02	Dismissal for an unexpected reason	946	0***	0
04	Finish the contract in a defined period	88	9.72	0.93
04S	End the contract in a defined period - special	237	0.14	0.06
05	Retirement	3605	3.82	15.83
05A	Retirement - independent employment	2193	0.02	0.06
06	Suspension of the independent employment for a period equal to or greater than 90 days	648	0.33	0.21
07	End of the temporary contract of the worker in Port	971	0.01	0.01
10	Rescission with indemnity of temporary worker not FGTS optionee	5058	0	0.04
23	Death of the holder of the account	344	2.18	0.08
23A	Death of the holder of the account - independent worker	539	0	0
26	Rescission without indemnity payment or end of the formal period (worker claim - not optionee)	2393	0.10	0.17
27	Payment of the deposit that deals with art. 73 of the FGTS regulation	10123	0	0
80	AIDS patients	1036	0.10	0.12
81	Malignant Neoplasia patients	3803	0.06	0.24
86	Account related without credit of deposit for 3 years, removed from 14/JUL/90	643	4.82	3.87
87	Permanence of the account related for 3 years without credit of deposit, with the right to 3% benefit.	113	0.76	0.62
87N	Permanence of the account related for 3 years without credit of deposit, without the right to 3% benefit.	96	8.90	0.97
88	Judicial determination	1270	1.66	2.08
88P	Judicial determination - for payment of alimentation of pension	1470	0.03	0.32
88R	Juristic determination for changing the manner of contract	1383	0.04	0.07
91	House financing - payment for residential property (Type 1)	8935	0.96	7.90
92	House financing - payment for residential property (Type 2)	6714	0.49	3.96
93	House financing - payment for residential property (Type 3)	2030	0.40	1.29
95	House financing - in construction phase	4222	0.10	0.79

Table 1. Properties of withdrawals from the FGTS ([4]). * average yearly account operations of 27 withdrawals are 100% from 07/1994 to 09/2000; ** average yearly value of 27 withdrawals are 100% from 07/1994 to 09/2000, US$1.0 = BRL$2,20 (exchange rate in February 2006, as an example); *** Zero in this table means that the percentage is less than 0.01%.

1% of the total. The sum all of 17 items in Group 1 constitutes just 2.16% of the total withdrawal value. b) Group 2 (medium quantity) includes 7 series (Codes 04, 23, 86, 87N, 88, 92, 93), in which the average yearly number of operations or value is more than 1% but less than 5% of the total. The sum of all of the items in Group 2 and the output of Group 1 accounts for 16.06% of all of the withdrawal value. c) Group 3 (large quantity) includes 3 series (Codes 01, 05, and 91), in which the average yearly number of operations or value is more than 7%.

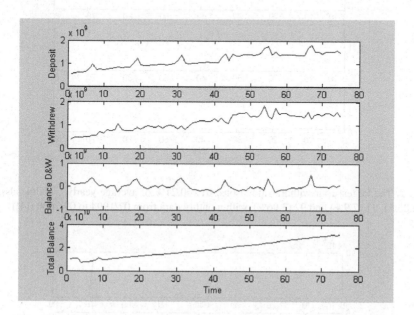

Fig. 1. Deposits, Withdrawals, and the Difference between the former two and the Balance of the FGTS — Monthly data from 07/1994 to 09/2000 ([4])

2.2 Nonlinearity

A high order of nonlinearity is present among the withdrawal variables. This may also increase the difficulties associated with applying conventional signal processing methods to the data. The deposit total (DT), total withdrawals (TW), the difference between DT and TW, and the Balance of the FGTS (there is still some other income in the balance which will not be discussed in this paper) are shown in Fig. 1. In Fig. 2, the first four largest withdrawal series can be seen: Codes 01, 05, 91 and 92, in which the values change from BRL\$ 5 million to BRL\$ 200 million. The four smallest withdrawal series 01S, 02, 07, and 23A are shown in Fig. 3, in which the values change from BRL\$ 0 to BRL\$ 1 million. It is obviously very challenging to derive regular models for such variables so as to reduce the amount of data.

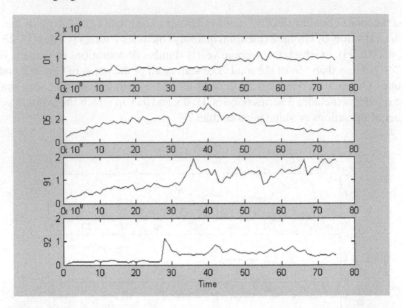

Fig. 2. The largest four withdrawal reasons: 01 (60.21% of average yearly withdrawals), 05 (15.83%), 91 (7.9%) and 92 (3.96%), with monthly data from 07/1994 to 09/2000 ([4])

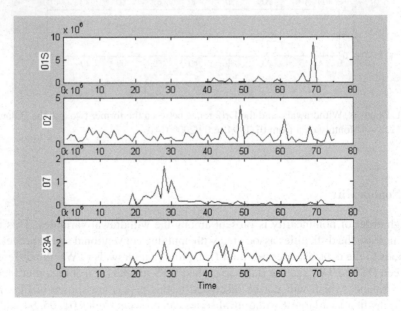

Fig. 3. The smallest four withdrawal reasons: 01S (0.02% of average yearly withdrawals), 02 (<0.01%), 07 (≤ 0.01%) and 23A (<0.01%), with monthly data from 07/1994 to 09/2000 ([4])

2.3 Open System

The FGTS is an open system. Its deposits, financial applications and credit for public construction, withdrawals, administration fees and others depend on the country's social, economic and political situation. For example, the withdrawal caused by dismissal is closely related to the unemployment rate. The AIDS patients' withdrawal rate has the closest relationship with the health condition of the population and the policies of the government. Since 1996, the Brazilian Ministry of Health has developed two projects to supply free treatment to AIDS patients (AIDS I [1] and AIDS II [3]). As a result, the death rate resulting from AIDS in Brazil has been reduced by 12.5%. Between 1996 and 1998, 14 out of 100,000 Brazilians were diagnosed with AIDS. However in 1999, this number fell to 11.2. This result has directly influenced the withdrawals from the FGTS (code 80). The governments expenses are shown in Table 2. The average monthly withdrawal for AIDS patients was US$1.2265 million in 1995, US$ 1.1126 million in 1996, and a lower US$1.0349 million in 1997. We can also observe that the number of AIDS cases increased by 12.78% from 1995 to 1996, and by 1.88% from 1996 to 1997, and fell by 2.90% from 1998 to 1999. One can draw two conclusions from these results: 1) The actions of the government have effectively reduced AIDS cases in Brazil; 2) The Ministry of Health has spent money to treating AIDS patients while the FGTS's withdrawal rate (caused by AIDS patients) has remained stable. FGTS funds are obtained from the Ministry of Finance, and therefore the government is saving money to some extent.

Year	1994	1995	1996	1997	1998	1999	2000
AIDS cases in Brazil*	18424	20168	22745	23173	23119	18288	8596
Government treatment cost**	2.6758	4.5450	8.7667	9.4417	1.1079	5.130	7.2361
Withdrawal from the FGTS by AIDS patients***	0.6716	1.2265	1.1126	1.0349	1.1620	0.8711	0.9991

Table 2. The Cost to the Ministry of Health for AIDS Patients and Withdrawals from the FGTS. *[1, 3]. **[1, 3] USD, millions, monthly average . ***[4] USD, millions, monthly average ; in 1994, from July to December; in 2000, from January to September. We do not analyze withdrawals from the FGTS by AIDS patients in 1999 and 2000 using the USD, because in this period the exchange rate from $BRL to USD is complicated.

2.4 Difference between Quantity and Value of the Operation

The quantity of accounts in operation by employees and the value in these accounts are not always in proportion. For example, withdrawal from the contract (04) accounts for 9.72% of the average yearly operations, but the value in the account for these people is only 0.93% (see Table 1). Futhermore, for retirement (05), 3.82% is in yearly operations, yet 15.83% of withdrawals are averaged over a one-year period, which is the second largest in the whole time series. Intensive analysis of this combination for the administration of accounts could be an interesting topic for further data mining research.

The complicated properties of the withdrawal means that we can neither merely discard any cause of the withdrawal nor make a simple combination to replace all of them. The main objective of this paper is to reduce the dimensions of withdrawal to a reasonable level and preserve as much information as possible. The basic idea is to combine the series with small values into one, and to make it comparable with large groups while capable of reproducing the original small value time series. Figure 4 shows the combination tree. There are four series to describe the withdrawal from the FGTS: 01, 05, 91 and a combination of others. Every final sequence of data will take at least 7% of the total average yearly amount of total withdrawals.

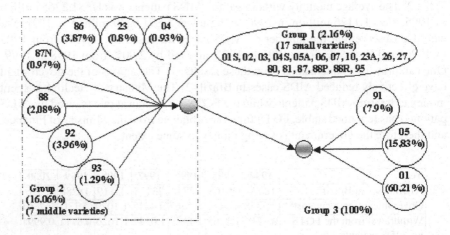

Fig. 4. Combination tree

3 Methods

The change in the employees' withdrawals over time and causes can be expressed as $X(t) = [x_1(t), x_2(t), \ldots, x_m(t)]$, where $t = 1 \sim n$, is the observation time, n is the total number of the data observed, and $x_i(t)$ $(i = 1 \sim m)$ is monthly withdrawals based on m reasons. The dimension-reduction during the pre-processing stage of this multivariate time series requires the use of the following mapping $g : \Re^m \to \Re^p (p < m)$ to map X_{mxn} to a p-dimensional space and to preserve as much information as possible at each point. To be able to map back to the original space, a second mapping $h : \Re^p \to \Re^m$ will be used. The optimal g and h are searched to ensure that the reconstruction error $\|X - h(g(X))\|$ will be minimal. To do this, two methods are used: principal component analysis and nonlinear principal component analysis.

3.1 Principal Component Analysis (PCA)

Principal Component Analysis is a well-understood and useful method for modeling data sets. When applied to an m-dimensional data set X, it performs forward and backward mapping with a linear transform,

$$V = W^\tau X \tag{1}$$

$$X^* = WV \tag{2}$$

where $W = [w_1, w_2, \ldots, w_p]$, is the linear transform, V is a p-dimensional feature vector representation of X, X^* is the reconstructed X.

If the vectors of W are chosen to be the p eigenvectors corresponding to p being the largest eigenvalues of $X^\tau X$, then the approximation error

$$\|X - WW^\tau X\| \tag{3}$$

will be minimized [15].

3.2 Nonlinear Principal Component Analysis (NLPCA)

Nonlinear principal component analysis also attempts to find mappings between a multidimensional data set and a lower-dimensional feature-space while minimizing the reconstruction error, but allows the mappings to be nonlinear. Instead of using (1) and (2), NLPCA uses a nonlinear mapping function to get feature vectors

$$V = g(X) \tag{4}$$

and another nonlinear mapping function to reconstruct the original data

$$X^* = h(V) \tag{5}$$

Neural networks are very suitable for realizing such nonlinear mappings. In order to do this, a feed-forward neural network with three hidden layers is trained with its input and desired output both as the original data set X ([10]). The second hidden layer is designed to have a lower dimension than the input and output layers. Therefore the output in this layer can be seen as a low-dimensional representation of the input X.

The advantage of NLPCA over PCA is that it is capable of representing and learning more general transformations. This is necessary when one wishes to eliminate correlations between dimensions within a set of data, or when the lower-intrinsic dimensionality of a data set arises from a nonlinear relationship between different dimensions of the data set. However, NLPCA also has important disadvantages compared to PCA, such as the feature vector no longer having a physical meaning as in the case of eigenvectors, more computation time and a local optimal solution. A successful example may be Hsieh's work ([7]). He used NLPCA with ANN for the monthly Pacific Sea Surface Temperature (SST) data analysis. A NLPCA model which was developed in MATLAB by Hsieh's Group ([8]) is used as the main reference in this research.

4 Dimension Reduction

PCA and NLPCA were applied to reduce the dimensions of 27 time series of withdrawals from the FGTS. Firstly, PCA is used to try to eliminate some unimportant variables. Then NLPCA is used to combine the multivariables. The results show that NLPCA is superior to PCA in our applications.

4.1 Parameters and Criteria

As mentioned in Fig. 4, the sequence of the combination is as follows: form 1 vector from Group 1 (with 17 time series), another from Group 2 (with 7 time series) and the final vector from Group 1 to form 1 vector.

When using NLPCA, the architecture of the five-layer neural network is formed to extract a 1-D (one-dimensional) approximation to the data set ([10, 13, 7, 11]). In Group 1, the first (input) and fifth (output) layers each contain 17 neurons (Fig. 5). Layers 2 and 4 are called the encoding and decoding layers, respectively, in which there are 5 neurons. The third layer is referred to as the bottleneck layer which just contains a single neuron. The output of this neuron is what we need, an 1D approximation of 17 vectors. We simply refer to this structure by 17:5:1:5:17. In Group 2, the architecture of the network is formed as 8:3:1:3:8.

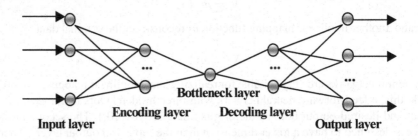

Fig. 5. The architecture of the five-layer neural network for NLPCA

There are three approaches used to normalize the variables ([7, 8]): 1) do not normalize at all; 2) scale all variables by removing the mean and dividing by the standard deviation of each variable; and 3) scale all variables by removing the mean and dividing by the standard deviation of the 1st variable in the Group (or second, third, ...). In probability theory and statistics, the coefficient of variation (Cv) is a measurement of dispersion of a probability distribution ([16]). It is defined as the ratio of the standard deviation σ to the mean μ: $Cv = \sigma/\mu$. The coefficient of variation is a dimensionless number that allows comparison of the variation of populations that have significantly different mean values. We use this index to help us define the strategy of the normalization. Table 3 shows the calculation of the index Cv for a set of data from Group 1 and Group 2. Just to take an example, the data is from January of 1999 and the value is expressed in BRL$.

Group	Number of data	Mean (μ)	Standard deviation (σ)	Coefficient of variation (Cv)
1	17	1993154	3492482	1.7522
2	8-1 = 7	21701762	14230461	0.6557

Table 3. The coefficient of variation Cv from data for Group 1 and Group 2.

It is clear that the coefficient of variation (Cv) for Group 1, 1.7522, is larger than that for Group 2 of 0.6557.

When the varieties have a large range, such as in the case for Group 1, a poor convergence can be expected and just for the original data we use the above-mentioned technique for normalization: we scale all variables by removing the mean and dividing by the standard deviation of each variable, which is what has been done for Group 1.

When the variables have a lower coefficient of variation, we can scale all variables by removing the mean and dividing by the standard deviation of the one variable of the Group. In the case of Group 2, the variables are normalized by the mean and standard deviation of the second variable (or by the mean and standard deviation of the first variable).

We use MSE_train (training mean square error), MSE_test (testing mean square error), J_train (minimum cost function $J = ||X - X^*||^2$ from training) and J_test (minimum cost function $J = ||X - X^*||^2$ from testing) as criteria to measure the quality of network training ([5]). We use at least two steps to determine the learning rate and the threshold value. First, we use 0.2 as the learning rate, to see the training process and the situation regarding the convergence. We then use 0.01 as the learning rate to train the network to get more precise results. By applying the same process, we define the stop condition case by case, i.e. the threshold value used to terminate the learning (convergence) process. With this procedure, there are two advantages of our training ([8]):

1. The initial weight and bias are randomly selected by the neuron network, and influence the convergence of the learning process. If the initial data are not suitable, we may re-start the process.
2. It can be beneficial to prevent overtraining by fitting the noise in the data.

Usually, training is stopped if the MSE increases in the test data by more than the threshold. To avoid the local minima in the cost function, we also use an ensemble of optimization runs from random initial weight parameters. The best member of the ensemble is selected as the solution. In this paper, we train the network 20 times to select the best result.

The criterion used to verify the quality of the results of the dimension reduction is based on the correlation coefficient between the output of the method (NLPAC and others) and the sum of all of the varieties of that Group.

4.2 Using PCA to Reduce the Dimensions

As the first step, we use PCA to pre-process the 17 variables of Group 1. We take the vectors with a contribution of more than 10% in Group 1. PCA reduces the 17 variables to 2 (see Fig. 6a). If we increase that level to 20% or decrease it to 1%, PCA will give one vector or 15 vectors, respectively, to represent 17 variables.

We then use PCA to pre-process 7 variables and the sum of Group 1 (17 time series). Figure 6b gives the 2 feature vectors that PCA extracted when the contributing level is set to be 10%. To get fewer feature vectors such as one, the contributing level should be set to 20%. If we wish to preserve more information and select a contribution level of 1% , the output of PCA shows 8 variables. In this case, PCA cannot eliminate anything.

From the above results, we need not mention the quality of processing using PCA for the FGTS. We cannot eliminate 20% of the information to get just one variety to represent both Groups 1 and 2. If we wish to preserve 99% of the information of the group, the quantity of varieties is more than 8 in both Groups.

4.3 Using NLPCA to Reduce the Dimensions

We have 75 points of data for each of the 27 time series. 80% of them are used to train the network and the remaining 20% are used for the tests. In order to avoid the local minima problem, we train the NLPCA 20 times and use the one with the minimum MSE as the best feature vector.

NLPCA for Group 1

By using a 17:5:1:5:17 neural network for Group 1, NLPCA can generate one time series to represent 17 variables. Figure 7 shows the best one selected from 20 times of training. After 25346 interactions, the MSE_train is 0.5441 and the MSE_test is 0.4675. The MSE_test is less than the MSE_train. The correlation coefficient of regression between the output of NLPCA and the sum of all 17 series is 0.8486. From the figure, we can observe that at some special point as in 01/1997, the result for 88R from NLPCA cannot reach the real point. Table 4 shows the distribution of the data of 88R (Juristic determination for changing the manner of contract) from October 1996 to March 1997. The value for January 1997 is 270 times that for December 1996 and 15.8 times thar for February 1997. This large variation may help to explain the lower correlation coefficient, but the reason for this sharp change is still being studied.

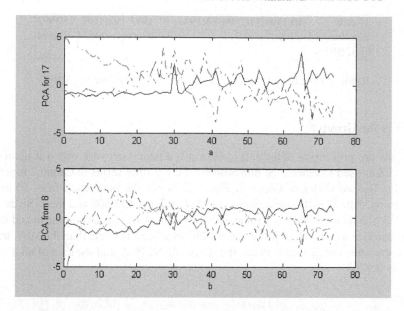

Fig. 6. PCA results for Groups 1 and 2 with a 10% rate of elimination. The solid line shows the sum of all variables in the group. a) 2 vectors (dashed lines) to represent 17 variables in Group 1; b) 3 vectors (dashed lines) to represent 8 variables in Group 2.

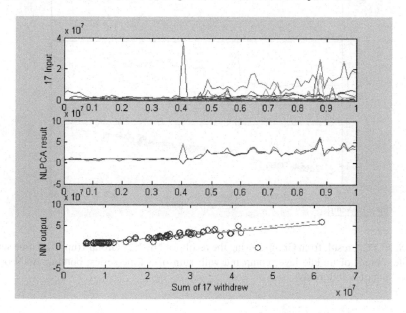

Fig. 7. NLPCA result from Group 1 (upper: 17 time series; middle: output of middle layer compared with the sum of 17 time series; bottom: NN output versus the sum of withdrawals)

Month	10/1996	11/1996	12/1996	01/1997	02/1997	03/1997
Withdrawal $ 88R, BRL$	310903	286914	140539	37987606	2400623	196894

Table 4. Distribution of withdrawal of 88R from 10/1996 to 03/1997

NLPCA for Group 2

After the pre-processing of the data in Group 1, a neural network with a structure of 8:3:1:3:8 is used to reduce the dimensions of the 7 time series in Group 2 together with the feature vector of Group 1. Figure 8 shows the best result from 20 times of training. After 18902 interactions, the MSE_train is 12.0508 and the MSE_test is 18.4052 (the reason for the big value is that we do not use the largest mean and standard deviation to normalize all variables). The MSE_test is larger than the MSE_train. The correlation coefficient between the output of NLPCA and the sum of all 8 variables is 0.9765.

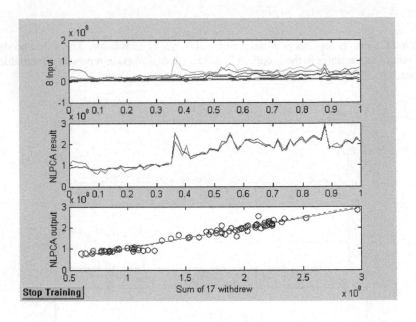

Fig. 8. NLPCA result from Group 2 using the result for NLPCA Group 1(upper: 8 time series; middle: output of middle layer compared with sum of 8 time series; bottom: ANN output versus sum of withdrawals)

We also use the sum of the 17 variables instead of the output of the NLPCA of Group 1 to improve the correlation. Figure 9 shows this modification. After 23117 interactions, the MSE_train is 12.1096 and the MSE_test is 17.2324 (the big value also arises because we do not use the largest mean and standard deviation to normalize all variables). The correlation coefficient between the output of NLPCA and the sum of all 8 variables is 0.9805. The result is better than in Fig. 8. This means that NLPCA is sensitive to the quality of the input.

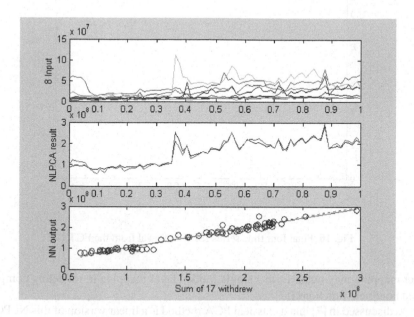

Fig. 9. NLPCA result from Group 2 using sum of variables of Group 1 (upper: 8 time series; middle: output of middle layer compared with sum of 8 time series; bottom: ANN output versus sum of withdrawals)

4.4 Discussion on PCA and NLPCA

As mentioned in 4.2, the PCA method is not suitable for the dimension reduction in the case of analyzing withdrawals from the FGTS. Using PCA, we cannot reduce the variables of Group 1 and Group 2 to one that can well represent the main feature of the data set. From 4.3, the NLPCA method is suitable for the dimension reduction of withdrawals from the time series. With NLPCA, we can get one time series to represent 17 in Group 1 with a correlation coefficient of 0.8486, and get one to represent 8 in Group 2 with a correlation coefficient of 0.9765. These results may not be the optimum, but at least they are the best among 20 trainings.

The fundamental difference between PCA and NLPCA is that NLPCA allows a nonlinear mapping from the n-dimension to the u-dimension where $n > u$, as PCA only allows a linear mapping. To perform NLPCA, the ANN in Fig. 5 contains 3 "hidden" layers of variables between the input and output layers of variables. NLPCA here generalizes easily to more than one hidden layer mapping, as 3 hidden

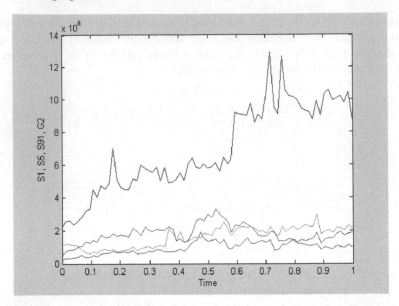

Fig. 10. Final four time series for withdrawal from the FGTS

layer mapping may outperform a single hidden layer mapping in modeling complicated nonlinear functions ([7]).

As discussed in [7] that a classical PCA method is a linear version of this NLPCA
can be readily seen by replacing all the transfer functions with the identity function,
thereby removing the nonlinear modeling capability of NLPCA. Then the forward
mapping from the n-dimension to the u-dimension involves only a linear combination
of the original variables as in the PCA. This fact explains the basic reason for the
result.

5 Conclusions

The main objectives in the development of the Actuarial System of the FGTS are
nonlinearity testing, feature extraction, correlation and causality analysis among the
variables of the FGTS, prediction and others. As an initial research effort, this paper
has just focused on the aspects of feature extraction and dimension reduction in regard to the data set. After some experiments involving 27 time series of withdrawals,
we reach the following conclusions:

1. Using NLPCA, 24 time series are combined with one vector which is expected
   to represent 16.06% of the values of average yearly withdrawals. Together with
   Codes 01, 05 and 91, these four time series are shown in Fig. 10.
2. The elimination methods, such as the PCA method, are not suitable for dimension reduction in the case of analyzing withdrawals from the FGTS. Compared

with NLPCA, using PCA, we can not reduce the variables in Group 1 and Group 2 to one that can well represent the main feature of the data set.

3. The NLPCA method is suitable for the dimension reduction in the withdrawals in the time series of the FGTS. With NLPCA, we can get one vector to represent 17 time series in Group 1 with a correlation coefficient of 0.8486, and get one to represent 8 time series in Group 2 with a correlation coefficient of 0.9765. These results may not be the optimum, but at least they are the best among the results from 20 trainings of ANN.

4. The results from Group 1 and Group 2 show that there are high order correlations between the output from NLPCA and the sum of the time series from this Group. The reason for this should be studied in depth in further research.

5. The outside influence on the FGTS is significant even if we just analyze the case of withdrawal by AIDS patients. The politics of government for the free treatment of these kinds of persons has a good effect on society, especially in terms of reducing the cost of the FGTS. We will continue to study the social, economic and political effects on the FGTS.

Further research will continue to analyze the property of withdrawals, deposits, financial applications and 3% yearly interest for every account in the FGTS and the relationship among them. We will formally test the nonlinearity of the data set and analyze correlation and causality using the data mining method. In order to efficiently predict the future behavior of the FGTS, a dynamic model will be constructed based on the results of this paper.

Acknowledgements

The authors are grateful to the Brazilian Curator Council of the FGTS and Caixa Econômica Federal, for providing the financial support and the data used in this paper, and to Prof. William W. Hsieh for making the source code for the NLPCA algorithm available. The authors would also like to thank the reviewers, namely, Mr. Bueno Borges de Souza, Mr. Antonio Magni and Editors of this book, for their helpful comments.

References

1. Ministério da Saúde, Secretaria de Projetos Especiais de Saúde, Coordenação Nacional de DST e AIDS, Execução Financeira do Projeto 3659/br - PROJETO DE CONTROLE DA AIDS E DST Brasília-DF, Abril 1997.
2. Ministério do Trabalho and Conselho Curador do FGTS (2000), O Que é o Fundo de Garantia do Tempo de Serviço?, maio 2000.
3. Ministério da Saúde, Secretaria de Projetos Especiais de Saúde, Coordenação Nacional de DST e AIDS. Relatório de Implementação e Avaliação - Aids II - dezembro/1998 à maio/2001 Acordo de Empréstimo - BIRD / 4392/BR - Brasília-DF, Maio 2001.
4. Caixa Econômica Federal, Relatório de FGTS - 2002. Accessed in February 2006.

5. Back AD, Weigend AS (1997) A first application of independent component analysis to extracting structure from stock returns. Int. Journal of Neural Systems 8(4):473–484
6. Comon P (1994) Independent component analysis, a new concept. Signal Processing 36(3):287–314
7. Hsieh WW (2001) Nonlinear principal component analysis by neural networks. Tellus:599–615
8. Hsieh WW (2005) Neuralnets for multivariate and time series analysis (neumatsa): a user manual. http://www.ocgy.ubc.ca/ william/Pubs/NN.manual.pdf Accessed in February 2006
9. Jain AK, Duin RPW, Mao J (2000) Statistical pattern recognition review. IEEE Trans. Pattern and Machine Intelligence 22:4–34
10. Kramer MA (1991) Nonlinear principal component analysis using auto-associative neural networks. AIChE Journal 37(2):233–243
11. Kung SY (1993) Digital neural networks. Prentice-Hall
12. Lesch RH, Caille Y, Lowe D (1999) Component analysis in financial time series. In: Proceedings of the IEEE/IAFE 1999 conference on computational intelligence for financial engineering:183–190
13. Monahan AH (2000) Nonlinear principal component analysis by neural networks: theory and application to the Lorenz system. J Climate 13:821–835
14. Stamkopoulos T, Diamantaras K, Maglaveras N (1998) ECG analysis using nonlinear PCA neural network for ischemia detection. IEEE Trans. Signal Processing 46(11):3058–3067
15. Wang XZ (1999) Data mining and knowledge discovery for process monitoring and control. Springer-Verlag, Great Britain:30–38
16. Wikipedia. Coefficient of variation. http://en.wikipedia.org/wiki/Coefficient of variation. Accessed in February 2006

Estimating Female Labor Force Participation through Statistical and Machine Learning Methods: A Comparison

Omar Zambrano[1], Claudio M. Rocco S[2], and Marco Muselli[3]

[1] Inter-American Development Bank, Washington D.C., USA
    Omar_Zambrano@ksg05.harvard.edu
[2] Universidad Central Venezuela, Facultad de Ingeniería, Caracas, Venezuela
    crocco@reacciun.ve
[3] Istituto di Elettronica e di Ingegneria dell'Informazione e delle Telecomunicazioni
    CNR, Genova, Italy
    marco.muselli@ieiit.cnr.it

Female Labor Force Participation (FLFP) is perhaps one of the most relevant theoretical issues within the scope of studies of both labor and behavioral economics. Many statistical models have been used for evaluating the relevance of explanatory variables. However, the decision to participate in the labor market can also be modeled as a binary classification problem. For this reason, in this paper, we compare four techniques to estimate the Female Labor Force Participation. Two of them, Probit and Logit, are from the statistical area, while Support Vector Machines (SVM) and Hamming Clustering (HC) are from the machine learning paradigm. The comparison, performed using data from the Venezuelan Household Survey for the second semester 1999, shows the advantages and disadvantages of the two methodological paradigms that could provide a basic motivation for combining the best of both approaches.

Key words: Female Labor Force Participation, Probit, Logit, Support Vector Machines, Hamming Clustering

1 Introduction

Labor force participation, as well as its determinants, is perhaps one of the most relevant theoretical issues within the scope of studies of both labor and behavioral economics. Moreover, it can be argued that, at least to some extent, the labor participation decision making process is consubstantial to some of the basic theoretical constructions of the economic discipline, including the traditional approach to aggregate supply and the more comprehensive general equilibrium models with micro foundations ([21]).

In general, early theoretical models on labor force participation were circum-scribed to the individual decision sphere of the allocation of limited time between work and leisure. In this basic framework, since the individual's endowment of time is finite, the ultimate distribution is given by the utility maximizing bundle of wages (the market value of work) and spare time, which is given by the relative price among those two goods ([21]). Later, this basic framework was extended to use the family, instead of the individuals, as the basic decision making unit for the labor market, which makes interactions and comparative advantages among family members mat-ter for individual labor decision purposes ([3]). The specialized literature has found as an empirical regularity a stable statistical relationship between labor force partic-ipation and variables related to the afore-mentioned relative price: the conditions of the labor markets, the wages of other family members, education levels, the fertility rate, and marital status, among others.

In this context, the study of female labor force participation (FLFP) became rel-evant for its specificity since it can be implied that the FLFP is affected by exclusive genre circumstances. Thus, variables like maternity, the number and ages of chil-dren, and specific patterns in marital status or the partner's income can be assumed to be exclusive determinants of FLFP ([6]). Seminal articles on theoretical models for female labor force participation are considered to be those led by Mincer ([17]) and Cain ([6]). Since Mincer and Cain, the empirical literature has found abundant economic and non-economic explanations for the FLFP phenomenon. The main eco-nomic determinants are related to conditions in labor markets for women (wages, part-time jobs availability) [4, 1], maternity and the number of infant children ([4]), the income of the partner ([4]), and the level of education ([4, 1, 9]). There are also references to technological conditions, such as the so-called "revolution" caused by the availability of technologically superior capital goods in the production function of the home, that has greatly impacted the woman's domestic productivity and, there-fore, stimulated a higher FLFP ([1, 9, 16]). Regarding non-economic factors, socio-cultural changes in the women's role in society are often mentioned ([20]).

Regarding the methodological aspects, most of the reviewed studies preferred a multivariate limited variable estimation approach (Logit/Probit) [1, 11, 2] to address the finding of such relationships. Additionally, it can be found that the use of ex-treme value estimations and data panel models were complementary techniques of the Logit/Probit models ([9, 11, 2]).

However, the decision to participate in the labor market is modeled as a dichoto-mous random variable, which takes the value of $+1$ if the individual participates in the labor market and -1 if it does not. Consequently, the analysis involved in estab-lishing the motivations for FLFP can also be performed by a classification method, which is able to retrieve a binary functional dependence, starting from a subset of examples.

Currently the most promising classification approach is that offered by Support Vector Machines (SVM) [10, 7]; indeed, SVMs are able to achieve high levels of prediction accuracy in a wide variety of applications. On the other hand, a compre-hension of the mechanisms involved in FLFP can be obtained by applying rule gen-eration methods, which provide a set of intelligible rules underlying the classification problem at hand. Among these techniques, Hamming Clustering (HC) [19, 18] offers a good tradeoff between the generalization ability and comprehensibility of the resulting rule set.

By focusing on the possibility of modeling the FLFP by using such approaches, the main idea of this paper is to compare the advantages and disadvantages of the classical statistical paradigm (represented by a general Probit or Logit model) with the machine learning paradigm (represented by Support Vector Machines and Hamming Clustering).

To the best of our knowledge, there are no reports on the use of machine learning techniques such as SVM or HC models as binary classifiers applied to the FLFP issues. In addition and also to the best of our knowledge, there are no studies that address the issue and the particularities of the FLFP phenomena in the Venezuelan case.

Section 2 contains an overview of the classifiers to be compared. The results of the example analyzed are presented in Sect. 3. Finally, Sect. 4 presents the conclusions.

2 Classifiers to be compared

2.1 Probit and Logit

Probit and Logit are statistical techniques used for estimating the effects of a set of independent variables (X) on a binary dependent variable (y). Probit and Logit avoid several statistical problems with linear probability models and generally yield results that make more sense. The inadequacies of the linear probability model suggest that a nonlinear specification is more appropriate. A natural candidate is an S-shaped curve bounded in the interval zero-one. One such curve is the cumulative normal distribution function corresponding to the Probit model. An alternative S-shaped curve is the logistic curve corresponding to the Logit model. Then the goal of Logit and Probit is to model: $\Pr(y = 1|X) = F(X\beta)$, where β is the vector of parameters associated with each of the independent variables ([11]). The parameter estimates give the partial effect of a coefficient with the effects of other variables being controlled (the *ceteris paribus* condition). The interpretation of these estimates allows the Decision-Maker (DM) to evaluate the overall model and to infer some conclusions.

For example, the DM can interpret the sign of the parameter estimates, the marginal effect of an explanatory variable on y or its probability or the marginal effect of an explanatory variable given a set of values for the explanatory variables.

2.2 Support Vector Machines

Suppose we have N training data points $(X_1, y_1), \ldots, (X_N, y_N)$, where X_i, $i = 1, \ldots, N$, is a vector of input variables and y_i is the corresponding participation decision. Denote with S^+ (resp. S^-) the convex hull of the points X_i with output $+1$ (resp. output -1). Thus, if S^+ and S^- are linearly separable, we can think of constructing the optimal hyperplane $w \cdot X + b = 0$, which has the maximum distance from these two convex hulls. The quantities w and b are usually referred to as the weight vector and bias ([10]). The problem can be mathematically formulated as:

$$\min_{w,b} \quad \frac{1}{2} w^T w$$
$$\text{subj to} \quad y_i(w \cdot X + b) \geq 1$$

This is a convex, quadratic programming problem involving the unknowns (w, b). It can be equivalently solved by searching for the values of the Lagrange multipliers α_i in the Wolfe dual problem. In this case we have:

$$w = \sum_i \alpha_i y_i X_i$$

Only those points, which lie closest to the hyperplane, have $\alpha_i > 0$ and contribute to the above sum. These points are called *support vectors* and capture the essential information about the training set at hand.

Once we have found the optimal hyperplane, we simply determine which side of the decision boundary a given test pattern X^* lies and assign the corresponding class label, using the function $\text{sign}(w \cdot X^* + b)$.

If the two convex hulls S^+ and S^- are not linearly separable, the optimal hyperplane can still be found by accepting a small number of misclassified points in the training set. A regularization factor C accounts for the trade off between the training error and the distance from S^+ and S^-.

To adopt nonlinear separating surfaces between the two classes, we can project the input vectors X^i into another high dimensional feature space through a proper mapping $\Phi(\cdot)$. If we employ the Wolfe dual problem to retrieve the optimal hyperplane in the projected space, it is not necessary to know the explicit form of the mapping Φ. We only need the inner product $K(X, X') = \Phi(X) \cdot \Phi(X')$, which is usually called the *kernel function* ([10]). Different choices for the kernel function have been suggested; they must verify Mercer's condition ([7]), as is the case for the Gaussian radial basis function kernel:

$$K(X, X') = \exp\left(\frac{-\|X - X'\|^2}{2\sigma^2} \right)$$

Classifiers obtained using this method are called *Support Vector Machines (SVM)*. The need to properly choose the kernel is a limitation of the support vector approach. In general, the SVM with lower complexity should be selected.

2.3 Hamming Clustering

Hamming Clustering (HC) is a rule generation method, based on Boolean function reconstruction, which is able to achieve performances comparable to those of the best classification techniques. The decision function built by HC can be expressed as a collection of intelligible rules in the **if-then** form underlying the classification problem. In addition, as a byproduct of the training process, HC is able to determine redundant input variables for the analysis at hand, thus allowing a significant simplification in the data acquisition process.

Since HC operates on binary strings, problems involving numerical or nominal variables can be solved by previously coding the values assumed by each input into a Boolean form. With this objective in mind, ordered attributes have to be previously discretized, by dividing their domain into a collection of adjacent subintervals. The choice of a suboptimal set of cutoffs to be used as boundary values for these subintervals can be performed by adopting proper discretization , e.g. [13], [15], [5].

For example, in the analysis of FLFP phenomena described in the next section, the variable WAGE_PARTNER (regarding the income of the woman's partner) is continuous and lies in the range [0,8000000]. The application of the technique described in [5] produces 8 cutoffs, namely, 175000, 275000, 325000, 452500, 550000, 650000, 900000 and 1350000, which determine 9 intervals coded by the first 9 positive integers $\{1, \dots, 9\}$.

Note that the cutoffs are not equi-spaced, since the discretization method tries to catch the input variability, by refining regions where the classification process is more critical. Since nominal attributes, for which no ordering is defined, can be directly coded via positive integers, after the discretization step every sample (X_i, y_i) in the training set is transformed into a pair (U_i, y_i), with U_i being a vector of positive integers.

Now, the application of HC requires that every U_i be properly coded by a binary string Z_i. To achieve this, standard binary coding cannot be employed, as it does not maintain information about ordering and distance. As a consequence, two close input values can be unreasonably put away by binarization.

A possible way of avoiding this undesirable effect is to adopt a binary coding that possesses the two following properties:

- it must be an *isometry*, i.e., $d_b(\lambda(u), \lambda(v)) = \alpha d(u, v)$, α being a constant, whereas d and d_b are the distances in the original (positive integers) and in the transformed (binary strings) space, respectively;
- it must be *full order* preserving, i.e., $u \leq v$ if and only if $\lambda(u) \leq \lambda(v)$.

If the Hamming distance, given by the number of different bits, is employed as the metric d_b for the transformed space, a binary coding λ for ordered variables that satisfies the two properties above is the *thermometer code*, which sets to 1 the ith bit if and only if $i < u$.

In this way the value 350000 for WAGE_PARTNER, which belongs to the fourth interval (325000,452500] and is associated with the positive integer $u = 4$ after discretization, will be coded by the binary string 11100000. Note that 8 bits (the same as the number of cutoffs) are required to realize the thermometer code for the variable WAGE_PARTNER.

As for nominal inputs, a good choice is given by the *only-one code*. This code sets to 1 the ith bit if and only if $i = u$. In this way, the positive integer 4 is coded by

00010000, supposing that the corresponding variable can assume at most 8 different values (the same as the number of bits in the binary string).

By concatenating the binary strings obtained after coding each input variable, every sample (X_i, y_i) in the training set is transformed into a pair (Z_i, y_i), which can be viewed as a row in the truth table of a Boolean function f to be reconstructed by HC.

To this end, HC proceeds by grouping together binary strings that belong to the same class and are close to each other according to the Hamming distance. A basic concept in the procedure followed by HC is the notion of the *cluster*, which is a string of elements in the set $\{0, 1, *\}$, $*$ being a don't care symbol. By expanding the $*$ symbols in a cluster, we obtain the collection of all the binary strings having the same values in a fixed subset of components. As an example, the four binary strings '01001', '01101', '11001', '11101' form the cluster '$*1 * 01$', since all of them only have the values 1, 0, and 1 in the second, the fourth and the fifth components, respectively.

It can be shown that every cluster can be directly translated into an intelligible rule involving the original variables of the classification problem. Input attributes including only don't care symbols in the corresponding portion of the cluster do not appear as antecedents in the rule. Thus, the Boolean function reconstruction performed by HC automatically selects the relevant features for the problem at hand.

The procedure employed by HC does not involve the tuning of any parameter and consists of the following four steps:

1. Choose at random an example (Z_i, y_i) in the training set.
2. Build a cluster of points including Z_i and associate that cluster with the class y_i.
3. Remove the example (Z_i, y_i) from the training set. If the construction is not complete, go to Step 1.
4. Simplify the set of clusters generated and build the corresponding set of intelligible rules.

To improve the accuracy of the resulting classifier, at Step 2 clusters that cover as many training samples belonging to class y_i as possible and containing more don't care symbols are to be preferred. However, a complete exploration of all of the possible configurations requires an excessive computational burden. Sub-optimal results are obtained by employing a greedy procedure, called the *Maximum Covering Cube (MC)* criterion ([19]).

This criterion sequentially introduces a don't care symbol in the position that reduces the Hamming distance from the highest number of training examples belonging to class y_i, while avoiding to cover patterns associated with the opposite class. Several trials on artificial and real-world classification problems have established the good properties of the MC criterion.

The repeated execution of Steps 2–3 leads to a redundant set of clusters, whose simplification can improve the prediction accuracy of the final set of rules. To this end a greedy technique called *minimal pruning* can be adopted: it extracts the clusters that cover the maximum number of examples in the training set one at a time. At each extraction only the examples not included in the clusters already selected are considered. Breaks are tied by examining the whole covering.

2.4 Performance of a Classifier

The performance of a binary classifier (BC) is measured using sensitivity, specificity and accuracy ([22]):

$$\text{sensitivity} = \frac{TP}{TP + FN}, \quad \text{specificity} = \frac{TN}{TN + FP}$$

$$\text{accuracy} = \frac{TP + TN}{TP + TN + FP + FN}$$

where:

TP: Number of True Positive classified cases (BC correctly classifies),
TN: Number of True Negative classified cases (BC correctly classifies),
FP: Number of False Positive classified cases (BC labels a case as positive while it is negative),
FN: Number of False Negative classified cases (BC labels a case as negative while it is positive.)

Sensitivity gives the percentage of correctly classified participation events, whereas specificity provides the percentage of correctly classified non-participation events. In order to select the best model, we used the Noise/Signal Ratio (NSR) [12]:

$$\text{NSR} = \frac{1 - \text{sensitivity}}{\text{specificity}}$$

This index measures the false signals as a ratio of the good signals issued. A good model selection rule was established to choose the model that minimizes the value of NSR.

3 Example

We used data from the Venezuelan Household Survey (VHS) of the second semester 1999. This survey publishes official data on the main socioeconomic indicators, labor issues, household structure and human development variables, from a set of stratified representatives of Venezuelan households.

We choose a data set of 2,497 women from the economically active population, between 15 and 64 years old, and belonging to the higher quintile of the income distribution. From this data set, 1,876 samples were used during the training phase, and the rest were used for the testing phase. We selected the following explanatory variables:

AGE (*discrete*): Number of years of age.
AGE2 (*discrete*): AGE squared.

SINGLE (*Boolean*): Woman's marital status: 1 when the woman has no domestic partner, 0 otherwise.

SCHOOL (*discrete*): Last school year achieved and approved.

HOUSE_HEAD (*Boolean*): 1 when the individual woman is the head of her household, 0 otherwise.

SCHOOL2 (*discrete*): SCHOOL squared.

SCHOOL_LEVEL (*discrete*): Last educational level achieved: 1 = less than primary, 2 = primary, 3 = secondary, 4 = college and 5 = graduate school level completed.

WAGE_PARTNER (*continuous*): Wages and income from other sources gained by the woman's household domestic partner.

WAGE_OPP (*continuous*): Estimated opportunity cost for the woman relative to domestic work as a point estimate of a Mincer regression ([17]). It can be interpreted as an indicator of the economy's wage conditions.

Even if the number of children less than six years old is a widely suggested candidate as a determinant of female labor force participation, it was not included in the study. The target subset of women in the study is that belonging to the higher quintile in the income distribution, so there might be close substitutes (probably domestic workers) for the child care chores of the mothers among this group. All variables were normalized for SVM and HC.

3.1 Logit/Probit Model Results

The results of the econometric models (Tables 1 and 2 for the Probit and Logit specifications, respectively) show that all the estimated coefficients for both models are statistically significant ($p < 0.05$) and have the expected sign, except for WAGE_PARTNER.

Table 1. Results of the Probit specification

Variable	Coefficient	Std. Error	Z-Statistic	Prob.
AGE	0.065845	0.018763	3.509315	0.0004
AGE2	−0.000947	0.000228	−4.154941	0.0000
HOUSE_HEAD	0.244931	0.116785	2.097276	0.0360
SCHOOL	0.137365	0.041423	3.316141	0.0009
SCHOOL2	−0.013298	0.002606	−5.102038	0.0000
SCHOOL_LEVEL	0.374222	0.077280	4.842430	0.0000
SINGLE	0.533183	0.100506	5.304969	0.0000
WAGE_PARTNER	0.000000	0.000000	−2.863354	0.0042
WAGE_OPP	0.000000	0.000000	18.27651	0.0000
C	−2.692425	0.492388	−5.468091	0.0000

The relative magnitudes as well as the sign of the estimated coefficients are good proxies of the relevance of each of the explanatory variables. As previously men-

Table 2. Results of the Logit specification

Variable	Coefficient	Std. Error	Z-Statistic	Prob.
AGE	0.080228	0.033755	2.376801	0.0175
AGE2	−0.001213	0.000413	−2.936611	0.0033
HOUSE_HEAD	0.399916	0.201530	1.984399	0.0472
SCHOOL	0.266310	0.076020	3.503150	0.0005
SCHOOL2	−0.026688	0.004874	−5.476072	0.0000
SCHOOL_LEVEL	0.713473	0.140188	5.089400	0.0000
SINGLE	0.925895	0.185486	4.991739	0.0000
WAGE_PARTNER	0.000000	0.000000	−1.930788	0.0535
WAGE_OPP	0.000013	0.000000	16.77774	0.0000
C	−4.488251	0.882635	−5.085058	0.0000

tioned, Logit and Probit models allow the DM to analyze several determinant effects. In general, Logit models are interpreted more easily.

For example, the Logit estimate for women's marital status is approximately 0.926. An exponentiation of it gives 2.524, which is the estimated effect on the odds ([14]). This marginal effect suggests that the odds for those who were single to have been classified as participating are about 2.524 times as high as those who were married, other things being equal.

Instead of examining the marginal effect of a variable on the odds, it is also possible to evaluate the marginal effect of a variable on the probability of the event. The partial derivative of $\Pr(y = 1)$ with respect to the selected variable or the change-in-probability method suggested in [5] can be used to quantify this effect. For example, for the women's marital status variable, being single increases the probability of participation in about 17% of the cases.

Table 4 shows the performance of the Probit and Logit classifiers, during training and testing. Since the dependent variable is binary, the results of testing are evaluated as:

If the predicted probability is ≤ 0.5, then output is $+1$, -1 otherwise

One important point that has to be considered when using regression-based approaches is the possible presence of high correlation among variables. In our case, some pairs of variables such as AGE and AGE2, or SCHOOL and SCHOOL2, present high correlation, which could affect final results. Indeed, a direct computation reveals that the correlation among AGE and AGE2 is 0.97, whereas the correlation among SCHOOL and SCHOOL2 is 0.95. On the contrary, all the other pairs show a value of correlation of less than 0.5.

Highly correlated variables could suggest the presence of multicollinearity, a situation that could affect the regression's interpretation. Since multicollinearity is a matter of degree, some diagnostics can be used to estimate the possible effects. For example [11] suggests the use of the condition number $\phi = \lambda_{max}/\lambda_{min}$, where λ_{max} and λ_{min} are the maximum and minimum eigenvalues of the correlation matrix, respectively. In particular, if ϕ exceeds 1000, or $\sqrt{\phi}$ exceeds 30, the effect of multicollinearity should be considered. In our case, the eigenvalues and the square roots of condition numbers are presented in Table 3. So, it can be concluded that, even if there are suggestions of multicollinearity, its effects do not seem too important in this case.

Table 3. Eigenvalues and square roots $\sqrt{\phi}$ of the condition numbers

Eigenvalue	$\sqrt{\phi}$
3.5718	
1.8114	1.404
1.5889	1.499
0.8005	2.112
0.6387	2.365
0.4132	2.940
0.1414	5.025
0.0226	12.574
0.0115	17.625

Table 4. Performance results for considered classifiers

TRAINING	LOGIT	PROBIT	SVM	HC
Accuracy %	86.39	84.24	88.90	**91.25**
Sensitivity %	90.05	87.63	93.31	**95.44**
Specificity %	75.69	79.78	74.31	**85.61**
NSR	0.1315	0.1551	0.0900	**0.0533**
TESTING	LOGIT	PROBIT	SVM	HC
Accuracy %	89.39	88.59	88.79	**91.80**
Sensitivity %	93.51	92.05	94.98	**97.28**
Specificity %	75.69	77.08	80.49	**73.61**
NSR	0.0857	0.1031	0.0624	**0.0370**

3.2 SVM and HC Model Results

In our simulations we used LIBSVM [8] (integrated software that implements SVM) which allows choosing among different kernels. The best results were achieved using a Gaussian kernel with $C = 5000$ and $\sigma = 2.247$, which has identified 612 support vectors; its performances are shown in the fourth column of Table 4. These classification indexes are better than those obtained by Logit or Probit, but SVM does not provide any information regarding the importance of the explanatory variables. Even if the examples of the training set labeled as support vectors are recognized to be border points between the two classes, it is not clear how this information be used to infer some valuable conclusions regarding the problem at hand.

An intelligible model is instead provided by HC, whose performances are reported in the last column of Table 4.

Through the discretization and the binarization steps HC has transformed each example of the training set into a binary string of length 65. Then, two separate Boolean function reconstructions have produced **52** and **24** intelligible rules for output class 1 (labor participating woman) and 0 (not participating woman), respectively. Each rule is associated with a relevance value depending on how many examples of the training set it explains.

For example, the 10 more relevant rules for output class 1 are:

1. **if** SINGLE $= 1$ **and** HOUSE_HEAD $= 1$ **and** WAGE_OPP > 110000 **then** labor participating
2. **if** AGE ≤ 27 **and** SINGLE $= 1$ **and** WAGE_OPP > 41000 **then** labor participating
3. **if** AGE ≤ 29 **and** SCHOOL ≤ 15 **and** WAGE_PARTNER ≤ 660000 **and** $110000 <$ WAGE_OPP ≤ 345000 **then** labor participating
4. **if** AGE ≤ 28 **and** SCHOOL > 7 **and** $110000 <$ WAGE_OPP ≤ 305000 **then** labor participating
5. **if** $30 <$ AGE ≤ 56 **and** HOUSE_HEAD $= 1$ **and** SCHOOL ≤ 15 **and** WAGE_PARTNER ≤ 275000 **and** $110000 <$ WAGE_OPP ≤ 305000 **and** SCHOOL_LEVEL > 1 **then** labor participating
6. **if** AGE ≤ 28 **and** SINGLE $= 1$ **and** WAGE_OPP > 265000 **then** labor participating
7. **if** $36 <$ AGE ≤ 45 **and** WAGE_PARTNER ≤ 175000 **and** $9500 <$ WAGE_OPP ≤ 285000 **then** labor participating
8. **if** AGE ≤ 44 **and** HOUSE_HEAD $= 1$ **and** WAGE_PARTNER ≤ 175000 **and** $285000 <$ WAGE_OPP ≤ 450000 **then** labor participating
9. **if** $46 <$ AGE ≤ 58 **and** HOUSE_HEAD $= 1$ **and** WAGE_OPP > 110000 **and** $1 <$ SCHOOL_LEVEL ≤ 4 **then** labor participating
10. **if** $34 <$ AGE ≤ 57 **and** HOUSE_HEAD $= 1$ **and** SCHOOL ≤ 9 **and** $110000 <$ WAGE_OPP ≤ 355000 **and** SCHOOL_LEVEL > 1 **then** labor participating

By analyzing these rules, together with the other 42 for the same class, it is possible to derive a comprehensible model that points out some motivations and conditions for FLFP. As an example, note that rules 2 and 6 highlight the threshold of 26 years old for a rapid increase in the opportunity cost WAGE_OPP. This reflects the existence of laws and rules for the inclusion of young women in the working world.

It is important to note that the SVM and HC models are not affected by the possible presence of high correlation among variables.

4 Conclusions

This paper has presented an approach for comparing classifiers for the FLFP problem, that belong to the statistical and machine learning paradigms.

Probit and Logit models provide relevant indicators for each of the explanatory variables. In terms of predictive ability, the Logit specification is found to perform slightly better than the Probit specification. Nevertheless, additional analysis could be required to determine whether the statistical hypotheses are fulfilled or not (for example, correlation among variables), in order to obtain a better understanding of the estimated coefficient of significance.

The predictive ability of SVM models is better than that of Probit/Logit models. However, it is very difficult to interpret the information included in the support vectors. Moreover, a trial-and-error procedure is required to select the best parameters. On the other hand, HC does not require any parameter tuning and gives the best performance values. It is also able to provide useful rules for explaining the role of the explanatory variables. Finally, both machine learning techniques are insensitive to possible correlation among pairs of variables.

Both paradigms present advantages and disadvantages. The fact that neither approach is superior could provide a basic motivation for combining the best of both approaches.

Acknowledgements

The authors are grateful to the anonymous referees for their comments and valuable suggestions on an earlier version of this paper.

References

1. Bar M, Leukhina O (2005) Accounting for labor force participation of married women: the case of the U.S. since 1959. http://bss.sfsu.edu/mbar/Research/Paper2.pdf
2. Beaudry P, Lemieux T (1999) Evolution of the female labor force participation rate in Canada, 1976-1994. Applied Research Branch, Human Resources Development Canada, W994E
3. Becker G (1965) A theory of the allocation of time. The Economic Journal 75(299):493–517
4. Blau F, Ferber M (1986) The economics of women, men and work. Prentice-Hall
5. Boros E, Hammer PL, Ibaraki T, Kogan A, Mayoraz E, Muchnik I (2000) An implementation of logical analysis of data. IEEE Transactions on Knowledge and Data Engineering 12:292–306
6. Cain G (1965) Married woman in the labor force. University of Chicago Press
7. Campbell C (2000) An introduction to Kernel methods. In: Howlett RJ, Jain LC (eds) Radial basis function networks: design and applications. Springer Verlag, Berlin

8. Chang CC, Lin CJ (2001) LIBSVM: a library for support vector machines. http://www.csie.ntu.edu.tw/~cjlin/libsvm
9. Costa D (2000) From mill town to board room: the rise of women's paid labor. The Journal of Economic Perspectives 14(4):101–122
10. Cristianini N, Shawe-Taylor J (2000) An introduction to support vector machines. Cambridge University Press
11. Gujarati DN (2004) Basic econometrics. 4th Ed. McGraw-Hill/Irwin:341–386
12. Kaminsky G, Lizondo S, Reinhart C (1998) Leading indicators of currency crisis. IMF Staff Papers, No. 45
13. Kohavi R, Sahami M (1996) Error-based and entropy-based discretization of continuous features. In: Proceedings of the second international conference on knowledge discovery and data mining:114–119
14. Liao TF (1994) Interpreting probability models: logit probit and other generalized linear models. Sage University, Thousand Oaks, CA
15. Liu H, Setiono R (1997) Feature selection via discretization. IEEE Transactions on Knowledge and Data Engineering 9:642–645
16. McConnell C, Brue S (1997) Labor economics. McGraw-Hill
17. Mincer J (1962) Labor force participation of married woman. In: Aspects of Labor Economics, Universities NBER Studies Conference, No. 14, Princeton University Press:63–97
18. Muselli M, Liberati D (2000) Training digital circuits with hamming clustering. IEEE Transactions on Circuits and Systems I 47(4):513–527
19. Muselli M, Liberati D (2002) Binary rule generation via hamming clustering. IEEE Transactions on Knowledge and Data Engineering 14:1258–1268
20. Rau W, Waziensky R (1999) Industrialization, female labor force participation and modern division of labor by sex. Industrial Relations 38(4):504–521
21. Sachs J, Larraín F (1994) Macroeconomics in the global economy. Prentice Hall
22. Veropoulos K, Campbell C, Cristianini N (1999) Controlling the sensitivity of support vector machines. In: Proceedings of the international joint conference on artificial intelligence. Stockholm, Sweden:55-60

An Application of Kohonen's SOFM to the Management of Benchmarking Policies

Raquel Florez-Lopez

University of Leon, Department of Economics and Business Administration, Campus de Vegazana s/n, Leon, Spain
raquel.florez@unileon.es

The DEA model provides scores regarding firms' efficiency, but it does not obtain an overall map about each unit's position, in order to identify competitive clusters and improve the design of complete benchmarking policies. This lack makes the interpretation of DEA results difficult, together with its real applications for the management of firms.

To overcome this problem, this paper proposes combining *DEA and SOFM models* to reach a graphical representation of the situation of units in terms of efficiency and competitive strategies. This hybrid proposal is evaluated through a well-known public dataset on insurance agencies.

Key words: Benchmarking, Self Organizing Feature Map, DEA, Efficiency, Competitive Strategies, U Matrix

1 An Introduction to Efficiency

1.1 Concept and Components of Efficiency

In the current competitive environment, the evaluation of efficiency is a topic of increasing interest to firms in their guest for survival and profitability.

Efficiency is usually conceived of as a measure that relates both resources and results. In this way, a procedure or production system is said to be efficient if it is able to produce the maximum level of outputs from a certain level of inputs, or if it employs the minimum level of inputs to obtain some specific outputs ([17]).

The first quantitative approach to the efficiency concept was provided by [10], who distinguished two components inside the economic concept of efficiency: the *technical one* and the *allocative one* (Fig. 1).

- Given a particular mix of productive factors, a production process is technically efficient if the maximum level of outputs is reached while supporting the minimum costs (in terms of input consumption). In addition, the presence of technical

inefficiency could be merged from the excessive use of some inputs (pure technical inefficiency) or the selection of a suboptimal size (scale inefficiency) [3].
• A production process is allocativelly efficient if optimal input proportions have been selected given relative prices.

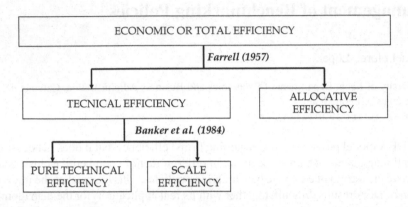

Fig. 1. Components of efficiency

By focusing on *technical efficiency*, [10] proposed a method for measuring the efficiency of firms within an industry by estimating the production function of firms which were 'fully-efficient' (i.e., a frontier production function). As a consequence, each unit's efficiency can be evaluated in connection with other homogeneous units, such that the efficiency measure is a relative and not absolute concept that indicates the deviation observed with regard to those units identified as being efficient.

Data Envelopment Analysis (DEA) is one of the most useful 'frontier' methods used in the evaluation of the relative efficiency of units. Besides, in recent years DEA has been extensively applied in the performance evaluation and benchmarking analysis of universities, financial firms, or schools, among others [14, 19, 22].

1.2 Data Envelopment Analysis

Data Envelopment Analysis (DEA) is a nonparametric technique that analyses the technical efficiency of decision making units (DMUs). A DMU is defined as the entity responsible for transforming inputs into outputs, and whose performance is evaluated.

The DEA model considers the amount of common inputs $(X_1, X_2, ..., X_m)$ and outputs $(Y_1, Y_2, ..., Y_s)$ associated with a group of DMUs, and obtains the efficiency score for the i-th DMU as follows:

$$Efficiency_{DMU_i} = \left(\frac{weighted\ sum\ of\ outputs}{weighted\ sum\ of\ inputs} \right)_{DMU_i} \tag{1}$$

According to this score, DEA model classifies each DMU as 'efficient' or 'inefficient', through its comparison with all possible linear combinations of the remaining DMUs in the sample. The group of efficient DMUs forms the efficient frontier (B, E, F, G in Fig. 2), and the distance to this frontier is employed to identify inefficient behaviour (A-A', C-C', D-D' in Fig. 2).

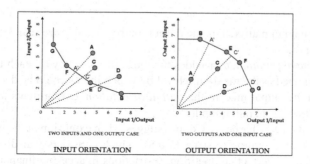

Fig. 2. Efficient frontier representation in DEA

For each inefficient DMU, DEA identifies a set of efficient individuals that can be used as benchmarking references. In addition, a measure is provided regarding the proportional input reduction (input orientation) or output increase (output orientation) that each DMU needs to become efficient.

To obtain previous scores, different approaches can be followed. Charnes, Cooper & Rhodes proposed the following model (CCR), solved through a dual problem [4], which assumes constant returns to scale (CRS).

Let each DMU_i be characterized by input-output data collected in the row vector (X_i, Y_i). Let X, Y denote the matrixes of the input and output data (respectively) for all DMUs in the sample (where N is the sample's size). The relative efficiency score of a DMU_i is obtained by solving the following linear programming model:

$$Min\ \theta\ ('Input\ orientation')$$
$$subject\ to$$
$$\lambda Y - s^+ = y_i$$
$$\lambda X + s^- = \theta X_i \quad (2)$$
$$\lambda, s^+, s^- \geq 0$$
$$\theta \in (0, 1]$$

$$Max \; \varphi \; (\text{'}Output \; orientation\text{'})$$
$$subject \; to$$
$$\lambda Y - s^+ = \varphi y_i$$
$$\lambda X + s^- = X_i \tag{3}$$
$$\lambda, s^+, s^- \geq 0$$
$$\varphi \in [1, \infty)$$

where X is the input matrix, Y is the output matrix, θ and φ are scalars, and λ is the weight vector.

In the *input orientation*, θ provides the index of efficiency for each DMU, which must be interpreted as the maximum level by which inputs could be decreased without a shift in the output mix. In the *output orientation*, φ represents the maximum growth of outputs from initial inputs.

Later on, Banker, Charnes & Cooper suggested an extension of the model (BCC) [3] toward variable returns to scale (VRS), which considers that diverse circumstances (such as imperfect competition, restrictions in accesing financial resources, etc.) can cause units not to operate at the efficient scale.

Thus they modified the linear programming model to introduce a restriction of convexity, such that:

$$e'\lambda = 1 \tag{4}$$

where e is a unitary vector (all components are equal to 1).

The BCC-efficiency scores are also called 'pure technical efficiency scores', since they eliminate the 'scale component' of the efficiency measurement.

In considering both proposals, [7] defined the 'scale efficiency' (SE) as the ratio of the 'global technical efficiency' (GTE) score (measured by the CCR model) to the 'pure technical efficiency' score (PTE) (measured by the BCC model):

$$CCR_{global \; technical \; efficiency} \div BCC_{pure \; technical \; efficiency} =$$
$$= Scale \; efficiency \leq 1 \tag{5}$$

This decomposition provides information regarding the sources of inefficiency, and indicates whether it is caused by inefficient operations ($PTE < 1$), by disadvantageous conditions displayed by the scale efficiency ($SE < 1$) or by both.

In the presence of scale inefficiency, the DMU's nature must be questioned to determine if it is operating in the area of 'increasing returns to scale' (IRS) or 'decreasing returns to scale' (DRS). To measure this, a new DEA analysis is carried out (the BCC model), with the restriction of *non-increasing returns to scale* (NIRS). Then the punctuations from the pure VRS and NIRS models are compared, such that:

$$If \; VRS_{technical \; efficiency} = NIRS_{technical \; efficiency} \; then \; DRS$$
$$If \; VRS_{technical \; efficiency} \neq NIRS_{technical \; efficiency} \; then \; IRS \tag{6}$$

Figure 3 compares the CCR (constant returns to scale) and BCC (variable returns to scale) models, providing an input-output frontier that has piece-wise linear characteristics with *(a)* increasing returns to scale occurring in the first solid line segment

(A-B), followed by *(b)* decreasing returns to scale in the second (B-D) and third (D-E) segments, and *(c)* constant returns to scale (B). DMUs named A, B, D and E are considered to be efficient in the BCC model, but the CCR model only regards the B unit as efficient.

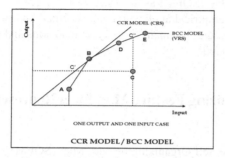

Fig. 3. Differences between the CCR and BCC DEA models

Traditionally, DEA has qualified many units as being efficient, except where the combined number of inputs and outputs is small relative to the sample size. As a consequence, very specialized units can be considered to be efficient due to there being only one input or output. In order to avoid this problem, [2] presented an extension of the original model to provide more information regarding the behaviour of efficient units. They compared each efficient unit with a linear combination of the rest of the efficient units, such that if the DMU was able to increase the consumption of its inputs and remained efficient (or alternatively, decrease its outputs), it would obtain a 'superefficiency index' higher than 1.

In conclusion, DEA scores are a useful tool that provides benchmarking references for inefficient units, and could orientate future improvement strategies.

Nevertheless, one of the main limitations of DEA is the lack of a graphical representation of each unit's position relative to the group, if multiple inputs and outputs are presented, which could be very interesting for the detection of competitive clusters[1]; additionally, for each i-th inefficient unit, DEA provides a list of efficient DMUs as reference, but the combination of strategies from these benchmarks usually brings near the i-th unit to other firms which were not initially identified but which are its final competitive references. A graphical representation of the firms' position could inform about these movements but DEA is only able to represent the efficient frontier in the presence of one input and two outputs (or one output and two inputs, depending on the model's orientation). Regarding this, see Fig. 2.

To overcome this problem, we propose combining the DEA results and self-organised neural nets. Kohonen's Self Organizing Feature Map (SOFM) provides

---

[1] Reference [9] proposed two-dimensional graphs for the representation of scores, but no distances among units were obtained. Additionally, [16] considered a gradient approach for a single unit.

a topographical representation of a group of individuals ([15, 16]), and allows a high dimensional structure to be presented as a two-dimension topology; from this representation, clusters of data can be detected, which is able to simplify the analysis of the DEA results.

The remainder of this article is structured as follows. First, the use of the Self Organizing Feature Map (SOFM) as an instrument for efficiency representation is analysed. Second, an empirical application is performed on a well-known database on agencies of an insurance company. Finally, conclusions and suggestions for further research are provided.

2 The Self Organizing Feature Map for a Representation of Efficiency

Kohonen proposed the Self Organizing Feature Map (SOFM), a competitive, unsupervised and self organizing neural net, based on the establishment of competitions and mutual links between neighbouring cells (neurons) [15, 16].

The SOFM net is organised in two different layers (Fig. 4), and comprises two different stages:

1. *Learning or Training Stage*: In this phase each output cell is trained to identify some typical patterns, so that neighbouring cells are represented near individuals. To achieve it, each time an individual $x(t)$ is presented to the input layer, the net obtains a 'winner output cell' c (the nearest output neuron to the pattern). Then c modifies its typical m parameters (weights), and other neighbouring neurons (i) also do so:

$$m_{i,k}(t+1) = m_{i,k}(t) + \alpha(t)h\left(|i-c|, t\right)\left(x_k(t) - m_{i,k}(t)\right), \quad if\, i \in N_c(t)$$
$$m_{i,k}(t+1) = m_{i,k}(t), \quad if \quad i \notin N_c(t)$$

   where k is an input variable, $h\left(|i-c|, t\right)$ is a function that establishes the 'neighbourhood zone' or $N_c(t)$, and $\alpha(t)$ is a parameter known as the 'learning rate' such that $0 < \alpha(t) < 1$.

2. *Operation or Working Stage*: In this phase each cells acts as a specific feature detector. Each time a new individual is presented to the net, the model assigns it to an only cell, obtained through the calculation of the distance between the input data and the weight vector m for each output neuron; the neuron with the minimum distance obtains the new unit ([15, 16]).

Additionally, SOFM arranges clusters into different regions of the lattice, which can be displayed through the U-matrix methods or UMM ([25, 26, 27]). The simplest UMM focuses on calculating, for each n-th neuron, the sum of the distance of its weight vector $[w(n)]$ to the weight vectors of the set of immediate neighbours on the map $[NN(n)]$, the so-called U-height ([25]):

$$U - height(n) = \sum_{m \in NN(n)} d(w(n) - w(m)). \tag{7}$$

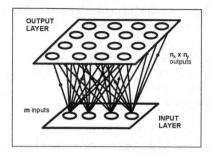

Fig. 4. The SOFM model

The U-matrix is a display of the U-heights on top of the grid positions of the cells on the map. The landscape can be interpreted as follows: if there are hills or walls, then the neighbouring weights are quite distant, i.e., the process states differ significantly. If a depression or valley can be seen, then the process states are quite similar ([26]).

In this paper, the SOFM is proposed for the topographical representation of both efficient and inefficient DMUs. To obtain it, some analogies must be made:

- DMUs act as $x(t)$ individuals on the SOFM map.
- To measure efficiency, all combinations of outputs and inputs must be considered.
- Each SOFM input variable will be obtained as the quotient between one output and one input; both previously normalised to reduce bias.

Once the SOFM is developed, the relative weights for the output cells will be analysed to obtain a final score for each DMU, which will be compared to the DEA results. Additionally, a cluster analysis on competitive groups will be performed using the U-matrix.

Finally, the benchmarking strategies proposed by DEA will be studied, and their consequences in relation to inefficient DMUs' positions inside the map will be observed.

3 Empirical Application

To test the SOFM's performance in the representation of benchmarking strategies, a well-known dataset [2] has been evaluated ([23]), which considers the efficiency of 63 agencies of an insurance company relative to the launching of a new contract (Table 1).

Inputs refer to several types of clients that are related to the current insurance coverage; besides, the potential new premiums have been included, which depend on the clients' current coverage, too. Outputs consider the aim of the insurance agencies:

---

[2] Accesible at http://www.wiso.uni-dortmund.de/lsfg/or/scheel/data/scheel1.txt

Table 1. Inputs and outputs of insurance agencies

Inputs	Outputs
No. 'type A' of clients	No. new contracts
No. 'type B' of clients	Sum of new premiums (DEM)
No. 'type C' of clients	-
Potential new premiums (DEM)	-

to sell as many contracts as possible, and to obtain the highest premiums possible (in Deutsche Marks or DEM) [3].

According to [23], a DEA model has been established, using the BCC alternative (variable returns to scale) joined to the input orientation and the "superefficiency" index (Table 2).[4]

Table 2. DEA results

	(Super)efficiency	Inefficiency
No. of DMUs	11	52
Min DEA score	1.029	0.292
Max DEA Score	∞	0.976
Average DEA Score	-	0.651
Std. deviation	-	0.209

Even if this information is valuable, due to both efficient and inefficient units being identified next to the benchmarking references, the insurance company is not able to solve some problems, such as:
- *How many different efficient policies could be identified from these agencies?*
- *Which agencies are developing a similar competitive strategy (input-output mix)?*
- *How should managers be moved from efficient to inefficient agencies to improve the firms' overall efficiency?.*
To solve these and similar questions, it is necessary to have information regarding the relative distances and neighborhoods between DMUs. We evaluate a 2-dimensional SOFM which represents the main relationships between agencies, and considers the presence of 63 individuals, as defined by four inputs and two outputs.

Nevertheless, the efficiency of each agency is not directly measured from these gross numbers, but from relationships among outputs and inputs. In this way, if the map tries to represent the firms' relative efficiency, the original data must be transformed into 8 different quotients ([0,1] normalised) [28]:

$V1 = O1/I1$; $V2 = O1/I2$; $V3 = O1/I3$; $V4 = O1/I4$;
$V5 = O2/I1$; $V6 = O2/I2$; $V7 = O2/I3$; $V8 = O2/I4$.

---

[3] A discussion on the effect of the number of variables in DEA can be consulted in [12, 14].
[4] Infinity means that efficiency is preserved under arbitrary proporcional increase of inputs. EMS software.

Each variable shows the capacity of each input for obtaining each particular output; the greater the ratio, the higher the firm's efficiency.

Regarding the map's shape, an 8x12 lattice has been selected, using Sammon's Mapping ([16, 20]). The number of neurons exceeds the sample size, due to the topographical map being used to represent the relative positions of patterns; in this case, [16] recommends using at least as many cells as patterns, and preferably some more cells, to avoid the massive inclusion of multiple DMUs inside the same neuron, which prevents one from visualizing distance among them.

A decay learning rate has been used, from $\alpha=0.9$ (early training) to $\alpha=0.1$ (late training). The 'neighborhood radio' has been adjusted too, from 13.04 (initial maximum Euclidean distance) to 1 (actualization of the winner cell and its four nearest neighbours) and a two-stage learning process has been applied (rough and fine learning).

Figure 5 shows the results on the map obtained for the 63 agencies (in bold and bigger, efficient units). Below, there is a contour graph for each output cell's average score, obtained from its 8 weights (see Annex 1, Table 3). The axes' units refer to the SOFM architecture (8x12 lattice).

The analysis of the previous map allows us to observe that efficient firms obtain a higher average-weight (0.47) than inefficient ones (0.23). This weight has been obtained as follows:

$$Average\ weight(ef.\ DMUs) = \frac{\sum_{i=1}^{K}(weight\ for\ efficient\ DMU(i))}{K}$$

$$Average\ weight(innef.\ DMUs) = \frac{\sum_{j=1}^{L}(weight\ for\ inefficient\ DMU(j))}{L}$$

$$(8)$$

where each DMU's cell refers to the SOFM unit where the efficient or inefficient DMU is situated; the average weight for this cell is considered (Annex 1, Table 3).

Besides, efficient units are mainly located at the borders of the map, and inefficient ones are nearer to the centre, not far from the usual image of the efficient frontier (Fig. 2, output orientation).

In addition, it is possible to observe that efficient firms have different strategies between them (see Fig. 5 and Table 3); for example, n.6 is located very far from entity n.47, and the inputs and outputs mix shows the reason: n.6 employs minimum inputs, and its outputs are quite limited too, such that only input 1 and output 2 have modest values. Nevertheless, agency n.47 employs many resources and obtains high outputs too (it is focused on input 2 and output 1). Even if common sense tells us that n.6 is having a worse performance than n.47, n.6 has the lowest values for inputs and outputs thus DEA considers it as "efficient" in order to complete the frontier; nevertheless, it is not a real efficiency but a extreme "VRS effect" in DEA model. The SOFM model allows us to identify this situation, if the weights are compared.

Additionally, SOFM identifies n.63 DMU as the most efficient unit, and the analysis of inputs and outputs confirms it: from minimum inputs (especially I1 and I3), it reaches some of the highest levels of outputs, that is to say, it has developed the most

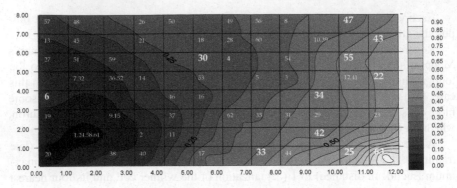

Fig. 5. SOFM for efficient and inefficient DMUs

competitive strategy of all agencies; nevertheless, DEA can not provide this sort of information.

Other interesting efficient agencies are n. 22, 43, 47 and 55, which are located in close proximity on the map. DEA simply identifies them as efficient units, but the neural net is able to verify that their competitive positions are quite similar (focused on inputs 1, 2 and 4, and on output 2).

Previous results can be completed through the U-matrix visualization (Fig. 6). The smaller the distances (clearer zones), the closer the competitive strategies between DMUs. To avoid bias among neurons at the borders of the map, an average U-height has been obtained, which considers the relative number of immediate neighbors on the map:

$$[U - height(n)]_{average} = \frac{U - height(n)}{card[NN(n)]} \tag{9}$$

From the U-heights, several clusters have been identified; each cluster fills a 'valley' inside the U-matrix (low heights), being surrounded by 'mountains' (higher heights). To identify clusters, we propose the following algorithm:

$Set=\{DMU_1, ..., DMU_N\}$
For $i = 1$ to N
Random k, $k \in Set$
$Group_i = DMU_k$
$here$:
$Incl_i = \emptyset$
For $j = 1$ to card($Group_i\_neighbours$)
    If $Qual(Group_i \cup DMU_j \geq Qual(Group_i)$ then
    $Incl_i = Incl_i \cup DMU_j$
    End if
Next j
If $Incl_i \neq \emptyset$ then
$Group_i = Group_i \cup Incl_i$

Goto *here*:
Else
$Set = Set - \{Group_i\}$
Next i

where N is the number of DMUs, $Group_i\_neighbours$ are cells surrounding the group, $DMU_j \in Group_i\_neighbours$; a cell is said to be a neighbour if the Euclidean distance to (at least) one cell inside the group is not greater than $\sqrt{2}$. For each group, a measure of clustering quality is provided, as follows:

$$Qual(Group_i) = \frac{1}{Intheight(Group_i)} \cdot Extheight(Group_i) \qquad (10)$$

where *Extheight* is the average U-height of neighbouring cells, and *Intheight* is the average U-height of cells inside the i-th group.

Figure 6 summarizes the most important clusters which were identified by the previous algorithm.

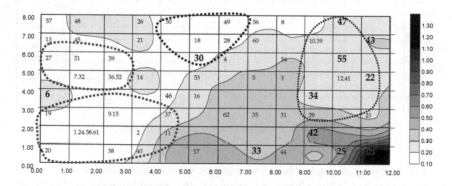

Fig. 6. U-Matrix and competitive clusters

As can be observed, the most efficient units obtain the highest heights, that is to say, they develop quite specific strategies to reach final outputs. In this way, DMUs n.42, n.25, and especially n.63, conform to individual clusters, such that their behavior appears to be very different compared with their neighboring DMUs.

Additionally, n.6 is clearly separated from the other units too, due to its production mix being quite rare (minimum inputs and outputs).

Regarding agencies n. 22, 34, 47 and 55, the U-matrix confirms few differences among them, such that they conform to an efficient cluster (*Qual*=1.5) which also includes some inefficient firms, n. 10, 12, 29, 39, 41) and only n.43 seems to have a particularly different strategy (Fig. 6, fine dotted line).

Regarding the inefficient units, three different groups can be identified (Fig. 6, thick dotted lines); firstly, units n. 7, 27, 32, 36, 51, 52, and n.59 conform to a cluster (*Qual*−1.5), being characterized by a quite low efficiency score. Secondly, units n. 1,

2, 9, 11, 15, 19, 20, 24, 37, 38, 40, 58, 61 build another cluster (*Qual*=1.6), which includes the most inefficient firms inside the map. Thirdly, DMUs n. 18, 28, 30, 49, and 50 are a different cluster (*Qual*=1.3), nearer to the efficient positions. The analysis of weights inside each cluster allows us to understand each group's particular input and output mix; many similarities can be found and, as consequence, benchmarking policies should be quite similar for units inside each cluster.

To check the relative effects of the benchmarking proposals on distances among agencies, we have developed an additional SOFM, using the data proposed for the benchmark coefficients, without slacks. These new individuals have been positioned on the original map, to discover the projected movements of firms' positions (Fig. 7). Some arrows have been included, which indicate the expected movement of DMUs if they follow DEA's recommendations; each arrow departs from the original position and arrives at the new predicted site. In addition, several formats have been used (related to arrows arriving at each previous cluster).

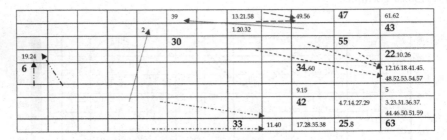

Fig. 7. SOFM after benchmarking proposals

This new map shows that benchmarking proposals really improve the inefficient agencies' scores, as DEA affirms (new value: 0.46), but additionally the SOFM provides information regarding the real units of reference after movements, and the novel competitive strategies.

As far as the inefficient competitive clusters are concerned, units from group n.1 (DMUs n. 7, 27, 32, 51, 52, 57, 59) are majority displaced to the rightbottom corner of the map, near to efficient units n.22 and 63. DMUs from the second group (n. 1, 9, 15, 20, 24, 38, 58, 61) are moved in a greater part to the medium-right zone of the map, not far from efficient DMUs n.34 and 42. Finally, agencies inside or near the third inefficient group (n. 18, 28, 49, 50, 56) are more diversified, and they finally appear to be closely located to efficient units n. 47, 25 and 63.

Previous information is relevant, for example, for the staff management: a manager from agency n.47 could supervise future decisions of agencies n.56 and n.49; a manager from agency n.33 could direct future competitive policies for n.40 and n.11, and so on.

4 Conclusions

From the analysis of the above results, three main conclusions may be highlighted:

- The DEA's benchmarking proposals allow the internal management of entities to be guided, identifying their strong and weak points.
- Nevertheless, the presence of multiple inputs and outputs prevents a direct graphical representation of DEA scores from being obtained, which greatly reduces the interpretation of the results and the efficient execution of improvement actions.
- To overcome this problem, the application of a SOFM model, using quotients between outputs and inputs as explanative attributes, together with a new U-matrix segmentation algorithm, complements DEA results and allows us to identify similarities among efficient and inefficient units, and additionally recognizes individuals that, being characterized as efficient by the DEA model, have very particular behaviors, in that they achieve a 'theoretical' but not practical efficiency.

As for future developments, the effect of DEA weight restrictions on inputs and outputs will be included in the SOFM model ([1, 12, 19, 24]); moreover, the influence of both DEA input and output orientations should be analysed, together with other DEA extensions as 'window analysis', additive models, alternative 'super-efficiency' measures or fuzzy measures of efficiency ([5, 7, 8]). Finally, a sensitivity analysis should be performed, too [11].

References

1. Allen R, Athanassopoulos A, Dyson RG, Thanassoulis E (1997) Weights restrictions and value judgments in DEA: evolution, development and future directions. Annals of Operations Research 73:13–34
2. Andersen P, Petersen NC (1993) A procedure for ranking efficient units in data envelopment analysis. Management Science 39(10):1261–1264
3. Banker RD, Charnes A, Cooper WW (1984) Some models for estimating technical and scale inefficiencies in data envelopment analysis. Management Science 30(9):1078–1092
4. Charnes A, Cooper WW, Rhodes E (1978) Measuring the efficiency of decision making units. European Journal of Operational Research 2(6):429–444
5. Charnes A, Cooper WW, Golany B, Seiford LM, Stutz J (1985) Foundations of data envelopment analysis for a Pareto-Koopmans efficient empirical production function. Journal of Econometrics 30:91–107
6. Charnes A, Cooper WW, Lewin AY, Seiford LM (eds) (1994) Data envelopment analysis: theory, methodology, and applications. Kluwer, Boston
7. Cooper WW, Seiford LM, Lawrence M, Tone K (2000) A comprehensive text with models, applications, references and DEA-solver software. Kluwer Academic Publishers, Norwell
8. Dia M (2004) A model of fuzzy Data Envelopment Analysis. INFOR 42(4):267–279
9. El-Mahgary S, Lahdelma R (1995) Data envelopment analysis: visualizing the results. European Journal of Operational Research 85:700–710
10. Farrell MJ (1957) The measurement of productive efficiency. Journal of the Royal Statistical Society Series A 120(III):253–281

Coord.	V1	V2	V3	V4	V5	V6	V7	V8	Aver.	Coord.	V1	V2	V3	V4	V5	V6	V7	V8	Aver.
(1,1)	0.021	0.026	0.009	0.012	0.019	0.063	0.024	0.058	0.029	(7,1)	0.114	0.078	1.000	0.092	0.130	0.205	0.997	0.211	0.353
(1,2)	0.050	0.068	0.006	0.036	0.048	0.136	0.026	0.102	0.059	(7,2)	0.193	0.198	0.774	0.210	0.146	0.254	0.794	0.243	0.352
(1,3)	0.052	0.085	0.000	0.043	0.071	0.201	0.032	0.148	0.079	(7,3)	0.273	0.313	0.541	0.320	0.166	0.307	0.599	0.280	0.350
(1,4)	0.058	0.034	0.007	0.015	0.161	0.298	0.087	0.257	0.115	(7,4)	0.202	0.341	0.363	0.333	0.119	0.308	0.392	0.270	0.291
(1,5)	0.073	0.144	0.013	0.098	0.114	0.291	0.065	0.229	0.128	(7,5)	0.236	0.566	0.216	0.517	0.076	0.245	0.118	0.199	0.272
(1,6)	0.087	0.256	0.020	0.181	0.065	0.282	0.042	0.198	0.141	(7,6)	0.141	0.639	0.132	0.489	0.037	0.285	0.080	0.193	0.250
(1,7)	0.086	0.284	0.015	0.201	0.058	0.278	0.033	0.193	0.143	(7,7)	0.281	0.580	0.093	0.500	0.127	0.398	0.089	0.305	0.297
(1,8)	0.217	0.432	0.009	0.282	0.087	0.270	0.016	0.165	0.185	(7,8)	0.206	0.478	0.134	0.455	0.128	0.443	0.159	0.373	0.297
(2,1)	0.077	0.082	0.099	0.079	0.044	0.098	0.012	0.094	0.086	(8,1)	0.204	0.305	1.000	0.324	0.114	0.239	1.000	0.230	0.427
(2,2)	0.055	0.040	0.021	0.026	0.007	0.012	0.015	0.013	0.024	(8,2)	0.184	0.369	0.771	0.356	0.083	0.253	0.646	0.219	0.360
(2,3)	0.053	0.097	0.032	0.070	0.021	0.083	0.033	0.065	0.056	(8,3)	0.180	0.370	0.755	0.354	0.075	0.243	0.598	0.208	0.348
(2,4)	0.065	0.174	0.015	0.126	0.035	0.149	0.026	0.111	0.088	(8,4)	0.194	0.518	0.613	0.504	0.057	0.222	0.417	0.190	0.339
(2,5)	0.105	0.219	0.051	0.188	0.045	0.158	0.048	0.128	0.118	(8,5)	0.216	0.739	0.410	0.729	0.024	0.170	0.136	0.147	0.321
(2,6)	0.130	0.253	0.043	0.219	0.064	0.200	0.050	0.162	0.140	(8,6)	0.271	0.676	0.218	0.634	0.073	0.273	0.106	0.223	0.309
(2,7)	0.191	0.353	0.005	0.214	0.092	0.267	0.016	0.159	0.162	(8,7)	0.340	0.556	0.118	0.557	0.141	0.353	0.102	0.310	0.310
(2,8)	0.303	0.567	0.013	0.352	0.094	0.275	0.013	0.156	0.222	(8,8)	0.185	0.489	0.194	0.503	0.108	0.424	0.213	0.382	0.312
(3,1)	0.092	0.107	0.144	0.109	0.063	0.139	0.017	0.133	0.120	(9,1)	0.295	0.534	1.000	0.558	0.096	0.272	1.000	0.249	0.500
(3,2)	0.056	0.087	0.068	0.075	0.018	0.063	0.064	0.057	0.061	(9,2)	0.185	0.469	0.727	0.455	0.112	0.418	0.862	0.260	0.448
(3,3)	0.039	0.139	0.090	0.113	0.013	0.098	0.076	0.079	0.081	(9,3)	0.120	0.565	0.688	0.507	0.058	0.402	0.604	0.320	0.408
(3,4)	0.079	0.188	0.066	0.159	0.031	0.131	0.057	0.105	0.102	(9,4)	0.185	0.617	0.563	0.599	0.069	0.353	0.428	0.298	0.389
(3,5)	0.133	0.249	0.091	0.236	0.046	0.147	0.071	0.127	0.137	(9,5)	0.193	0.651	0.480	0.656	0.035	0.215	0.217	0.189	0.330
(3,6)	0.152	0.293	0.057	0.247	0.074	0.229	0.062	0.179	0.162	(9,6)	0.378	0.774	0.234	0.769	0.085	0.273	0.112	0.236	0.358
(3,7)	0.219	0.354	0.030	0.267	0.117	0.291	0.042	0.208	0.191	(9,7)	0.304	0.644	0.186	0.654	0.123	0.401	0.154	0.257	0.353
(3,8)	0.249	0.584	0.017	0.367	0.103	0.390	0.025	0.227	0.245	(9,8)	0.262	0.533	0.178	0.551	0.153	0.469	0.201	0.423	0.346
(4,1)	0.054	0.100	0.177	0.098	0.040	0.129	0.204	0.121	0.116	(10,1)	0.295	0.586	0.974	0.604	0.142	0.436	1.000	0.390	0.553
(4,2)	0.060	0.154	0.141	0.157	0.027	0.121	0.124	0.114	0.112	(10,2)	0.142	0.308	0.497	0.303	0.183	0.581	0.993	0.512	0.440
(4,3)	0.061	0.188	0.134	0.165	0.024	0.129	0.110	0.108	0.115	(10,3)	0.154	0.427	0.442	0.442	0.134	0.530	0.638	0.481	0.406
(4,4)	0.155	0.333	0.168	0.322	0.058	0.179	0.127	0.157	0.187	(10,4)	0.242	0.623	0.530	0.622	0.122	0.469	0.497	0.409	0.439
(4,5)	0.132	0.416	0.158	0.399	0.022	0.138	0.074	0.118	0.182	(10,5)	0.275	0.692	0.466	0.674	0.117	0.429	0.366	0.364	0.423
(4,6)	0.198	0.370	0.082	0.328	0.093	0.245	0.062	0.193	0.196	(10,6)	0.323	0.775	0.269	0.768	0.124	0.462	0.213	0.398	0.417
(4,7)	0.311	0.405	0.030	0.338	0.183	0.373	0.049	0.284	0.247	(10,7)	0.232	0.713	0.219	0.737	0.112	0.511	0.205	0.458	0.399
(4,8)	0.197	0.601	0.022	0.383	0.113	0.504	0.038	0.299	0.270	(10,8)	0.264	0.639	0.137	0.596	0.148	0.530	0.153	0.436	0.363
(5,1)	0.114	0.146	0.574	0.192	0.056	0.133	0.493	0.149	0.232	(11,1)	0.312	0.668	1.000	0.683	0.184	0.584	1.000	0.519	0.619
(5,2)	0.106	0.233	0.310	0.264	0.040	0.149	0.237	0.151	0.186	(11,2)	0.242	0.495	0.744	0.501	0.199	0.592	0.983	0.526	0.535
(5,3)	0.104	0.315	0.214	0.274	0.040	0.195	0.166	0.156	0.183	(11,3)	0.168	0.583	0.525	0.567	0.122	0.584	0.648	0.502	0.462
(5,4)	0.190	0.273	0.188	0.270	0.094	0.231	0.189	0.206	0.206	(11,4)	0.300	0.703	0.463	0.677	0.147	0.511	0.428	0.431	0.458
(5,5)	0.226	0.355	0.168	0.356	0.093	0.211	0.134	0.190	0.217	(11,5)	0.333	0.744	0.428	0.706	0.160	0.529	0.387	0.440	0.466
(5,6)	0.281	0.503	0.075	0.447	0.114	0.310	0.064	0.245	0.255	(11,6)	0.361	0.840	0.341	0.801	0.175	0.605	0.316	0.502	0.493
(5,7)	0.271	0.504	0.043	0.403	0.153	0.425	0.058	0.310	0.271	(11,7)	0.282	0.765	0.223	0.733	0.155	0.620	0.235	0.517	0.441
(5,8)	0.262	0.530	0.046	0.432	0.168	0.512	0.071	0.377	0.300	(11,8)	0.268	0.735	0.087	0.625	0.147	0.593	0.101	0.447	0.375
(6,1)	0.174	0.180	1.000	0.276	0.076	0.137	0.814	0.176	0.354	(12,1)	1.000	0.633	1.000	0.741	1.000	1.000	1.000	1.000	0.922
(6,2)	0.143	0.209	0.652	0.269	0.062	0.149	0.529	0.167	0.273	(12,2)	0.261	0.742	0.654	0.709	0.196	0.677	0.687	0.572	0.562
(6,3)	0.166	0.328	0.308	0.310	0.092	0.271	0.316	0.232	0.253	(12,3)	0.178	0.754	0.615	0.705	0.106	0.641	0.652	0.524	0.522
(6,4)	0.127	0.360	0.178	0.338	0.073	0.313	0.190	0.264	0.231	(12,4)	0.223	0.849	0.473	0.779	0.122	0.675	0.487	0.542	0.519
(6,5)	0.349	0.370	0.156	0.392	0.155	0.260	0.140	0.243	0.258	(12,5)	0.268	0.943	0.333	0.852	0.138	0.709	0.324	0.559	0.516
(6,6)	0.286	0.522	0.070	0.463	0.113	0.316	0.060	0.249	0.260	(12,6)	0.308	0.965	0.321	0.919	0.137	0.643	0.281	0.529	0.513
(6,7)	0.240	0.575	0.053	0.437	0.108	0.392	0.055	0.269	0.266	(12,7)	0.341	1.000	0.306	0.999	0.132	0.581	0.234	0.502	0.512
(6,8)	0.220	0.457	0.078	0.404	0.150	0.468	0.112	0.372	0.283	(12,8)	0.305	0.868	0.197	0.812	0.140	0.587	0.167	0.474	0.444

Table 3. Appendix 1. SOFM weights [(x,y coordinates)]

11. Hughes A, Yaisawarng S (2004) Sensitivity and dimensionality tests of DEA efficiency scores. European Journal of Operational Research 154:410–422
12. Jahanshahloo GR, Soleimani-Damaneh M (2005) A note on simulating weights restrictions in DEA: an improvement of Thanassoulis and Allen's method. Computers & Operations Research 32:1037–1044
13. Jenkins L, Anderson M (2003) A multivariate statistical approach to reducing the number of variables in data envelopment analysis. European Journal of Operational Research 147:51–61

14. Kao C, Liu SH (2004) Predicting bank performance with financial forecasts: a case of Taiwan commercial banks. Journal of Banking and Finance 28:2353–2368
15. Kohonen T (1990) The self-organising map. Proceedings of the IEEE 78(9):1464–1480
16. Kohonen T (1997) Self-organising maps. Springer-Verlag, Berlin Heidelberg New York
17. Lovell CAK (1993) Production frontiers and productive efficiency. In: Fried HO, Novell CAK, Schmidt SS (eds) The measurement of productive efficiency, techniques and applications. Oxford University Press, New York
18. Maital S, Vaninsky A (1999) Data envelopment analysis with a single DMU: a graphic projected-gradient approach. European Journal of Operational Research 115:518–528
19. Paradi J, Schaffnit C (2004) Commercial branch performance evaluation and results communication in a Canadian bank? a DEA application. European Journal of Operational Research 156:719–735
20. Sammon JW (1969) A nonlinear mapping for data structure analysis. IEEE Transactions on Computers C-18(5):401–409
21. Sarrico CS, Dyson RG (2004) Restricting virtual weights in DEA. European Journal of Operational Research 159:17–34
22. Seiford LM (1996) Data envelopment analysis: the evolution of the state of the art (1978-1995). Journal of Productivity Analysis 7:99–137
23. Scheel H (1999) On continuity of the BCC efficiency measure. In: Westermann G (ed) Data envelopment analysis in the public and private sector. Gabler, Wiesbaden
24. Thompson RG, Langemeier LN, Lee CT, Lee E, Thrall RM (1990) The role of multiplier bounds in efficiency analysis with application to Kansas farming. Journal of Econometrics 46:96–108
25. Ultsch A (1993) Self-organized neural networks for visualisation and classification. In: Opitz O, Lausen B, Klar R (eds) Information and classification: concepts, methods and application. Springer, Dortmund, Germany:307–313
26. Ultsch A (1993) Self-organized feature maps for monitoring and knowledge acquisition of a chemical process. In: Proceedings of the international conference on artificial neural networks:864–867
27. Ultsch A (2003) U-matrix: a tool to visualize clusters in high dimensional data. Technical Document, University of Marburg
28. Zhu J (1998) DEA vs. principal component analysis: an illustrative study of the economic performance of Chinese cities. European Journal of Operational Research 111:50–61

Trading Strategies Based on K-means Clustering and Regression Models

Hongxing He[1], Jie Chen[1], Huidong Jin[1], and Shu-Heng Chen[2]

[1] CSIRO Mathematical and Information Sciences
GPO Box 664, Canberra, ACT 2601, Australia
Hongxing.He,Jie.Chen,Warren.Jin@csiro.au
[2] AI-ECON Research Center, Department of Economics
National Chengchi University, Taipei, Taiwan 11623
chchen@nccu.edu.tw

This paper outlines a data mining approach to the analysis and prediction of the trend of stock prices. The approach consists of three steps, namely, partitioning, analysis and prediction. A commonly used k-means clustering algorithm is used to partition stock price time series data. After data partition, linear regression is used to analyse the trend within each cluster. The results of the linear regression are then used for trend prediction for windowed time series data. Using our trend prediction methodology, we propose a trading strategy TTP (Trading based on Trend Prediction). Some results of applying TTP to stock trading are reported. The trading performance is compared with some practical trading strategies and other machine learning methods. Given the volatility nature of stock prices the methodology achieved limited success for a few countries and time periods. Further analysis of the results may lead to further improvement in the methodology. Although the proposed approach is designed for stock trading, it can be applied to the trend analysis of any time series, such as the time series of economic indicators.

Key words: Data Mining, Clustering, k-means, Time Series, Stock Trading

1 Introduction

Trend analysis and prediction play a vital role in practical stock trading. Experienced stock traders can often predict the future trend of a stock's price based on their observations of the performance of the stock in the past. An early sign of a familiar pattern may alert a domain expert to what is likely to happen in the near future. They can then formulate their trading strategy accordingly. Can we gain such knowledge automatically using data mining techniques ([6])? There have been studies on efficiently locating previously known patterns in time series databases ([1, 11, 3]). The search for and matching of similar patterns have been studied extensively in time series analysis ([5, 9]). Patterns in long time series data repeat themselves due to seasonality or other unknown underlying reasons. Early detection of patterns similar to those that have occurred in the past can readily provide information on what will follow. This information will be able to help decision-making in regard to the trading strategy in stock market trading practice.

In this paper, we report an approach to the pattern matching of stock market time series data and apply it to stock trading practice. We use ten years of historical data to form training data. The k-means clustering algorithm is then applied to the training data to automatically create partitions. k clusters or representative patterns are formed. Each of these is presented as a time series, approximated by its cluster center. Each time series is then divided into two parts. The first part is used for pattern matching while the second part is used to decide the trend of the cluster. Binary classes in terms of trend are assigned to clusters. We use linear regression modeling to decide the classification of the representative patterns. The "UP" class is assigned to clusters with a positive gradient and the "DOWN" class is assigned to clusters with a negative or zero gradient. For each test time series, we look for the best match in all clusters. The trend class of the matched cluster is regarded as the future trend of the test series. Finally, we use the predicted trend of the test time series in our trading strategy to determine the trading decisions.

The paper is organised as follows. Section 2 explains the method for forming windowed time series for training and test data. Section 3 describes our methodology applied in trend analysis and its application to trading data matching and trend prediction. Section 4 explains two trading strategies used in our experiments. Section 5 gives the experimental designs used to run the simulation of this study. Section 6 shows some results and makes a comparison with some other trading strategies. Section 7 concludes the paper and lists possible future directions.

2 Time Series Data Preparation

We follow [3] closely to create training data by sliding a fixed-length time window from time t_b to t_e. The following $N = t_e - t_b$ time series are created with window length w_{tr}.

$$s_1 : p_1, p_2, ..., p_{w_{tr}}$$
$$s_2 : p_2, p_3, ..., p_{w_{tr}+1}$$
$$\cdots$$
$$s_N : p_N, p_{N+1}, ..., p_{w_{tr}+N-1}$$

where $p_i (i = 1, 2, \cdots, w_{tr} + N - 1)$ are stock prices at time i. We therefore create an N by w_{tr} matrix or a data set with N data records and w_{tr} attributes. Note that all attributes take continuous values and conventional data mining methods can be applied directly.

We divide the windowed time series into two parts, the antecedent part and the consequent part (see Fig. 1). The antecedent data of length $w_{te} = w_{tr} - w_{lm}$ is used

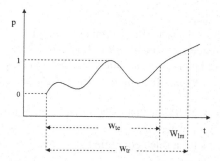

Fig. 1. Schematic view of windowed time series and normalisation

to decide the cluster index. The consequent part of length $w_{lm} = w_{tr} - w_{te}$ is used to decide the classification of the cluster. In order to do the trend pattern matching, we normalise each windowed series individually. The windowed time series used for the clustering algorithm is normalised in such a way that the first w_{te} part of a series is normalised to fall between 0 and 1. The data is normalised in this way to ensure that the time series to be matched in order to decide the cluster index are on the same scale. Fig. 1 is a schematic view of a windowed time series.

3 Methodology for Trend Analysis

Our data mining approach consists of the following steps.

1. Initialisation.
   - Select window lengths w_{tr} and w_{te} for the antecedent and the consequent part of time series, respectively.
   - Select a training period.
     In this paper, we consider a ten-year training period. For example, a training sample starts w_{tr} days before the first trading day of the year 1991 and ends on the last trading day of the year 2000.
   - Select a test period.
     The test period is set to 2 years long. For example, in the above-mentioned example, the corresponding test period is 2001-2002. The test period then starts from the first trading day of 2001 to the last trading day of 2002.
2. Data Mining.
   - Create N training series of window length w_{tr} from the training period.
   - Normalise each time series individually such that the first w_{te} values of the time series fall between 0 and 1.
   - Partition the training data into k clusters, which are represented by their cluster centers.
   - Classify all the clusters into two distinct classes using a linear regression model. A model is built based on the last w_{lm} values of each cluster center. Class "UP" is labeled if the gradient is positive and "DOWN" otherwise.

3. Test model on test data.
   - Form a test series dataset with the window length w_{te}. Normalise them individually. Consequently, values will fall between 0 and 1.
   - Assign a cluster label $c_i = j$ to time series s_i in the test data such that cluster $j(j = 1, 2, \cdots, k)$ has the smallest Euclidean distance to the normalised series s_i.
   - Assign the class ("UP" or "DOWN") of cluster j to time series s_i, where time series s_i has cluster label j.
   - Calculate returns for a selected trading strategy.

Some details are given in the following subsections.

3.1 Unsupervised Learning Using k-means Clustering

k-means clustering is an algorithm to group objects based on attributes or features into k groups ([10]). $k > 1$ is a positive integer. The input of the k-means algorithm is the training data set with N records each with w_{tr} attributes (in our case). The grouping is done by minimising the cost function defined in (1), that is, the sum of distances between data and their corresponding cluster centres.

$$\text{Cost} = \sum_{j=1}^{k} \sum_{i=1}^{N} D(s_i, \text{Centre}(j)) \delta(c_i, j) \tag{1}$$

The Kronecker delta function $\delta(c_i, j)$ means that only members of cluster j are included in the sum. Thus, the purpose of k-means clustering is to partition the data into a number of groups automatically in such a way that data records within the same cluster are similar and data records belonging to different clusters are dissimilar.

The k-means clustering procedure can be stated as follows:

Step 1: Initialise k cluster centres randomly. Assign all the data records in the training set to their nearest cluster centres.

Step 2: Update cluster centres using (2).

Step 3: Update cluster label assignment for all the data records in the training set.

Repeat steps 2 and 3 until convergence is achieved, i.e., until a pass through the training data causes no new assignments.

$$\text{Centre}(j, m) = \frac{\sum_{i=1}^{N} p_{i,m} \delta(c_i, j)}{\sum_{i=1}^{N} \delta(c_i, j)} \tag{2}$$

In (1) and (2), c_i is the cluster label for the ith record, N is the total number of records, $p_{i,m}, m = 1, 2, \cdots, w_{tr}$ is the mth attribute of the ith record and $j = 1, 2, \cdots, k$ stands for the jth cluster.

It is well known that k-means clustering is a greedy search for the minimum cost function [6, 8]. The local minimum rather than the global one is reached as a consequence. In order to obtain a good data partition, we run a number of independent training procedures (each with a different random number). The resultant clustering with the lowest cost out of these runs is used.

3.2 Classification of Clusters

As stated earlier, we use a linear regression model to determine the trends of clusters. Extracting the trend from the slope of the model is straightforward. This model is also more robust than other complex models.

In linear regression [2], a dependent variable is fitted by a straight line expressed by (3). The constants a and b are determined by minimising the mean square error. In our case, the constants a and b are given by (4) and (5), respectively.

$$y = a + bt \tag{3}$$

$$a = \frac{\sum_{i=1}^{t_{lm}} y_i}{w_{lm}} - b \frac{\sum_{i=1}^{t_{lm}} t_i}{w_{lm}} \tag{4}$$

$$b = \frac{\sum_{i=1}^{t_{lm}} t_i y_i - \sum_{i=1}^{w_{lm}} t_i \sum_{i=1}^{t_{lm}} y_i / t_{lm}}{\sum_{i=1}^{t_{lm}} t_i^2 - (\sum_{i=1}^{t_{lm}} t_i)^2 / t_{lm}} \tag{5}$$

Trend class "UP" is assigned to clusters with $b > 0$, and "DOWN" to other clusters.

3.3 Pattern Matching

For a test time series $s_i = s_{i,1}, s_{i,2}, \cdots, s_{i,w_{te}}$, we assign a cluster label as given by (6)

$$cl(i) = \arg \min_{j} MSdis(Centre(j), s_i) \quad j = 1, 2, \cdots, k \tag{6}$$

where $cl(i)$ is the cluster label of test time series s_i. The mean square distance between time series s_i and the cluster centre of j is expressed by (7).

$$MSdis(Centre(j), s_i) = \frac{\sum_{m=1}^{w_{te}} (Centre_m(j) - s_m(i))^2}{w_{te}} \tag{7}$$

Since the test time series and cluster centre time series are both normalised to $(0,1)$, the distance indicates their difference in shape. The test series is then assigned a trend class ("UP" or "DOWN") by simply assigning the trend class of the cluster closest to it.

4 Trading Strategies

In this section we introduce two trading strategies. The first strategy is naive trading, where the future trend is not taken into consideration. The second is the same as the first except that the future trend prediction is used in the trading decision.

If $\pi_t = 1$:
>   if $p(t)(1 - c) > p(t_{\text{prev\_buy}})(1 + c)$
>   Action = Sell
>   else :
>   Action = Stay

If $\pi_t = -1$:
>   if $p(t)(1 + c) < p(t_{\text{prev\_sell}})(1 - c)$
>   Action = Buy
>   else :
>   Action = Stay

Fig. 2. Naive Trading (NT)

4.1 Naive Trading (NT)

We call our trading strategy "naive trading" because it is very simple. In NT, we buy the stock if we are not holding a share and the purchase cost is lower than the value at which we sold previously. By the same token, we sell the stock if we hold a share and we can make profits from that sale. That is, we sell the stock if the value received exceeds the value at which we bought previously. The trading strategy is expressed in Fig. 2.

In Fig. 2, c is the trading cost. π_t is the state of the stock holding at time t ($\pi_t = 1$ for holding, -1 for not holding). $p(t_{\text{prev\_buy}})(1 + c)$ is the cost of buying in previous buying action. $p(t_{\text{prev\_sell}})(1 - c)$ is the value received in the previous selling action. We initialise the trading on the first day of the time period by buying a unit of stock.

4.2 Trading based on Trend Prediction (TTP)

As illustrated in Fig. 3, TTP is a slight variation of NT. The only difference is that we consider the forward trend of the stock price. Intuitively, we would buy a stock when the "UP" trend is found and sell it when the "DOWN" trend will follow. Since we try to enter the market as soon as we can, we only use the trend information to select the time of selling. We sell the share only if the trend prediction is downward. In other words, instead of selling a stock at any profit, we hold it until a maximum profit is reached.

5 Experimental Design

5.1 Training and Test Periods

In order to compare our trading strategies with the strategies studied in [4], we use five stock indexes which were used in [4] with the same trading periods and testing periods as indicated in Table 1.[1]

---

[1] Reference [4] also shows the results of the 21 technical trading strategies, which have actually been used by investors in financial securities firms. These strategies are basically

If $\pi_t = 1$:

    if $p(t)(1 - c) > p(t_{prev\_buy})(1 + c)$ and $Trend(t) =$"DOWN"

        Action = Sell

    else :

        Action = Stay

If $\pi_t = -1$:

    if $p(t)(1 + c) < p(t_{prev\_sell})(1 - c)$

        Action = Buy

    else :

        Action = Stay

Fig. 3. Trading based on Trend Prediction (TTP)

Table 1. List of Three Test Time Periods and their Corresponding Training Periods

	Test Period	Training Period
1	1999–2000	1989–1998
2	2001–2002	1991–2000
3	2003–2004	1993–2002

5.2 Parameter Values

The values of the parameters used by k-means clustering are summarized in Table 2. The performance and efficiency of the algorithm can depend on the number of clusters and the number of runs. While low values of these two parameters may make the derived results less robust, high values of them can cause the computation to be very time-consuming. The values chosen here are the results from a few pilot experiments. The lengths of the windowed time series and its constituents (the antecedent part and the consequent part) are decided on pilot experiments as well. The decision on the length of the antecedent part of the windowed series can determine the patterns to be recognized, whereas the length of the consequent part can affect the statistical errors of the regression model.

6 Experimental Results

6.1 Accuracy Rate

The essential idea in this paper is whether we can meaningfully cluster the windowed financial time series based on their associated geometrical patterns. The clustering

---

made up of the historical data on prices and trading volumes. Since the data on trading volumes are not available from some markets, their testing is inevitably limited to those markets whose data are sufficient, which includes the US, UK, Canada, Taiwan and Singapore. This is the main reason why we only consider the stocks of these five countries in this study. Nonetheless, in the case of Japan, since the trading volume data are available for the period 2003-2004, the results for Japan for that period also become available. We therefore consider six countries, instead of five, in the period 2003-2004.

Table 2. List of Parameters and their Values

Name	Description	Value
k	Number of clusters	50
N_{run}	Number of k-mean runs	20
w_{tr}	Length of each windowed series	50
w_{te}	Antecedent part of each windowed series	40
c	Transaction cost rate	0.005

Table 3. The Accuracy Rate of the Trend Prediction

	US	UK	Canada	Taiwan	Singapore	Japan	Mean
1999-2000	52.1	53.0	53.9	52.9	52.0	NA	52.8
2001-2002	50.2	48.6	51.7	49.9	49.1	NA	50.2
2003-2004	56.3	51.1	50.0	52.4	51.7	52.4	52.3

work can be useful if it helps us predict the future from the past. In other words, we can perform better conditional expectations when provided with the geometric patterns. Our design of the TTP trading algorithm is in effect based on this assumption. Therefore, it would be important to ask whether clustering does help predict the trend.

In Table 3, we report the accuracy rate achieved by our trend-prediction algorithm, i.e., the prediction based on the sign of the regression coefficient (see Eqs. 3–5). The overall accuracy rate is 51.8% over about a total of 7,500 predictions. While the 1.8% margin over the accuracy rate of random guessing, i.e., 50.0%, is small, it is statistically significant at a significance level of 0.05.

Furthermore, if we look at countries by countries and periods by periods, we find that out of the 16 scenarios, there are only three scenarios (the UK, Taiwan and Singapore), all of them happening in the period 2001-2002, for which the accuracy rate is below 50%. For the rest, the accuracy rates are all above 50%. Therefore, our proposed trend prediction algorithm based on k-means clustering does bring us some prediction power, although it is somewhat marginal. We shall come back to this point again in the last section.

6.2 Results of the Total Return

Given the little prediction power, it would be interesting to see whether we can take advantage of it. Tables 4 to 6 list the returns from using the TTP strategy for selected markets in the three time periods. In addition, we also compare the performance of our trading strategies with the NT strategy and those studied in [4], which include the Buy-and-Hold (B&H) strategy and the trading strategies developed by machine intelligence, specifically, genetic programming (GP).

In Tables 4 to 6. The row headed by B&H is the total return earned by simply using the B&H strategy, the row headed by GP1 refers to the mean total return of the 50 GP runs without short sales, whereas the row headed by GP2 refers to the

Table 4. The Total Return of Stock Trading for 1999–2000

Rule	US	UK	Canada	Taiwan	Singapore
B&H	0.0636	0.0478	0.3495	-0.2366	0.3625
GP 1	0.0655	0.0459	0.3660	0.1620	0.1461
GP 2	0.0685	0.0444	0.3414	0.5265	0.1620
TTP	0.1778	0.1524	0.0541	-0.22	0.4654
NT	0.0786	0.1560	0.0207	-0.1480	0.0524

Table 5. The Total Return of Stock Trading for 2001–2002

Rule	US	UK	Canada	Taiwan	Singapore
B&H	-0.3212	-0.3682	-0.2395	-0.1091	-0.2998
GP 1	-0.3171	-0.3625	-0.1761	0.0376	-0.3123
GP 2	-0.3231	-0.3658	-0.2367	-0.0470	-0.2939
TTP	-0.3196	-0.3560	-0.2413	0.0327	-0.2636
NT	-0.3190	-0.3545	-0.2345	0.0511	-0.2636

same thing but with short sales.[2] The performances of B&H, GP1 and GP2 are all borrowed from [4], and are duplicated in Tables 4 to 6. The rows headed by TTP and NT give the mean total return by taking an average over the 20 runs.

Based on the results shown in these tables, we would like to first ask whether the TTP strategy outperforms the NT strategy. Notice that the NT strategy is a very conservative strategy: it basically does not recommend any transaction which may result in an immediately realized loss. Based on its "stubborn" rule without any stop-loss design, it can be easily locked in and can trigger a very risky decision. Furthermore, since it only cares about the occurrence of the current realized loss, and cares neither about future gains nor future losses, it does not learn anything from the past, and hence is not intelligent. Can the TTP strategy which has little power in predicting future trends beat this naive strategy?

Out of the 16 scenarios which we have examined, TTP loses six times to NT. While, from these numbers, TTP is still by and large dominant, NT does not perform in a way that is as inferior as one might expect. Even though in many cases the accuracy rate of trend prediction is over 50%, TTP can still give way to NT, which means that, not only in prediction, but also in profits, clustering only has a marginal contribution to the trading design.

The second thing that we would like to look at is to compare our proposed trading strategy with some of the other trading strategies developed using different computational intelligence tools, such as genetic programming. Genetic programming applies the ideas of biological evolution to a society of computer programs. From one generation to another, it follows the survival of the fittest principle to select from the existing programs, and then operates these selected programs via some genetic oper-

---

[2] The *total return* means the return earned over the entire investment horizon [0,T] per unit of investment. So, say, $R = 0.05$ means that a one-dollar investment will earn five cents as a total over the entire investment horizon [0,T]. For details, see [4].

Table 6. The Total Return of Stock Trading for 2003–2004

Rule	US	UK	Canada	Taiwan	Singapore	Japan
B& H	0.3199	0.1888	0.3625	0.3434	0.5311	0.3054
GP 1	0.3065	0.1797	0.3109	0.3631	0.2512	0.0212
GP 2	0.3109	0.1817	0.3389	0.2740	-0.0183	-0.1792
TTP	0.1461	0.0983	0.0049	0.2239	0.0351	0.0044
NT	0.0302	0.0100	0.0049	0.0324	0.0234	0.0025

ators, such as reproduction, crossover and mutation. Each program in GP can serve as a trading strategy.

The representation of trading strategies developed by GP is largely determined by the primitives, i.e., the function set and the terminal set. The standard choice of these primitives makes the resultant trading strategies more like rule-based trading strategies, which may or may not be associated with the geometry-based strategies. Therefore, the comparison between GP and k-means can provide us with some insight into different ways to think of trading strategies. Besides, some severe limitations of using GP have been observed in [4]; therefore, it would also be interesting to know whether when GP performs particularly badly there are other alternatives that can take its place. In the latter, we are actually inquiring into the cooperative relationship rather than just the competitive relationship between two intelligent machines.

Our results generally show that, out of 16 scenarios, GP1 wins 10 times, whereas TTP picks up the remaining six. In particular, in the period 2003-2004, GP1 consistently dominates TTP. Of course, one should always be careful when making comparisons between two different intelligent machines, since there are many different variants determined by different control parameters. Therefore, while the specific results seem to favor GP1 over k-means, one can hardly obtain a decisive result given the limited evidence and limited trials. In these experiments, there is no uniform dominance for either GP1 or k-means.

Finally, we also find that the performance of GP1 is also superior to NT.

7 Conclusions and Future Work

We have applied a data mining approach to analyze and predict the trend of stock prices and have developed trading strategies based on these predictions. The proposed trading strategy based on trend prediction using k-means clustering is applied to a few selected countries over some samples of financial time series. The results are compared with various existing trading strategies and GPs obtained earlier in [4]. Although the trend analysis method is simple and does not always achieve high accuracy, it has the following advantages:

1. It allows matching every testing time series to one of the representative patterns. Therefore, a decision regarding trading can always be made. This feature is not shared by other sophisticated search techniques, such as the motif, which can be

used to locate patterns in the history, but may not be able to match *every* testing time series, and hence is not always able to make a trading decision ([11]).

2. The computation resources required are an important issue in real world applications. We use a computer with an Intel(R) Xeon(TM) CPU (3.20 GHz) running the Linux operating system. The procedural language Python is used for programming. It takes about 40 minutes to finish training and testing on a ten-year training period followed by a two-year testing period. The huge saving in time makes it a competitive candidate in real world applications.

While the methodology developed in the work can correctly predict the trend of stock prices in some markets in some periods, it does not perform well on many occasions. The fundamental difficulty arises from the highly volatile nature of the stock price. The proposed trend-prediction algorithm is very simple, and, therefore, has its limitations. For the future, we propose the following directions to enhance its performance:

1. Improve the performance by optimizing the parameter settings. We may add a validation period to optimize the setting of various window lengths and the number of clusters.
2. Improve the linear regression model with a larger window length, and perhaps by allowing some overlaps between the antecedent part and the consequent part.
3. In this paper, the decision on the classification of clusters is made based on the sign of the regression coefficient. However, for those samples whose coefficient values are around zero, a slight difference can have a big effect on the final decision, be they up or down. We may consider using fuzzy mathematics or something equivalent to smooth this dichotomous decision so as to improve the accuracy of the trend prediction.
4. Improve computational efficiency by using sophisticated and scalable clustering techniques, such as [8, 7].
5. By introducing scale change to pattern matching we can discover similar patterns with different time scales.
6. In this paper, we use the trend prediction only for making selling decisions. With better and more accurate trend prediction, we may modify the trading strategy TTP by using the trend prediction for making buying decisions as well.
7. Combine our method with other techniques, such as GP, for better and more sophisticated trading strategies.

Acknowledgments

The authors are grateful to the authors of [4] for their permission to use their data and results in this paper. The authors also acknowledge Damien McAullay and Arun Vishwanath for their assistance in the preparation of the paper.

References

1. Agrawala R, Faloutsos C, Swami A (1993) Efficient similarity search in sequence databases. In: Proceedings of the 4th international conference on foundations of data organization and algorithms:13–15
2. Chambers JM, Hastie TJ (eds) (1992) Statistical models in s. Chapman & Hall/CRC
3. Chen SH, He H (2003) Searching financial patterns with self-organizing maps. In: Chen SH, Wang PP (eds) Computational intelligence in economics and finance. Springer-Verlag:203–216
4. Chen SH, Kuo TW, Hsu KM (2007) Genetic programming and financial trading: how much about "what we know"? In: Zopounidis C, Doumpos M, Pardalos PM (eds) Handbook of financial engineering. Springer. Forthcoming.
5. Ge X(1998) Pattern matching financial time series data. Project Report ICS 278, UC Irvine
6. Han J, Kamber M (2001) Data mining: concepts and techniques. Morgan Kaufmann Publishers, San Francisco, CA, USA
7. Jin HD, Leung KS, Wong ML, Xu ZB (2005) Scalable model-based cluster analysis using clustering features. Pattern Recognition 38(5):637–649
8. Jin H, Wong ML, Leung KS (2005) Scalable model-based clustering for large databases based on data summarization. IEEE Transactions on Pattern Analysis and Machine Intelligence 27(11):1710–1719
9. Keogh E, Smyth P (1997) A probabilistic approach to fast pattern matching in time series databases. In: Proceedings of KDD'97:24–30
10. MacQueen JB (1967) Some methods for classification and analysis of multivariate observations. In: Proceedings of 5-th Berkeley symposium on mathematical statistics and probability. Berkeley, University of California:281–297
11. Patel P, Keogh E, Lin J, Lonardi S (2002) Mining motifs in massive time series databases. In: Proceedings of the 2002 IEEE international conference on data mining:370–377

Comparison of Instance-Based Techniques for Learning to Predict Changes in Stock Prices

David B. LeRoux

Open Data Group, Suite 90, 400 Lathrop Ave, River Forest, IL 60305, USA
lerouxdave@gmail.com

This paper is a practical guide to the application of instance-based machine learning techniques to the solution of a financial problem. A broad class of instance-based families is considered for classification using the WEKA software package. The problem selected for analysis is a common one in financial and econometric work: the use of publicly available economic data to forecast future changes in a stock market index. This paper examines various stages in the analysis of this problem including: identification of the problem, considerations in obtaining and preprocessing data, model and parameter selection, and interpretation of results. Finally, the paper offers suggestions of areas of future study for applying instance-based machine learning in the setting of solving financial problems.

Key words: Tactical Asset Allocation, Stock Price Prediction, Instance-Based Learning, WEKA, Financial Data Mining

1 Introduction

The fields of finance and economics provide a fertile area for application of machine learning techniques. Vast amounts of data measuring many aspects of the economy and financial markets are readily available. While many theories exist on the causal relationships among measurable quantities, generally the relationships are poorly understood and the predictive powers of the models are often weak. The problem is made more difficult because of its non-stationary nature. This is true not only because of changing underlying factors in the economy, but also because knowledge of relationships can provide opportunities to financially exploit the information, which in turn changes the environment. This is particularly true with respect to predicting future changes in stock market prices where public information is readily incorporated into current price levels.

Machine learning has the ability to deal with large amounts of data, to rapidly explore many potential models and to adapt to changing environments. This paper illustrates the use of machine learning techniques to solve a common problem in finance using publicly available data and the WEKA open source software ([5]).

2 Identification of the Problem

The problem examined here is the prediction of the future change in a stock market index based on information available at the time of the prediction. Specifically, the problem is to use publicly available monthly economic index data from the Federal Reserve to predict changes in the S&P 500 stock index. An important consideration in defining this problem is to ensure that the data used in predicting the change in the stock market index are publicly available prior to the beginning date of the period for which the stock market change is measured. For example, it would not be proper to use the change in a September employment index as an input to a model to predict the change in the October S&P index because the September employment index is not available until near the end of October and thus would not be available at the time needed to make the prediction. For this reason, the problem has been constructed to use data current as of time t to estimate the change in the stock index between times $t + 1$ month and $t + 2$ months.

The problem examined is a classification problem: Will the S&P index increase by more than typically in the month following the month when all of the data is available? In order to provide a maximally challenging binary feature for testing, the question is whether the index will increase by more than the median amount of increase during the period under consideration. By defining the problem this way, exactly half the observations are correctly classified TRUE and half FALSE, so that a constant decision rule can do no better than 50% accuracy.

3 Obtaining and Pre-processing Data

The data source for this problem is the FRED II economic database maintained by the Federal Reserve Bank of St. Louis. This data source contains over 1,000 economic time series in categories of interest rates, inflation indexes, employment rates, monetary aggregates, population data, productivity rates, and many other financial categories. The data may be downloaded for all indexes in a single zipped file and extracted in ASCII format with each series in a separate file.

The first step in preprocessing the data is to select which indexes to use and to combine them into a single file with their index dates synchronized. For this example analysis, 14 indexes were selected: 5 involving interest rates of different maturities and credit spreads (GS1, GS10, MORT, AAA, and BAA), 7 involving business conditions (INDPRO, BUSINV, ISRATIO, PPIENG, PPIACO, TCU, and NAPM) and 2 involving employment (AWHI and UNRATE). The indexes were chosen to be a broad mix of important and widely publicized economic data. All of these indexes are monthly and have been calculated for many years. The individual files were combined into a single file with one record for each month. Months prior to the date when all of the indexes became available were discarded, resulting in a full table of indexes from 1/1/1992 through 6/1/2003, or 138 months of complete data.

The WEKA software has the ability to calculate additional features by performing arithmetic operations on the existing features. This may be done on the Preprocessing window using the AttributeExpression Filter or it may be done prior to importing the data to WEKA. Since much of the information content in economic indexes comes from the change in index value rather than the simple magnitude of the index, an additional feature was added for each of the above 14 indexes to show the rate of change of the index from the prior month to the current month.

Finally, the values of the S&P 500 index were obtained from the Standard & Poor's website. For each month, m, in the feature database, the following values related to the S&P 500 index were added: index at $m + 1$, index at $m + 2$, change in the index from $m + 1$ to $m + 2$, and a "normalized up/down indicator." This last feature takes the value "up" if the index rises by more than the median historical increase during the month from $m + 1$ to $m + 2$ and "down" otherwise. Of course, for the up/down classification problem, the values of the index at $m + 2$ must be excluded from the available features.

4 Model and Parameter Selection

Conceptually, instance-based or lazy-learner methods are simple, following the basic rule of classifying or estimating based on the correct values of similar instances in the known history. There are, however, many choices involved in selecting a particular instance-based model. In this section consideration is restricted to the k-nearest neighbor model as implemented in the WEKA software. Reference is made to the model and parameter selection options available in version 3.2.3 of WEKA. As will be seen, this software offers considerable flexibility and requires numerous choices in parameter selection. An active area of research is how to explore the parameter selection space in an efficient, automated way to identify the optimal parameters ([2], [4]). Section 6 of this paper discusses models beyond those offered in WEKA.

4.1 Metric and Feature Selection

In order to base our estimation or classification on similar past observations, we must define "similar." This is frequently the most important and difficult aspect in applying an instance-based model. A natural choice for similarity is to view each observation as a point in n-dimension space, where n is the number of features of each observation. Similarity can then be defined based on the distance between points using any metric, such as the Euclidean metric. There are several problems with this approach. First, without some form of normalization of the feature values, features with the largest values will dominate. The features may be normalized both as to size and dispersion, but this may not be optimal. Ideally, we would like to use training data to determine which factors are most important and to increase their importance in the similarity metric. A possible approach to this is discussed in Sect. 6. Without a method of automatically reducing the importance of features with little relevance, we are left with a problem related to the "curse of dimensionality." Factors with little relevance tend to increase the distance between points that are truly similar based on the factors that do matter. Without the ability to vary the weights on features within the similarity metric, we must restrict our features to those with high importance.

WEKA offers no choice of metric and uses the Euclidean metric applied to all numeric features. The feature values may be normalized either by applying a Normalization Filter before classification or by selecting normalization during classification. In either case the numeric attribute values are rescaled so that they range between 0 and 1. This is clearly better than using the raw data, which in this example can vary in size by several orders of magnitude between features. However, this form of normalization does not necessarily put all features on an equal footing. Suppose, for example, that the data of one feature has a single outlier. This form of normalization will put the outlier at either 0 or 1 and clump the other values near the other extreme. Care must be taken to eliminate outliers or use an external method to normalize data prior to importing it to WEKA.

WEKA offers a number of ways to identify the features that are most important to the task at hand. Upon selecting the AttributeSelection Filter on the Preprocessing screen, WEKA offers several Evaluators for selecting attributes. An alternative approach is to use the Linear Regression classifier to fit a linear model to the change in stock index variable and use one of the attribute selection methods offered there. The attributes chosen here have the most predictive value in a linear model estimating the change in future stock price, and so should be useful in the classification problem. This latter approach was used to limit the number of variables to the 8 with the most predictive value in a linear model. These are: GS1, MORT, INDPRO, TCU, UNRATE, SP, BUSINV_change, and TCU_change.

4.2 Number of Neighbors

The selection of the number of neighboring points to use is based primarily on evaluation of the noisiness of the data and the heterogeneity of the underlying function. If there is significant noise in the data, choice of a larger k value will cause the noise contributions to offset and will result in a better estimation. On the other hand, including more points broadens the radius of the neighborhood and includes points that are less representative of the point being classified.

Some insight into the relative importance of these two factors can be gained by considering the problem of estimating a continuous function, f, at x_0 by using a simple average of the known values of f at k-nearest neighbors, $x_1, x_2, ..., x_k$, where x_i are vectors of n feature values. Assume the feature values have been normalized and the exact function values are known at m training points uniformly distributed in the n-dimensional unit square. The average radius in n-dimension Euclidean space needed to obtain k points will be that of a sphere with volume equal to k/m. Using the formula for the volume of a sphere in n-space, $(1/(n/2)!)\pi^{(n/2)}r^n$ (in the case n is even) we can solve for the average radius required. If we have an estimate of the derivative of f in the region under consideration, we can use the radius to calculate an estimate of the error caused from the heterogeneity source. This, of course, will increase with k. The error from the noise source will decrease in proportion to $1/k$ base on the Central Limit Theorem. An estimate of the proportionality constant may be obtainable through repeated sampling of f at a single point. Once formulae have been obtained for the two sources of error, choose a value for k that makes the two sources close to equal.

Figure 1 illustrates this tradeoff in the sample problem. Using only a few neighbors makes for poor predictions due to the noisiness and weak correlations of the underlying data. Choosing too many neighbors sweeps in examples that are not representative of the case at hand. The choice of 25 neighbors is used in the remainder of this analysis. While there may be some bias in choosing the k for which the accuracy is highest, the graph suggests that the improved accuracy is due to the error reduction effects rather than model selection bias.

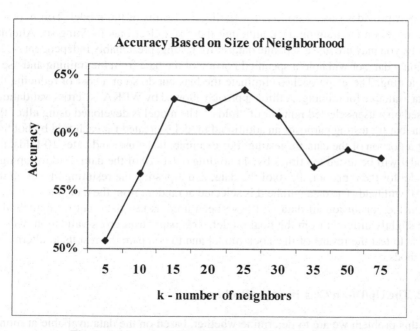

Fig. 1. Accuracy rates for choices of number of neighbors.

4.3 Weighting of Neighbor Contributions

Once we have selected the nearest neighbors to the point under consideration, we must decide how to use their results in estimating or classifying the current point. One possibility is to give equal weighting to each of the neighbors. It seems reasonable, however, to give more weight to the closer neighbors. WEKA allows three weighting choices: equal weighting, weights based on $1/d$ and weights based on $1-d$, where d is the distance from the neighbor to the point under consideration. Assuming the features have been normalized to the unit cube, the $1/d$ and $1-d$ weighting schemes produce weights in the ranges $[1/n, \infty]$ and $[0, 1]$ respectively, where n is the number of features. The $1/d$ weighting scheme will put virtually all the weight on a single very close point if one exists. This is not desirable in the case of noisy data as we have in the stock prediction example since we want to consider a large number of points to offset errors. The $1-d$ weighting produces the best results with the stock data.

5 Interpretation of Results

5.1 Testing Using WEKA

WEKA provides several options for testing the results of the model. You may test the model on the training data, although there is a clear bias in doing so. Alternatively, you may provide a separate dataset for testing, presumably independent of the training data, or withhold a specified portion of the data from the training and use it for testing. These approaches eliminate the bias but do so at a cost of reducing the data available for training. A third approach allowed by WEKA is "cross-validation" based on a user-selected number of "folds." The model is developed using all of the data, but for testing purposes an additional model is created for each fold by holding out a portion of the data for testing. For example, if the user indicates 10 folds, the model will be tested ten times by: 1) holding out $1/10$ of the data, 2) developing a model for the remaining $9/10$ of the data, and 3) testing the resulting model on the $1/10$ withheld. The data withheld is selected at random from the data not yet tested, so at the conclusion all data will have been used as test data, but on models that are slightly different from the final model. This paper uses cross-validation with 10 folds to test the results of the stock model and to compare the results to alternative methods.

5.2 The Up/Down Classification Problem

In this problem we are to determine whether, based on the data available at month m, the stock index will increase by more than the median amount during the period $m + 1$ to $m + 2$. Based on this definition, exactly half of the data points correspond to TRUE and half to FALSE. Table 1 shows the results of using the k-nearest neighbor approaches. The base case is the approach developed in the prior sections. It is shown with modifications discussed above and using two algorithms designed to improve performance. The classification accuracy is shown along with the statistical significance at which we could reject the null hypothesis of the classification being random.

All of the models provide results that are statistically significant at low alpha levels ($< .01$). Limiting the model to a small number of key features improves the

Table 1. Classification accuracies for several modifications of the k-nearest neighbor model. Base case uses 25 nearest neighbors, $(1-d)$ metric and feature selection.

MODEL	ACCURACY
BASE CASE	63.8%
NO FEATURE SELECTION	61.6%
$1/D$ METRIC	60.9%
WITH ADABOOST	63.8%
WITH BAGGING	63.0%

results, as does using the $(1-d)$ weighting in the metric. Neither AdaBoost nor Bagging improved the results of the simple k-nearest neighbor classifier.

Figure 2 shows a comparison of classification accuracy among various classifiers provided in WEKA. For each, the comparison is made based on using all feature data as well as selecting the key features.

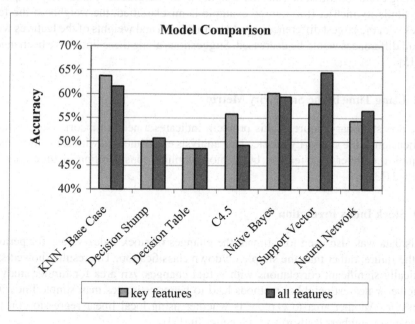

Fig. 2. Accuracy comparison of alternative classifiers provided by WEKA. Default parameters were used in the models other than KNN.

The simple k-nearest neighbor approach compares favorably to the alternative WEKA classifiers on the stock classification problem. The Support Vector Machine did perform slightly better than KNN when presented will all of the features and appears to be able to avoid the problems of too many features encountered by KNN.

Overall, it appears that the k-nearest neighbor approach applied to economic indexes is able to find information helpful in predicting stock market direction. Further study is needed before concluding that this information could be used in a successful trading system, since the magnitudes of gain and loss were not considered in this analysis.

6 Areas for Future Study

6.1 Evolving Metrics and Automatic Scaling of Features

One significant limitation of the WEKA software is the lack of flexibility in defining the metric. Even with more flexibility, it is difficult to know in advance which metric to use. An area of future study is the use of training data to learn an appropriate metric. One approach is to use the Euclidean metric except to apply a weight or "scaling factor" to the square of the difference of each feature. During repeated training cycles on the same data, the weights would be gradually adjusted to improve the similarity metric. If a training example is misclassified, the weights of the features with the largest differences would be increased and weights of the features with small differences would be decreased. Suggestions along these lines have been made by [5].

6.2 Using Time in the Similarity Metric

The non-stationary nature of this problem indicates a need to incorporate the time dimension in the similarity metric. This analysis experimented with using the month sequence number as a feature, but a more explicit consideration of time may be needed ([3]).

6.3 Stock Index Prediction

This data was also used to estimate the changes of stock index values for periods in the future, rather than the simple up/down classification. The results showed statistically significant correlations with actual changes. An area for further study is whether k-nearest neighbor methods lead to better estimates than simple linear regression. Another area to explore is whether using local linear regression on the k-nearest neighbors leads to an even better fit ([1]).

References

1. Atkeson CG, Moore AW, Schaal S (1997) Locally weighted learning. Artificial Intelligence Review 11:11–73
2. Maron O, Moore AW (1997) The racing algorithm: model selection for lazy learners. Artificial Intelligence Review 11:193–225

3. McCallum AK (1995) Instance-based utile distinctions for reinforcement learning with hidden state. In: Prieditis A, Russell SJ (eds) Proceedings of the twelfth international conference on machine learning. Morgan Kaufmann, San Fransisco, CA:387–395
4. Moore AW, Lee M (1994) Efficient algorithms for minimizing cross validation error. In: Cohen WW, Hirsh H (eds) Proceedings of the 11th international conference on machine learning. Morgan Kaufmann, San Fransisco, CA:190–198
5. Witten IH, Frank I (1999) Data mining: practical machine learning tools and techniques with Java mplementations. Morgan Kaufmann, San Fransisco, CA

Application of an Instance Based Learning Algorithm for Predicting the Stock Market Index

Ruppa K. Thulasiram[1] and Adenike Y. Bamgbade[2]

[1] Department of Computer Science, University of Manitoba, MB, Canada
`tulsi@cs.umanitoba.ca`
[2] Department of Computer Science, University of Manitoba, MB, Canada
`adenike@cs.umanitoba.ca`

Instance based learning is a class of data mining learning paradigms that applies specific cases or experiences to new situations by matching known cases and experiences with new cases. This paper presents an application of the instance-based learning algorithm for predicting daily stock index price changes of the S&P 500 stock index between October 1995 and September 2000, given the daily changes in the exchange rate of the Canadian Dollar, the Pound Sterling, the French Franc, the Deutsche Mark and the Yen, the monthly changes in the consumer price index, GDP, and the changes in the monthly rates of certificates of deposit. The algorithm is used to predict an increase, decrease or no change in the S&P 500 stock index between a business day and the previous business day. The predictions are carried out using the IB3 variant of the IBL algorithms. The objective is to determine the feasibility of stock price prediction using the IB3 variant of the IBL algorithms. Various testing proportions and normalization methods are experimented with to obtain good predictions.

Key words: Stock Market, Financial Forecasting, Computational Intelligence, Instance Based Learning, Stock Price Index

1 Introduction

Financial data are usually represented as time series. These time series display certain characteristics that make it difficult to derive relationships from them for forecasting future values of the time series ([22, 18, 24]). These characteristics are a high noise-to-data ratio, non-linearity, and a non-Gaussian noise distribution.

Stock index prices are represented in financial time series. The stock index data exhibit independent price variations from one step to another in the long run. However, some form of regularity exists in the short run price variations of the stock market ([11]). Data mining learning paradigms can be used to detect and learn from these short run regularities and predict the future behavior of stock index prices in the market. There are several computational intelligence techniques reported in the literature for various applications including those in economics and finance as briefly presented in the next section. In this study we have chosen an Instance Based Learning (IBL) algorithm and apply it to stock index prediction. To our knowledge IBL has not been used in financial applications before.

Instance based learning consists of a class of data mining learning paradigms that applies specific cases or experiences to new situations by matching known cases and experiences with new cases ([11]). The IB3 variant of the instance based learning algorithms is optimized for reduced storage and works well in noisy domains ([1]). This paper presents an application of the IBL algorithm for predicting daily stock index price changes in the S&P 500 stock index between October 1995 and September 2000, given the daily changes in the exchange rate of the Canadian Dollar, the Pound Sterling, the French Franc, the Deutsche Mark and the Yen, the monthly changes in the consumer price index, GDP, and the changes in the monthly rates of certificates of deposit. The IB3 variant of the IBL algorithm is used to predict an increase, decrease or no change in the S&P 500 stock index between a business day and the previous business day. The objective is to determine the feasibility of stock price prediction using the IB3 variant of the IBL algorithms. Various testing proportions and normalization methods are experimented with to obtain good predictions.

2 Background and Related Work

Financial forecasting is a time series prediction problem ([22, 18]). This prediction problem is a result of some properties of financial time series, such as poor signal-to-noise ratios, a non-Gaussian noise distribution and limited training data. Stock prices and indices are examples of financial time series.

According to the Efficient Markets Hypothesis (EMH) ([23]) and the Random Walk Hypothesis ([5]), forecasting from historical stock market time series is practically impossible. This difficulty arises as a result of the stochastic behavior of the price variations from one step to the next over the long run. This theory recognizes the possible existence of hidden short term regularities. However, these regularities do not take long to disappear. For a detailed study of these issues and further questions, we refer the readers to an interesting review [15] and the many references therein.

Computational intelligence techniques have been employed to exploit the above mentioned short term regularities in financial forecasting. Since our focus in this paper is on the proper application of computational intelligence techniques to finance, (a) we will concentrate only on the most relevant published work in this area; (b) the literature in finance theory is very vast and we will not do it justice by just selecting a few papers from general finance for the current purpose. However, to provide a motivation for the current research topic in the field of general finance, we refer the readers to [6, 17].

2.1 Time Series Forecasting

Reference [14] present the application of EpNet to the Hang Seng stock index forecasting problem. EpNet is a system which evolves generalized feed forward neural networks for predicting stock prices. The experimental results show that EpNet was able to evolve neural networks that were well generalized to the independent testing data. The results further showed that, compared with the actual stock index values, the evolved neural network captured almost all the changes in the time series. Reference [12] developed a feed forward neural network for predicting stock prices for companies. The results he obtained showed that the stock price movements, which he considered to be of more importance than the precise value of the stock market, were captured by the neural network predictions. Yao, et al's research into the prediction of the Kuala Lumpur composite index of Malaysian stocks shows that neural networks successfully predict the stock price changes ([26]). In addition, [26] were able to show that neural networks gave better results compared to the conventional ARIMA models. However, a general impediment of the neural network algorithm is the training time of the network, which is generally large. A recent study ([21, 20]) expedites the training by designing parallel algorithms for the neural network architecture. This study produces accurate results, that are more accurate than traditional regression models such as ARMA ([16]). The results from a comparative test of statistical and logical learning algorithms show that the Nearest Neighbor (NeNe) algorithm outperforms the feed-forward neural networks in terms of prediction accuracy ([9]). Soft computing using fuzzy and rough sets has been one of the tools of analysis in finance (see for example [7, 2]). In [7] the authors try to forecast future prices from past data using a new mathematical theory of Rough Sets ([19]) and have applied it to a data set from the New Zealand stock exchange. The authors claim that a reasonable prediction could be achieved with rough rules obtained from training data. In [2] fuzzy mathematics has been applied to the study of the option pricing problem in finance. Datamining, especially machine learning algorithms, is instanced based acquiring prominence in finance. In such problems as the detection of outliers in financial time series, the distance based mining algorithm (based on [10]) and statistics based algorithm ([13]) have recently been reported to predict outliers. A hybrid algorithm ([13]) has been shown to outperform these two algorithms by capturing almost all kinds of outliers. These studies have shown that data mining algorithms are simpler and easier to use than neural networks. Instance based algorithms are an extension of the Nearest Neighbor algorithm.

2.2 The IBL Algorithm

IBL is a supervised data-mining learning paradigm that classifies unknown cases by matching them with known cases. IBL algorithms are an extension of the nearest neighbor pattern classifier ([4]). Reference [1] present three variants of the instance based learning algorithms: IB1, which is the simplest extension to the k-Nearest neighbor classifier; IB2, which is an improvement over IB1 in terms of storage reduction, and IB3, which is an improvement over IB2 in terms of noise tolerance.

The main output of an IBL algorithm is a Concept Descriptor (CD). A CD includes a set of stored instances and in some cases, the classification and classification performance history of the instances. IBL algorithms do not construct extensional CDs, hence the set of instances in the CD may change after each training run. There are three basic components of the IBL algorithms:

- similarity function — this function computes the numerical value that shows the similarity between a query instance and the saved examples in the CD;
- classification function — this function uses the results from the similarity function and the classification performances of the saved instances in the CD to determine the classification of a query instance;
- the CD updater — maintains the instances in the CD. It updates their classification performances and determines which instances are acceptable, noisy or mediocre.

IBL algorithms classify new instances based on the CD, the similarity function and the classification function.

The algorithm is explained through the solution strategy in 3 phases: (1) the data pre-processing phase, (2) the training phase, and (3) the testing phase.

3 Predicting Stock Price Index Variation

The focus of this work is to predict the daily stock index price changes of the S&P 500 stock index using the IB3 algorithm. The IB3 algorithm is described as a pseudo code in this section. The S&P 500 stock index price will be predicted using its historical time series, the gross domestic product, the consumer price index, the exchange rates of the Canadian Dollar, the Deutsche Mark, the French Francs and the Japanese Yen and the monthly interest rates on bank certificates of deposit. These data values between October 1995 and September 2000 were used in this study. The exchange rates and the interest rates are examples of quantitative factors other than time series that affect stock price movement.

```
====================================================
CD <= 0
For each x in training set do
for each y in CD do
sim[y] <= similarity(x,y)
if there exists {y in CD | acceptable(y)}
then ymax <= some acceptable y in CD with maximal sim[y]
else
i <= a randomly selected value in {1|CD|}
ymax <= some y in CD that is the i-th most similar instance to x
for each y in CD do
if sim[y] >= sim(ymax)
then
update y's classification record
if y's record is significantly poor
then CD <= C - {y}

====================================================
The IB3 Algorithm
====================================================
```

Let D represent the instance space of the short run stock index times series with d instance objects, where d represents a record in the time series

$$D = \{d_i, ...\}, d_i = (d_{i1}, d_{i2}, ...d_{in}), i = 1, m$$

Each object d in the instance space is represented by an ordered set of n attributes. The first $n - 1$ attributes represent the predictor values while the nth attribute represents the classification of object d.

We need to select a set of objects from the instance space D such that given a target object d_t with $d_{tn} = \emptyset$, the value of d_{tn} can be predicted using the Euclidean distance between the known $n - 1$ attributes of d_t and the $n - 1$ attributes of all the selected instances from the instance space D. The Euclidean distance between d_t and each of the selected objects d_i in the selected set can be computed by the function $\vartheta(d_i, d_t)$

$$\vartheta(d_i, d_t) = \sqrt{\sum_{j=1}^{n-1} (d_{ij} - d_{tj})^2}$$

4 Experimental Framework

4.1 Data Pre-processing Phase

The S&P 500 stock index daily price time series data covering the period between October 1995 and September 2000 were collected. Seasonally adjusted *GDP* figures for the months during this period and the seasonally adjusted, monthly consumer price index(*CPI*) for all urban consumers for all items were also collected. The average daily figures of the *foreign exchange rates* of the US dollar to the Deutsche Mark, Yen, French Franc, and the Canadian Dollar were collected. The exchange rate values were based on the noon buying rates in New York City for cable transfers payable in foreign currencies. The daily rates on nationally traded *certificates of deposit* were also collected. These rates are determined each business day, with the exception of the GDP, CPI and certificates of deposit that are determined monthly. The S&P 500 stock index data were obtained from the Yahoo! finance ([25]), while the CPI, GDP, foreign exchange rates and interest rates on certificates of deposit were obtained from the records of the United States' federal reserves statistical release ([3]). The data were merged, normalized to the required format and stored in a Microsoft Access table. Each record in the table is an object instance. Each object instance is described by the changes in the closing stock price for the day, the changes in monthly GDP value, the monthly CPI, the changes in foreign exchange rates for the Deutsche Mark, Yen, French Franc and Canadian Dollar, the changes in the daily rates on certificates of deposit and the classification of the index change. We defined 3 disjoint index change classifications — increase, decrease, no change.

The important characteristics of the data are the period over which the data were generated and the significance of the factors used for the interpretation. Various factors such as economic growth, the political environment, bank interest rates, inflation, expectations regarding the future earnings of a corporation, trade with foreign countries and the exchange rate of foreign currencies affect stock price changes. Only the quantitative factors can be computed. Hence the data chosen for this work are based on the following assumptions: (1) Between October 1995 and September 2000, the U.S. enjoyed a stable political climate and economic growth. (2) The effect of trade with foreign countries and the currency rates were represented by the exchange rate changes involving the Canadian Dollar, Deutsche Mark, Yen and Pound Sterling. (3) The effect of inflation was represented by the changes in the consumer price index for all commodities.

4.2 Training Phase

The goal of the training phase is to generate a non-extensional CD. At the end of the training phase, the CD should contain a set of good examples for classification in the testing phase.

A portion of the data in the pre-processed, stored data is used for training, while the rest is used for testing. The portion of data used for the training (the training set) is varied for each testing run. The training starts with an initially empty CD and iterates over the steps described below for each instance in the training set:

- [Step 1]: The Euclidean distances between each instance from the training set and the instances currently in the CD are computed.
- [Step 2]: An "acceptable" instance in the CD with the shortest Euclidean distance from the training instance is assigned to the variable $ymax$. If none of the instances in the CD are acceptable, then a random number i is generated between the value 1 and the current length of the CD descriptor. The ith nearest neighbor of the training instance in the CD is assigned to the variable $ymax$.
- [Step 3]: If the classification of the training instance is the same as the instance $ymax$ in the CD, then the classification is correct; otherwise, the classification is wrong and the training instance is added to the CD.
- [Step 4]: The classification records of the instances in the CD are updated at this step. Instances with significantly poor records are removed from the CD.

At the end of the training phase the instances saved in the CD are the example instances that will be used for classifying the testing phase instances. Instance acceptability in the testing phase is based on a confidence interval of proportions test ([8]) as used by [1]. The confidence interval test is also used to determine if an instance is mediocre or noisy. The confidence intervals are constructed around the current CD instances, current classification accuracy, and the observed relative frequency of its classification category.

4.3 Testing Phase

The testing phase uses the examples saved in the CD after the training phase, the similarity function and the classification function of the IB3 algorithm to determine the classification of the test instances. The testing phase is a step operation, iterated over for each training instance. The Euclidean distance between the training instance and each instance in the CD is computed. The classification function uses the nearest neighbor method to assign the classification of the nearest CD instance to the testing instance. The nearest instance is the CD with the shortest Euclidean distance from the training instance. The proportion of the training data set and the normalization method were varied for various training runs.

5 Results

During experimentation, the normalization method and training data set proportions were varied for each test and training run. For each run, the level of significance for dropping an instance from the concept descriptor was set at 75%, while a significance level of 90% was set for accepting an instance into the concept descriptor.

The object instances were normalized linearly by their range or by their standard deviations during the testing and training runs. The training data set proportions were varied from 5% to 95% in steps of 5%. Testing was carried out on the instances that made up the proportion of the data set that was not used for training.

For each data set proportion, and normalization option at the set significance levels, 50 training and testing trials were carried out. The trials' best classification accuracy values were used for the results analysis.

The average classification accuracy of all the training and testing runs in the experiment was 51.8%. The average classification accuracy of the best accuracy values obtained from training and testing without normalization was 51.46%. Normalizing linearly (normalizing using the range) the average of the obtained best classification accuracies was 51.66%. For normalizations using the standard deviation, the average of the best classifications came to 52.25%.

In the figures below, the x-axis values are the test database proportions in percentages (0-100% increasing in steps of 10%), while the y-axis values are the classification accuracies in percentages (47-55% in Fig.1; 47-56% in Fig. 2; and 44-55% in Fig.3; all increasing in steps of 1%)

Figure 1 presents a graph of the best classification accuracies recorded from the testing and training trials normalized by standard deviations. The classification accuracies range between 50.5% and 54.25% for test properties that are less than 40% of the dataset. The classification accuracies of the training and testing runs carried out on more than 70% of the data set ranged between 53.75% and 51.75%.

Figure 2 presents the best classification accuracies for the testing and training trials using the linear normalization method. The classification accuracies increased steadily as the test data set proportion was increased from 10% to 20%. Large pro portions of about 65% and greater produced lower classification accuracies.

The best classification accuracies values of test and train trials that did not involve any form of normalization are shown in Fig. (3). We observe that classification accuracies improved rapidly as the test proportion increased to 10% of the dataset size. The classification accuracies, however, declined gradually as the the test size increased beyond 10% of the database.

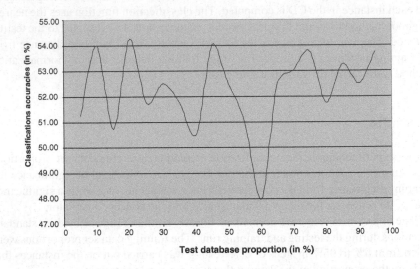

Fig. 1. Best Classification Accuracies for Trial Normalized by Standard Deviations

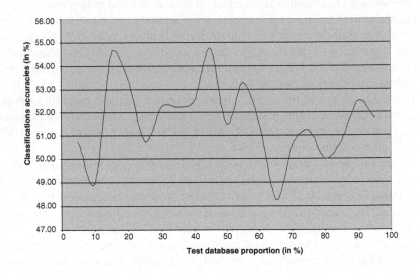

Fig. 2. Best Classification Accuracies for Trial Normalized Linearly

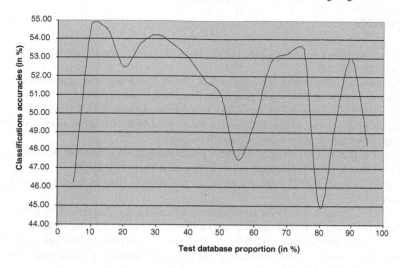

Fig. 3. Best Classification Accuracies for Trial with no Normalization

6 Conclusions

Compared with the 46% average classification accuracy value obtained from the use of IBL classifications in other domains ([1]), we can conclude that IBL can be successfully used for financial forecasting, and hence stock price prediction. The results obtained show that higher classification accuracies can be obtained by normalizing the instance objects during the training and testing phase. For test and training runs in which the instance objects are normalized using their standard deviations, 40% of the dataset or less will produce good classification results. Good classification results can be obtained from training 10% of the database if the instances are normalized linearly using their ranges. Testing and training runs which do not employ any form of normalization will yield good classification results for 10% of the instance database. Further research can be carried out in identifying the length of time that can be considered to be an appropriate short run period for use with the IBL algorithm to achieve higher accuracy.

Acknowledgement

The authors are grateful for the constructive comments from anonymous reviewers. The first author acknowledges the partial financial support from the Natural Sciences and Engineering Research Council of Canada and the University of Manitoba Research Grant Program.

References

1. Aha DW, Kibler D, Albert MK (1991) Instance-based learning algorithms. Machine Learning 6:37–66
2. Appadoo SS, Thulasiram RK, Bector CR (2004) Fuzzy algebraic approach to option pricing - a fundamental investigation. In: Proceedings (CD-RoM) of the Administrative Sciences Association of Canada (ASAC) conference, Quebec City, Canada
3. Board of governors of the Federal reserve system Federal reserve statistical release. http://www.federalreserve.gov/releases/H10/hist/
4. Cover T, Hart P (1967) Nearest neighbor pattern classification. Institute of Electrical and Electronics Engineers Transactions on Information Theory 13:21–27
5. Cowles A, Jones H (1937) Some a posteriori probabilities in stock market action. Econometrica 5:280–294
6. Dixit AK, Pyndick RS (1994) Investment under uncertainty. Princeton University Press
7. Herbert J, Yao J (2005) Time-series data analysis with rough sets. In: Proceedings (CD-RoM) of the computational intelligence in economics and finance, Salt Lake City, UT
8. Hogg RV, Tanis EA (2001) Probability and statistical inference. Prentice-Hall, Inc., New Saddle river, NJ, 6th edition
9. King R, Feng C, Sutherland A (1995) Statlog: comparison of classification algorithms on large real-world problems. Applied Artificial Intelligence 9(3):289–333
10. Knorr EM, Ng RT (1998) Algorithms for mining distance-based outliers in large datasets. In: Proceedings of the VLDB:392–403
11. Kovalerchuk B, Vityaev E (2000) Data mining in finance: advances in relational and hybrid methods. Kluwer Academic Publishers, Norwell, MA
12. Landt FWO (1997) Stock price prediction using neural networks. Master's thesis, Leiden University
13. Leung CK, Thulasiram RK, Bondarenko D (2005) The use of data mining techniques in detecting noise and pre-processing financial time series. In: Proceedings (CD-RoM) of the computational intelligence in economics and finance (CIEF), Salt Lake City, UT
14. Liu Y, Yao X (2001) Evolving neural networks for Hang Seng stock index forecast. In: Proceedings of the 2001 congress on evolutionary computation. IEEE Press:256–260
15. Lo A (2000) Finance: a selective survey. Journal of the American Statistical Association 95(450):629–635
16. Makridakis S, Wheelright S (1978) Forecasting methods and applications. John Wiley & Sons, New York, USA
17. Mendelbrot B (2004) The misbehavior of markets. Basic Books
18. Oliker S (1997) A distributed genetic algorithm for designing and training modular neural networks in financial prediction. In: Nonlinear financial forecasting proceedings of the first international nonlinear financial forecasting conference. Finance and Technology Publishing:183–190
19. Pawlak Z (1991) Rough sets-theoretical aspects of reasoning about data. Kluwer Academic
20. Rahman MR (2002) Distributed and multithreaded neural network algorithms for stock price learning. MSc Thesis, Department of Computer Science, University of Manitoba, Winnipeg, MB, Canada
21. Rahman MR, Thulasiram RK, Thulasiraman P (2002) Forecasting stock prices using neural networks on a Beowulf cluster. In: Akl SG, Gonzalez TF (eds) Proceedings of the fourteenth IASTED international conference on parallel and distributed computing and systems. IASTED Press:465–470

22. Refenes APN (ed) (1995) Neural networks in the capital markets. John Wiley & Sons, Chichester, England
23. Samuelson P (1965) Proof that properly anticipated prices fluctuate randomly. Industrial Management Review 6:41–49
24. Weigend AS, Abu-Mostafa YS, Refenes APN (1997) Decision technologies for financial engineering. World Scientific, New York, NY
25. Yahoo! Incorporated. Yahoo finance - historical prices. http://table.finance.yahoo.com
26. Yao J, Tan C, Pohyao H (1999) Neural networks for technical analysis: a study on klci. International Journal of Theoretical and Applied Finance 2(2):221–241

Evaluating the Efficiency of Index Fund Selections Over the Fund's Future Period

Yukiko Orito[1], Manabu Takeda[2], Kiyoaki Iimura[2], and Genji Yamazaki[2]

[1] Ashikaga Institute of Technology
268-1, Ohmae-cho, Ashikaga, Tochigi 326-8558, Japan
orito@ashitech.ac.jp
[2] Tokyo Metropolitan University
6-6, Asahigaoka, Hino, Tokyo 191-0065, Japan

It is well known that index fund optimization is important when hedge trading in a stock market. By "optimization" is meant the optimization of the proportion of funds in the index fund. Index funds consisting of a small number of listed companies are constructed in this paper by means of a genetic algorithm method based on the co-efficient of determination between the return rate of the fund price and the changing rate of the market index. The method is examined with numerical experiments applied to the Tokyo Stock Exchange. The results show that the index funds work well in forecasting over a future period when a market index has followed a downward or a flat trend. In addition, we reveal problems arising from this optimization in that the coefficient of determination depends on the characteristics of the scatter diagram between the index fund price and the market index.

Key words: Index Fund Optimization, Coefficient of Determination, Genetic Algorithms

1 Introduction

"*Index funds*" have been used very extensively in hedge trading, which is the practice of offsetting the price risk on any cash market position by taking an equal, but opposite, position in a futures market. At the stock selection level, suppose that we select N companies listed on a stock market and invest in a certain number of stocks of each of the N companies. It is well known that a group consisting of N companies will be very useful for hedge trading if the total rate of return of the group follows a similar path to the rate of change in the market index. This group is referred to as "*an index fund.*"

The best index fund is constructed by including all listed stocks comprising the market index in proportion to their weightings in the market index. When the market index is weighted by a great number of companies, however, it is hard to purchase stock in all these companies. On the other hand, the index fund requires rebalancing in order to reflect the changes in the composition of the market index over the fund's future period. However, the total price of the index fund is unknown, and so the implied cost of rebalancing is uncertain. When the number of companies is large, we have to make a large investment in rebalancing. In this context, it is preferred that the index fund consisting of N listed companies be constructed in such a way that N is small. Then we have the important problem of finding such a group of N companies.

In previous work on the portfolio selection problem, some heuristic methods have provided optimal portfolios to achieve a maximum return or to minimize risk. There are heuristic methods using genetic algorithms (see, e.g., [1] and [7]), tabu search ([1]) and simulated annealing ([1]). Index fund optimizations can be viewed as a combinatorial optimization problem to achieve maximum *"fitness value"* between the return rate of the fund price and the changing rate of the market index. The coefficient of determination between the total return rate of the index fund and the changing rate of the market index, R^2 (defined in Sect. 2), is usually used as a measure of how the return rate follows the changing rate.

On the Tokyo Stock Exchange, some securities firms provide index funds consisting of a large number of listed companies, or more than $N = 600$ companies, when we select the Tokyo Stock Price Index (TOPIX) as the market index. Reference [6] and [5, 4] applied GA methods to one year on the Tokyo Stock Exchange and reported that their methods led to the construction of index funds consisting of $N < 500$ companies with $R^2 > 0.96$. However, rather than try to optimize the proportion of funds in the index fund, they attempted to select N companies in the index fund from a group consisting of more than N companies.

In this paper, we propose a GA method to optimize the proportion of funds in the index fund such that R^2 is high. The results show that, based on this GA method, the index funds work well in forecasting over the fund's future period when the market index has followed a downward or a flat trend. However, we reveal a problem with this optimization in that the coefficient of determination R^2 depends on the characteristics of the scatter diagram between the index fund price and the market index.

2 Preliminaries

Suppose that we invest in a group consisting of N listed companies on a stock market, which starts at $t = 1$ and ends at $t = T$. The t is set on a data basis. It is assumed throughout the paper that the amount of money invested in each company belonging to the group is equal to the total available budget and that the group consisting of N companies is selected at $t = T$ before rebalancing. This means that the portfolio is unique for the group. In the field of regression analysis, the coefficient of determination has often been used as a measure of how well an estimated regression fits. As the coefficient approaches 1, the estimated regression will provide a better fit (for this, see, e.g., [2]). By analogy, the coefficient of determination between the return rate of the fund price and the changing rate of the market index is defined as

$$R^2 = \frac{\left(T\sum_{t=1}^{T}x(t)y(t) - \sum_{t=1}^{T}x(t)\sum_{t=1}^{T}y(t)\right)^2}{\left(T\sum_{t=1}^{T}x(t)^2 - \left(\sum_{t=1}^{T}x(t)\right)^2\right)\left(T\sum_{t=1}^{T}y(t)^2 - \left(\sum_{t=1}^{T}y(t)\right)^2\right)},$$

where $y(t)$ is the return rate of the index fund between $t = 1$ and $t = T$, and $x(t)$ is the changing rate of the market index between $t = 1$ and $t = T$. In this paper, R^2 is adopted as the fitness measure.

3 GA Method

The GA method consists of the following two steps:

3.1 Step 1

Suppose that a stock market consists of K listed companies, numbered as company 1, company 2, $\cdots$, company K. The first step of the GA method is to choose N companies from K companies according to the heuristic rule. The rules of [6] and [5] are based on "*trading volume*." In this paper, the rule is based on "*trading volume × closing price*."

For a company i in the market, the average of the company's volume $v_i(t) \times$ closing price $p_i(t)$ between $t = 1$ and $t = T$ is defined by

$$V_i = \frac{1}{T}\sum_{t=1}^{T}v_i(t) \times p_i(t).$$

Suppose that the V_is are assigned to the K companies in the market. Without loss of generality, we can renumber the K companies so that

$$V_1 \geq V_2 \geq \cdots \geq V_i \geq \cdots \geq V_K.$$

We note that the renumbered company i has the i-th highest V_i of all companies. Therefore the heuristic rule means that the set of company 1, company 2, $\cdots$, company N is chosen as the index fund.

3.2 Step 2

The second (final) step of the GA method is formulated as the problem of optimizing the proportion of funds in the index fund consisting of N companies, such that the R^2 is the highest in the R^2s of all subsets of the proportion of funds.

It is well known that GAs are useful for such optimization problems (see, e.g., [3]). Hence, we use a GA to optimize the proportion of the funds in the N companies.

For the GA, a gene which refers to the proportion of funds of company i in the index fund is defined by

$$\forall g_i \in [0, 1],$$

and a chromosome is denoted by

$$\bar{g} = \{g_1, g_2, \cdots, g_N\} \qquad \text{subject to} \sum_{i=1}^{N} g_i = 1.$$

The coefficient of determination R^2 is set as the *"fitness value of the GA."* The process of the GA is designed as follows:

1. **Beginning**
   On the 1st generation of the GA, we randomly generate 100 chromosomes in the initial population.
2. **Evaluation of the fitness value**
   Next we select one chromosome which has the highest fitness value, R^2 in the current population, say, $\bar{g}_{max}$.
3. **Crossover**
   After Step 2, which is the evaluation of the fitness value, we generate a random number r in $[0, 1]$ for each chromosome in the current population. If the r is less than the given crossover rate P_c, the crossover makes new offspring by exchanging the partial structure between the chromosome and another one selected at random. Then we recalculate g_i so that $\sum g_i = 1$. The exchange of the partial structure position is determined at random in both chromosomes.
4. **Mutation**
   Following the crossover process, we generate a random number r in $[0, 1]$ for each chromosome in the current population. If the r is less than the given mutation rate P_m, the mutation makes new offspring by replacing the partial structure of the chromosome. The partial structure position is determined at random and replaces g_i with a new random value in $[0, 1]$. Then we recalculate g_i so that $\sum g_i = 1$.
5. **Selection**
   After the crossover and mutation processes, suppose that there are M chromosomes, numbered $\bar{g}_1$ through $\bar{g}_M$. Let f_i be the R^2 for $\bar{g}_i$ and let p_i be the rate $f_i / \sum_{j=1}^{M} f_j$. The (cumulative) probability $q_i = \sum_{j=1}^{i} p_j$ is assigned to $\bar{g}_i$. We generate a random number r in $[0, 1]$. The $\bar{g}_i$ is selected as an element in the new population when $q_{i-1} < r \le q_i$. By repeating this procedure, we select 100 chromosomes in the new population. If the highest R^2 in the new population is less than the R^2 of the $\bar{g}_{max}$, one of the 100 chromosomes is randomly replaced with the $\bar{g}_{max}$. On the next generation of the GA, the new population consists of 100 chromosomes that were chosen by this selection process.
6. **Stop**
   Finally, the GA is broken off on the given final generation. If the number of generations is less than the final generation, the GA goes back to Step 2 which is the evaluation of the fitness value.

On the final generation, the chromosome $\bar{g}_{max}$ with the highest R^2 is obtained. For company i, the g_i of the $\bar{g}_{max}$ is the proportion of funds of the fund consisting of N companies. For a fixed number of N companies, the GAs are executed 20 times and 20 funds are given. We select one fund which has the nearest R^2 to the average of the 20 funds' R^2s. This is the proportion of funds in our index fund that is based on applying the GA method.

4 Numerical Experiments

We apply the GA method to the Tokyo Stock Exchange consisting of more than 1,500 listed companies from Mar. 11, 1997 to Dec. 21, 2001. In this section, the results for 27 cases, i.e., Case 1, Case 2, $\cdots$, Case 27, are shown. For each case, the data period in the numerical experiment is 200 days in length, i.e., $t \in [-99, 100]$. The period is shifted every 30 days between Mar. 11, 1997 and Dec. 21, 2001.

For each case, we obtain the index fund by applying the GA method to the data from $t = -99$ to $t = 0$ and evaluate the efficiency of the index fund over the fund's future period from $t = 1$ to $t = 100$. In this paper, the former data period $[-99, 0]$ is referred to as a "*past period*" and the latter $[1, 100]$ as a "*future period*."

4.1 Preliminary Experiments

We perform the preliminary experiments in order to set the number of companies N in the index fund and the date length T using the first step of the GA method. The crossover rate P_c or the mutation rate P_m of the GA in the experiments below is set as 0.9 or 0.05, respectively.

For the 27 case studies from Mar. 11, 1997 to Dec. 21, 2001, we first apply the GA method with $T = 100$ to the group consisting of $N = 200$ or $N = 400$ companies and optimize the proportion of funds of the index fund. The averages of the 27 coefficients of determination of the optimized index funds consisting of $N = 200$ or $N = 400$ are shown in Table 1, respectively.

Table 1. The averages of the 27 coefficients of determination of optimized index funds consisting of $N = 200$ or $N = 400$ companies for the 100th and 200th generations

Generation No.	$N = 200$	$N = 400$
100th	0.9450	0.9376
200th	0.9501	0.9456

Table 1 shows that the coefficient average values of index funds consisting of $N = 200$ for the 100th and the 200th generations are higher than the average values for $N = 400$. On the other hand, the computation time on the 100th generation is less than that on the 200th generation. In this context, the number of companies in the index fund is set as $N = 200$ and the final generation of the GA is set as the 100th in the experiments below.

By varying the date length T using the first step of the GA method, the average for the 27 coefficients of determination of the optimized index funds is shown in Table 2.

Table 2. The average of the 27 coefficients of determination of the optimized index funds as a function of T

T	Coefficient of Determination
25	0.9402
50	0.9412
75	0.9434
100	0.9450

From the table it can be seen that, the more that the date length T varies, the higher the coefficient rises. This means that good index funds need groups of companies with high volumes and high prices over a long past period. Hence, the date length T of the first step of the GA method is set as $T = 100$.

4.2 Movement of the Index Fund Price and Market Index

In the past period of each case study, the GA method with $T = 100$ optimizes the proportion of funds in the index fund. The coefficient of determination between the return rate of the index fund price and the changing rate of the market index over the past period of each case is shown in Table 3.

From Table 3, the coefficient of determination in each case study is higher than 0.88. The highest coefficient is the 0.9845 for Case 14, but the lowest coefficient is the 0.8814 for Case 20. For example, the movement of the index fund price and the movement of the market index for Case 14 or Case 20 are shown in Figs. 1(a) and (b), respectively. The time t in the past or the future period is the horizontal axis between $t = -99$ and $t = 100$. Let $Q(t)$ be the market index at time t and the TOPIX used as the market index in this paper. For Case 14 or Case 20, the movement in TOPIX normalized with $Q(0)$, i.e., $Q^*(t) = Q(t)/Q(0)$, is shown by a thin line in Fig. 1(a) or (b), respectively. On the other hand, let $A(t)$ be the total price of the optimized index fund at time t. The movement in the total price normalized with $A(0)$, i.e., $A^*(t) = A(t)/A(0)$, is shown by a thick line in Fig. 1(a) or (b), respectively. To investigate the difference between the 27 case studies over the future period, the average error between the index fund price and the market index from $t = 1$ and $t = 100$, i.e., $\frac{1}{100} \sum_{t=1}^{100} |A^*(t) - Q^*(t)|$, is shown in Table 4.

The index fund price for Case 14 follows a similar path to the market index over the past and the future periods in Fig. 1(a) and the coefficient of determination is high. On the other hand, the index fund price for Case 20 does not follow the market index in Fig. 1(b) and the coefficient of determination is lower than the coefficient

Table 3. The coefficient of determination between the return rate of the index fund price and the changing rate of the market index over the past period

Case	Coefficient of Determination	Case	Coefficient of Determination
1	0.9520	15	0.9836
2	0.9389	16	0.9694
3	0.9387	17	0.9429
4	0.9477	18	0.9300
5	0.9709	19	0.9073
6	0.9752	20	0.8814
7	0.9771	21	0.9021
8	0.9839	22	0.8839
9	0.9688	23	0.9221
10	0.9689	24	0.9124
11	0.9684	25	0.9073
12	0.9750	26	0.9142
13	0.9807	27	0.9275
14	0.9845		

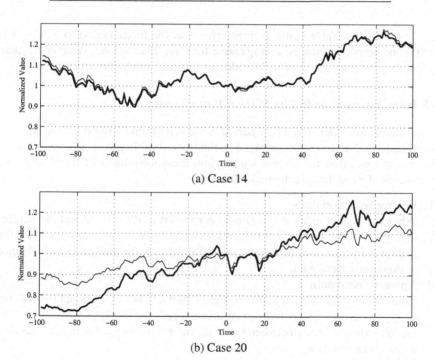

(a) Case 14

(b) Case 20

Fig. 1. The market index normalized with the value at $t = 0$ (thin line) or the total return of the optimized index fund normalized with the value at $t = 0$ (thick line) as a function of t

Table 4. The average error between the index fund price and the market index from $t = 1$ to $t = 100$ over the future period

Case	Error Average	Case	Error Average
1	0.0052	15	0.0164
2	0.0058	16	0.0454
3	0.0095	17	0.0517
4	0.0141	18	0.0074
5	0.0121	19	0.0155
6	0.0076	20	0.0562
7	0.0105	21	0.0244
8	0.0044	22	0.0217
9	0.0072	23	0.0534
10	0.0080	24	0.0503
11	0.0147	25	0.0489
12	0.0060	26	0.0086
13	0.0086	27	0.0143
14	0.0057		

for Case 14. From Table 4, the average error over the future period for Case 14 is 0.0057 and is smaller than the average error for Case 20 of 0.0562. What is the main difference between these results? We address this problem in the next section.

4.3 Index Funds Classified by Market Index Trend

When the market index over a past period is viewed as time series data, the data can be characterized as downward, upward or flat trend data. In this section, we classify the market index data for 27 case studies into these three kinds of trend data. The three kinds of trend data are defined as follows:

1. **Downward trend data**
   When the market index at $t = 0$ is lower than it is at $t = -99$ and the number of days when the market index decreases exceeds the number of days when the market index increases between $t = -99$ and $t = 0$, the market index is defined as downward trend data.
2. **Upward trend data**
   When the market index at $t = 0$ is higher than it is at $t = -99$ and the number of days when the market index increases exceeds the number of days when the market index decreases between $t = -99$ and $t = 0$, the market index is defined as upward trend data.
3. **Flat trend data**
   The market index that is not characterized by downward or upward trend data is defined as being characterized by flat trend data.

For each of these 27 case studies, the data trend classified by these rules is shown in Table 5.

Table 5. The case studies classified by downward, upward or flat trend data

Case	Data Trend	Case	Data Trend
1	upward	15	flat
2	upward	16	upward
3	upward	17	upward
4	downward	18	upward
5	downward	19	upward
6	downward	20	upward
7	downward	21	upward
8	downward	22	upward
9	flat	23	upward
10	downward	24	upward
11	downward	25	upward
12	downward	26	flat
13	downward	27	downward
14	downward		

From Table 5 and Table 3, the average of the coefficient of determination for the 11 case studies characterized by the downward trend is 0.9691 and the average of the coefficient characterized by the flat trend is 0.9515. These results suggest that the proposed GA method works well in optimizing the proportion of funds in the index fund when the market index exhibits a downward or a flat trend. On the other hand, the average of the coefficient for the 13 case studies characterized by the upward trend is 0.9222. The average of the coefficient is lower than in the case of the downward or the flat trend data. This means that the GA method does not optimize the proportion of funds in the good index fund when the market index has exhibited an upward trend.

In addition, the averages of the results over the future period for the downward, flat or upward trend data shown in Table 4 are 0.0089, 0.0107 or 0.0304, respectively. The error between the index fund price and the market index for the upward trend data of 0.0304 is larger than those for the downward and the flat trend data. Why, then, is the coefficient of determination low and the error large when the market index has been on an upward trend? In this section we address this problem.

The relationship between two variables can be shown in a scatter diagram. For example, two kinds of clusters of variables are plotted in Figs. 2(a) and (b).

It is well known that the coefficient of determination measures the clustering around a linear line. For instance, the plotted points in Fig. 2(a) are tightly clustered around a line. There is a strong linear association between the two variables and the coefficient of determination is high. On the other hand, the cluster in Fig. 2(b) is looser than that in Fig. 2(a) and the coefficient is lower than the coefficient for Fig. 2(a). As mentioned in Sect. 2, the coefficient of determination is used as a measure of fit between the rate of return on the index fund price and the change in the rate of the market index in this paper. The scatter diagram of the fund price and the market

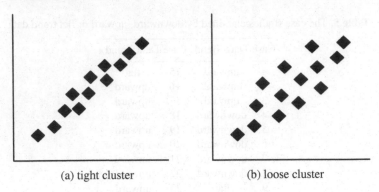

(a) tight cluster   (b) loose cluster

Fig. 2. Examples of scatter diagrams

index in Case 14 is characterized by a downward trend or in Case 20 is characterized by an upward trend as shown in Figs. 3(a) and (b), respectively.

The results show that the cluster for Case 14 in Fig. 3(a) is tighter than the cluster for Case 20 in Fig. 3(b). This means that the index fund price and the market index for Case 14 are correlated on the same stratum. However the correlations for Case 20 are weak. To improve the performance of the index fund in such a case study, we need to develop a new fitness value instead of the coefficient of determination.

5 Concluding Remarks

We have proposed the GA method in order to optimize the proportion of funds in the index fund and have applied this method to the Tokyo Stock Exchange.

The numerical experiments show that the GA method optimizes the proportion of funds in the index funds well when the market index exhibits a downward or a flat trend. However, we also reveal a problem in that the coefficient of determination depends on the characteristics of the scatter diagram between the index fund price and the market index.

Future work will include developing a new fitness value instead of the coefficient of determination to improve the performance of the index funds. We will be focusing on the tracking error of the fund price and the market index. Our findings will be revealed in future studies.

References

1. Chang TJ, Meade N, Beasley JE, Sharaiha YM (2000) A model for portfolio selection with order of expected returns. Computers & Operations Research 27:1271–1302
2. Downie NM, Health RW (1983) Basic Statistical Methods. Harpercollins College Div, 5th edition
3. Gen M, Cheng R (1997) Genetic algorithms and engineering design. Willy–Interscience

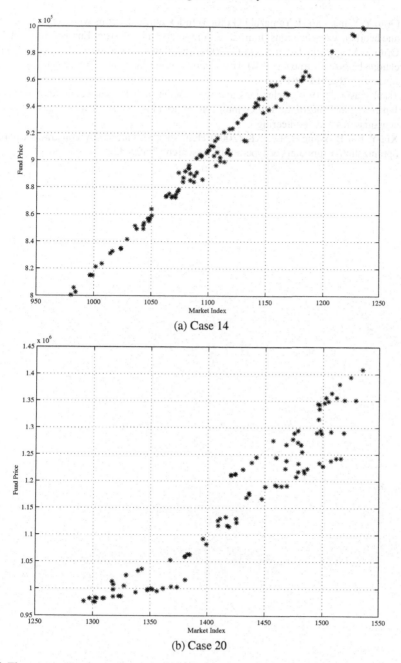

(a) Case 14

(b) Case 20

Fig. 3. The scatter diagram between the index fund price and the market index when the market index exhibits a downward trend or an upward trend

4. Orito Y, Yamamoto H, Yamazaki G (2003) Index fund selections with genetic algorithms and heuristic classifications. Journal of Computers and Industrial Engineering 45:97–109
5. Orito Y, Motoyama T, Yamazaki G (2004) Index fund selections with GAs and classifications based on turnover. IEEJ Transactions of the Institute of Electrical Engineers of Japan 124-10:2014–2018
6. Takabayashi A (1995) Selections and rebalancing of funds with genetic algorithms (in Japanese). In: Proc. of the 1995 winter conference of the Japanese association of financial econometrics and engineering
7. Xia Y, Liu B, Wang S, Lai KK (2000) Heuristics for cardinality constrained portfolio optimization. Computers & Operations Research 27:409–422

Failure of Genetic-Programming Induced Trading Strategies: Distinguishing between Efficient Markets and Inefficient Algorithms

Shu-Heng Chen[1] and Nicolas Navet[1,2]

[1] AI-ECON Research Center, Department of Economics, National Chengchi University, Taipei, Taiwan 11623, chchen@nccu.edu.tw
[2] LORIA-INRIA, Campus-Scientifique, BP239, F-54506 Vandoeuvre, France, nnavet@loria.fr

Over the last decade, numerous papers have investigated the use of Genetic Programming (GP) for creating financial trading strategies. Typically, in the literature, the results are inconclusive but the investigators always suggest the possibility of further improvements, leaving the conclusion regarding the effectiveness of GP undecided. In this paper, we discuss a series of pretests aimed at giving more clear-cut answers as to whether GP can be effective with the training data at hand. Precisely, pretesting allows us to distinguish between a failure due to the market being efficient or due to GP being inefficient. The basic idea here is to compare GP with several variants of random searches and random trading behaviors having well-defined characteristics. In particular, if the outcomes of the pretests reveal no statistical evidence that GP possesses a predictive ability superior to a random search or a random trading behavior, then this suggests to us that there is no point in investing further resources in GP. The analysis is illustrated with GP-evolved strategies for nine markets exhibiting various trends.

1 Motivation and Introduction

Computational intelligence techniques such as genetic programming[1], with their continuous advancement, persistently bring us something positive to expect, and incessantly push the application domain to more challenging issues. However, sometimes, the costs and benefits of using these advanced CI techniques are uncertain. Usually the benefits are not assured, while the costs are immediate. On the one hand, the CI techniques are frequently used as intensive search algorithms, which are inevitably computationally demanding, and take up a great amount of computational

---

[1] Although, in this paper, we solely focus on genetic programming, the general ideas and some specific implementations should also be applicable to other computational intelligence techniques used to induce trading strategies.

resources. On the other hand, whether or not there is a needle in the haystack remains dubious. For example, in the financial application domain, the lack of such a needle may be due to the efficient markets hypothesis or the no-arbitrage condition. Certainly, if such a needle does not exist at all, then all efforts are made to no avail. Given this asymmetry between costs and benefits, it would be economical, at the first stage, to test for the existence of such a needle before a fully-fledged version of the search is applied. We refer to this procedure as a *pretest*.

The pretest procedure proposed here is in a sense similar to the pretests used in econometrics where the estimator of an unknown parameter is chosen on the basis of the outcome of a pretest [9]. Pretesting, also known as "data-snooping" in finance, classically serves to select the right model that will be used later on for forecasting purposes (see [5, 20]). More broadly, pretesting can be considered to be a practice of a sequential decision-making process, which is used when the decision involves a great deal of uncertainty, and the costs of making a wrong decision are huge. [2] In this case, at the first stage, we would like to expend some limited resources on probing into gaining some initial information, e.g., the distribution of a very uncertain environment, while in the later stages, we will make our decision based on the gauged distribution.

The reasoning behind prestesting is very intuitive, and [11] is the first to apply this idea to the financial application of genetic programming (GP). Reference [11] proposed a measure known as the η statistic. The η statistic is a measure of predictability obtained by comparing the predictions regarding the actual data and the shuffled data.[3] Basically, by using a simple (vanilla) version of GP, one can first gauge the predictability based on η. When η is low or close to zero, it indicates that there is nothing to forecast. So, the use of fully-fledged GP is not advised. The virtue in doing this is to distinguish *two kinds of possibilities* when we see the failure of an initial attempt based on simple GP. First, the series itself has nothing to forecast; second, GP has not been used appropriately. Understanding this distinction can result in big differences in our second stage of the decision. In the former case, we may simply give up any further search to avoid wasting resources. In the latter case, we should keep on exploring different deliberations of GP to search for potential gains before a final conclusion can be reached. In either case, we have a clear-cut situation. However, when a pretest is absent, we become less conclusive: we are no longer sure whether the problem is due to the non-existence of the needle, or the improper use of GP.

---

[2] The problem of sequential decision making under incomplete knowledge has been studied by researchers in various fields, such as optimal control, psychology, economics, and game theory.

[3] The η statistics make use of *surrogate data*, that is, the data sharing statistical properties of the data under study but not the property that is tested for. Here, the property investigated is temporal dependence and, thus, by shuffling the original time series, the temporal dependencies, if any, are lost. The interested reader might refer to [16] and [18] for a good starting point on the use of surrogate data.

Unfortunately, in most financial trading applications of GP, a pretest has been largely neglected.[4] We think that this negligence may give rise to many inconclusive results. Typically, what happens is that the results from using GP are not very convincing, but the investigators always suggest directions for further improvement, leaving the actual conclusion regarding the effectiveness of GP undecided. Therefore, this study attempts to provide a practical pretesting procedure aimed at reducing the number of cases where the conclusion is inconclusive.

Needless to say, there are various ways of implementing different types of pretesting. For example, the η statistic mentioned above can be used as a pretest, as [11] did, but that is mainly applied to forecasting time series. That a series is to a certain extent predictable does not necessarily imply that we can develop profitable trading strategies. For example, the predictability horizon might be too short, the fluctuation might not be volatile enough to cover the round-trip transaction costs or, simply, the right trading instrument might not be available (e.g., no short selling in a downward oriented market) or else they are some regulation and rules (e.g., the "uptick rule" makes intraday trading with short selling more difficult). Consequently, the literature on forecasting with GP (e.g., [12, 17] and [6]) and the literature on trading with GP (e.g., [1, 14, 21] and [4]) are usually separated. Therefore, in this paper, we attempt to develop pretest procedures that are more suitable for trading purposes. However the correlation between the predictability[5] of a time series and the profitability of GP induced rules, and more generally of any trading strategies, is an intriguing and still open question, whose answer[6] constitutes, in our view, a major step towards efficient market timing decision tools.

More precisely, we will propose here several different styles of pretests, which when put together can help us decide whether there are hidden patterns to be discovered and whether GP is properly designed to do the job. The essential idea underlying all proposed pretests is to compare the performance of GP with random trading strategies or behavior. However, as we shall see in Sect. 2, just making trading strate-

---

[4] This may not be completely so. In fact, most earlier studies selected a risk-free investment (e.g., treasury bills) or, most often, the buy-and-hold strategy as the benchmark. However, the conclusion that "GP performs better than buy-and-hold in a bearish market and worse in a bullish market" is often found in the literature. However, nothing different can be expected since buy-and-hold is the worst possible strategy in a steadily decreasing market and the best possible strategy in a steadily increasing market. This shows the limits of choosing buy-and-hold as a benchmark.

[5] Numerous metrics, emerging from the fields of information theory, the study of dynamical systems and algorithmic complexity or statistics, have been devised to quantify the predictability of a system observed by the data it produces. One can mention the Lyapunov exponent, which is a measure of the rate of divergence of nearby trajectories and thus an indication of the short-term predictability, the Shannon entropy which measures the diversity of the data produced or the Grassberger-Crutchfield-Young statistical complexity which informs us of the amount of information which is relevant to the system's dynamic. The reader interested in predictability measures can refer to [2] and [19] for a comprehensive survey.

[6] Of particular interest is the work of [10] which is a significant step in that direction.

gies or trading behavior arbitrarily random is not sufficient to provide a fair and informative comparison. To do so, some constraints are expected, and the interesting point is how to impose these constraints properly.

The rest of the paper is organized as follows. Section 2 provides a detailed formulation of the four pretests. The first three are concerned with the trading strategies, whereas the last one is concerned with the trading behavior. Normally, trading behavior comes from trading strategies, and they cannot be separated; however, when randomness is introduced, differences between the two may arise. In particular, in the vein of algorithmic complexity, random trading strategies can imply trading behavior actually using knowledge, while random trading behavior presumably excludes such a possibility. We, therefore, intentionally distinguish between the two by referring to the former as *zero-intelligence strategies*, and the latter as *lottery trading*. Section 3 discusses how to use these proposed tests together to make a better judgment given the initial results we have. Section 4 illustrates the proposed pretests based on the real data and the experimental designs detailed in the appendix. Section 5 gives the concluding remarks.

2 Pretests: Description and Rationale

In this section, we describe a series of 4 pretests and discuss their purpose and implementation. Of the 4 pretests, we highlight 2 that are of particular interest and, as shown in Sect. 3, enable us to gain complementary knowledge on the data under study and on the efficiency of the GP's implementation. In the following, we consider GP with a validation stage before the actual testing of the out-of-sample data. Validation means that the best rules induced on the training interval are further selected on the unseen data, i.e., the validation period, before being applied out-of-sample. The validation step is a device to fight overfitting that has been widely used in earlier GP work (see for instance [1, 15]).[7] Note that our proposals, except for pretest 1 which explicitly requires validation, remain valid as they do for GP without the validation step.

2.1 GP versus Equivalent Intensity Random Search

The basic idea here is to compare the outcome of GP with an *equivalent intensity random search*. We say that two search algorithms are equivalent in terms of search intensity if their execution leads to the evaluation of the same number of *distinct* trading strategies for the training data. For instance, let us consider GP with the parameters chosen for this study: a population of 500 individuals evolved over 100 generations. In the first approximation, the equivalent random search (ERS) would consist of evaluating 50,000 randomly created solutions. In practice, search algorithms sometimes rediscover identical solutions over the course of their execution. This can

---

[7] The actual effectiveness of validation in this context is, however, still an open question. See [4] and [3].

simply be detected by keeping track of all created individuals since the beginning of the execution, and in doing so useless fitness evaluations can be skipped, which actually saves computing time when the fitness function is rather time-consuming. Since, computationally speaking, what is preponderant in our context is the fitness evaluation, we impose the restriction that our definition of equivalent search intensity only accounts for unique individuals, *i.e.*, individuals that require evaluation. We consider two solutions to be distinct if their expression is *syntactically different*[8], in our GP context, if the trees representing the programs are different.

The three following pretests compare GP with a random search both with and without a training and validation stage. In random search, the biologically inspired evolution process of GP is simply replaced by the creation of solutions at random. Since with random search the strategies do not benefit from the "intelligence" resulting from the evolution and learning process[9], we dub randomly created solutions as *zero-intelligence trading strategies*.

For each pretest i, we formulate the null hypothesis $\mathcal{H}_{i,0}$ that GP does not outperform the technique it is compared with at pretest i, where the alternative hypothesis is denoted by $\mathcal{H}_{i,1}$. The experiments will provide us with the answer to whether $\mathcal{H}_{i,0}$ should be rejected in favor of $\mathcal{H}_{i,1}$ or not. As usual, the chosen significance level of the test enables us to finely control the probability to falsely reject the null, that is in our case to come wrongly to the conclusion that GP is more effective than the technique it is compared with.

Pretest 1: GP versus Equal Search Intensity Random Search - both with a Training and a Validation Stage.

The implementation of the random search strategy is straightforward: parameters of GP are set in such a way that only the initial generation, where individuals are created at random, is used. The size of the initial population is adjusted so that the resulting search intensity is identical to the one for the regular GP.

---

[8] Two individuals can be syntactically different while being equivalent in the sense that they always lead to the same trading decisions, and the equivalence could thus also be defined in terms of semantics. With symbolic simplification using rewriting rules and interval arithmetic on the function arguments, we could detect that some syntactically different individuals are in fact semantically identical. However, there is no way of making sure that all duplicates will be detected and the implementation of this procedure would be so complex and time consuming at run time that, in our opinion, a definition based on semantics would be of little practical interest. Alternatively, the equivalence in search intensity could be defined in terms of equivalent running time. However, there is such a difference in complexity between a fully-fledged GP implementation and random search that it is hard to imagine how we can ensure that the two implementations have been optimized in a similar manner, while a better implementation of GP may for instance may lead us to come to an opposite conclusion.

[9] Comparing GP with random search informs us regarding the effectiveness of the GP operators. Further meaningful information regarding this issue could be obtained by comparing regular GP with an implementation that would favor crossover among the less fit solutions ("breed-the-worst"), as suggested in [13].

- **Hypothesis $\mathcal{H}_{1,0}$ cannot be rejected:** the first explanation that can be envisaged is that, GP or not, there is nothing essential to be learned from the past. In that case GP would strongly "overfit" the training data, possibly explaining that in the same cases its out-of-sample performance is worse than that with a random search. This can be due to the market being efficient or because the training interval exhibits a time series pattern which is significantly different from the out-of-sample period.[10] Another explanation is that the GP machinery is not working properly, for instance due to a wrong choice in the composition of the function and terminal sets, because the parameters controlling the GP run are inappropriate (e.g., a search intensity that would be insufficient), or the genetic operators are unable to create better-than-random individuals.
- **Hypothesis $\mathcal{H}_{1,0}$ is rejected in favor of $\mathcal{H}_{1,1}$:** there may be something to learn from the past and GP, with the chosen parameters, may be effective in that task.

Rejecting $\mathcal{H}_{1,0}$ is of course a first indication of the efficiency of GP but, as we will see in Sect. 3, further investigation may provide additional information to answer that question and rule out mere luck.

Pretest 2: GP versus Equal Search Intensity Random Search with a Training but without a Validation Stage.

Here, the best solutions found at random over the training interval are applied directly to the out-of-sample period. With regard to pretest 1, pretest 2 could give us some insight into how effective validation is as a device to fight against overfitting. However, since overfitting is unlikely to occur with random search, the rationale for using pretest 2 is unclear and it will not be further considered in this study. A more direct and effective way to evaluate the effect of the validation stage is simply to compare regular GP with and without validation.[11]

Pretest 3: GP versus Equal Search Intensity Random Search both without a Training and without a Validation Stage

In pretest 3, the selection of the strategies for the training set is removed: a large number of random strategies are created and applied directly out-of-sample. The performance is evaluated as the average performance (e.g., average total return) over the set of random strategies. Comparing the outcome of pretest 3 with regard to pretest 1 and regular GP tells us something about how effective the selection process is, and the extent to which a top performing rule on the training and validation sets will keep on performing well out-of-sample. If strategies selected by GP or random search on the training and validation intervals have some predictive ability out-of-sample, this will provide us with evidence that there is something to learn from the past. It is

---

[10] In [4], experiments have consistently highlighted that when training and out-of-sample data sets are very "dissimilar", for instance if the market exhibits opposite trends, then there is little chance that GP will perform well out-of-sample.

[11] For instance, as in the case of [4] and [8].

worth pointing out that the randomness of the strategies here is constrained by the GP language: rules can only be made with GP functions/terminals organized according to the constructs of the language and its typing scheme. For instance, it may happen that the GP language is not sufficiently expressive to define a rule consisting of buying and selling every other period. [12] In the remainder of this study, we will consider pretest 4, presented in Sect. 2.2, that is similar in spirit to prestest 3, but is more random in the sense that it does not possess the bias in randomness induced by the GP language.

2.2 GP versus Lottery Trading

We refer to *lottery trading* as a strategy that would consist of making the investment decision randomly on the basis of the outcome of a random variable. In its simplest form, the random variable would follow a Bernoulli distribution where the parameter p expresses the probability of taking a long position and $1 - p$ the probability of closing a long position or staying out of the market.

In our context, this requires refinement since we are interested in profitability and profitability takes into account transaction costs. Therefore, in order to allow a fair comparison with GP, we should make sure that the expected number of transactions for lottery trading is the same as for GP. We refer to the expected number of transactions per unit of time as the *frequency of a trading strategy*. Another important characteristic of a trading strategy is what we term its *intensity, i.e.* the number of periods where a position[13] "in the market" is held, over the length of the trading interval. We should also enforce lottery trading to have the same expected intensity as GP to avoid misleading results, for instance, in the case where, given its frequency, the intensity of lottery trading is not sufficient to cover the transaction costs with the volatility of the market under study.

We denote by F_{GP} and I_{GP}, respectively, the average frequency and average intensity observed for the set of GP-evolved rules applied to the testing interval over all GP runs, and N_{GP} is the number of transactions leading to F_{GP}. For the experiments made in the following, a sequence of investment decisions S_{LT} resulting from lottery trading is generated at random according to the following procedure:

- the intensity for lottery trading, I_{LT}, is uniformly chosen in $[I_{GP} \cdot (1 - \alpha), \min(1, I_{GP} \cdot (1 + \alpha))]$ where parameter α $(0 \leq \alpha \leq 1)$ introduces a con-

---

[12] Period refers to the granularity of time used for trading, for instance, one second or one day.

[13] Implicitly, we consider here the trading of a single instrument, e.g., an index, where two positions are possible at each point in time, i.e., be in or be out of the market if short selling is not possible, or with short selling as implemented in [4], holding a long position or a short position. These concepts can be extended to the case where there are three possibilities in each time period: holding a long position, holding a short position or staying out of the market. Similarly, intensity and the frequency of a strategy can be instantiated for each traded instrument.

trolled randomness.[14] In the first step, S_{LT} is made of the '0' positions (*i.e.*, out of the market) followed by the block of '1' positions (*i.e.*, in the market) corresponding to I_{LT},

- the number of transactions N_{LT} is uniformly chosen in the set of integer values that are even[15] in interval $[N_{GP} \cdot (1 - \alpha), N_{GP} \cdot (1 + \alpha)]$. The block of '1' is subdivided at random in $N_{LT}/2$ sub-sequences and each sub-sequence is inserted at random inside the block of '0'. This design avoids the problem of overlapping among the '1' sub-sequences that may occur with other schemes.

We formulate the pretest comparing GP and lottery trading and denote by $\mathcal{H}_{4,0}$ the null hypothesis that GP does not outperform lottery trading while the alternative hypothesis is $\mathcal{H}_{4,1}$.

Pretest 4: GP versus Lottery Trading

Obviously, if GP is not able to outperform lottery trading, it gives strong evidence that GP will not be good at evolving effective trading strategies with the data at hand. In Sect. 3, we shall discuss this point in more detail.

3 What do the pretests tell us ?

The outcomes of the pretests provide us with answers to the following two questions: Is there something essential to learn on the training data that can be of interest for the out-of-sample period? Does the GP implementation show some evidence of effectiveness in that task? Clearly, before actually trading with GP evolved programs, these two questions must be answered with reasonable certainty; the rest of this section explains how pretests may help in that regard.

3.1 Question 1: Is there something to learn ?

The null hypothesis $\mathcal{H}_{4,0}$ corresponding to pretest 4 has been presented in Sect. 2.2. We introduce pretest 5 that will be used in conjunction with pretest 4.

---

[14] Parameter α is intended to reproduce the variability of intensity and frequency observed over the sample of GP runs that lottery trading is compared with. In the simplest form presented here, this is implemented as a parameter α which is unique for intensity and frequency. It is of course possible to refine this scheme by individualizing the parameter for intensity and frequency, or by drawing at random the values of I_{LT} and N_{LT} according to the empirical distributions of intensity and frequency encountered over the sample of GP runs. This latter procedure is especially meaningful when the empirical distributions of intensity and frequency in GP significantly differ from the uniform distribution that is implicitly assumed here.

[15] N_{LT} has to be even since a "buy" transaction is followed by a sell transaction and no positions are left open.

Pretest 5: Equivalent Intensity Random Search with Training and Validation versus Lottery Trading

Here, we compare lottery trading to a random search with training and validation, and a search intensity equivalent to the one used for GP in pretest 4. The null hypothesis $\mathcal{H}_{5,0}$ is that the equivalent intensity random search does not outperform lottery trading for the out-of-sample data. Depending on the validity of $\mathcal{H}_{4,0}$ and $\mathcal{H}_{5,0}$, we can draw the conclusions that are summarized in Table 1:

	$\mathcal{H}_{4,0}$	$\mathcal{H}_{5,0}$	Interpretation
case 1	¬**R**	¬**R**	there is evidence that there is nothing to learn
case 2	**R**	¬**R**	there may be something to learn (weak certainty)
case 3	**R**	**R**	there is evidence that there is something to learn
case 4	¬**R**	**R**	there may be something to learn (weak certainty)

Table 1. Information drawn from the outcomes of pretest 4 and pretest 5 (¬**R** means that the null hypothesis $\mathcal{H}_{i,0}$ cannot be rejected while **R** means that the hypothesis is rejected in favor of the alternative hypothesis).

In case 1, the best solutions for the training intervals, obtained with 2 different search algorithms, do not perform better than lottery trading for the out-of-sample period. This suggests to us than there is nothing to learn. In case 2, GP outperforms lottery trading but random search does not; it is possible that there is something to learn, but that the selected random rules do not have a sufficient predictive ability. In any case, this leads us to a less certain conclusion than in case 3 where both search techniques outperform lottery trading. Finally case 4 is a special case where random search performs better than lottery trading but GP does not. The whole evolutionary process of GP has thus a detrimental effect and a possible explanation is that GP-induced solutions strongly overfit the training data despite the validation stage.

3.2 Question 2: Is the GP machinery working properly?

The second question we ought to ask is whether GP is effective. Of course, this cannot be answered with the data at hand if pretests 4 and 5 have shown that there is nothing to be learned (case 1 in Table 1). In addition, in case 4 of Table 1, we already know that GP is not efficient since, by transitivity, it is outperformed by the random search-based algorithm. Thus, the only two cases where one really needs to proceed to further examination are case 2 and case 3. The validity of the null hypothesis $\mathcal{H}_{1,0}$, which can be tested with pretest 1, gives a helpful insight into the answer: only if $\mathcal{H}_{1,0}$ should be rejected can we conclude that GP shows some real effectiveness. We would like to stress that rejecting $\mathcal{H}_{1,0}$ is far from implying profitability, but beating a mere random search algorithm on a difficult problem with an infinite search space is the bare minimum one can expect from GP.

4 Experiments

The aim of the experiments is to evaluate the extent to which the pretests proposed are reliable. The methodology adopted here is to check if the outcomes of the pretests are consistent with results already published in the literature. We call the software used in [4] GP1, which will constitute our benchmark, while GP2 is the GP implementation developed for this study. Although both programs have been developed by members of the AI-ECON Research Center, they have not been written by the same persons and do not share a single line of code. Furthermore, GP2, which is based on the *Open-Beagle* C++ library (see [7] and http://beagle.gel.ulaval.ca/), makes use of strongly-typed GP on the contrary to GP1. The GP2 control parameters, as close as possible to the ones used in [4] for GP1, are summarized in Table 1 (Appendix A).

The traded instruments are the indexes of 3 stock exchanges: the TSE 300 (Canada), the Nikkei Dow Jones (Japan) and the Capitalization Weighted Stock Index (Taiwan). They have been chosen among the 8 markets studied in [4] because they exhibit the main price evolution patterns that can be found in the set of 8 markets. The aim of GP is to induce the most profitable strategy, measured by the accumulated return, for trading the stock exchange index. The use of short selling is possible. We adopt what is done classically in the literature in terms of data-preprocessing and use normalized data that is obtained by dividing each day's price by a 250-day moving average.[16] In a way similar to what is usually done, we subdivide the whole data set into three sections: the *training*, *validation* and *out-of-sample* test periods. For each stock index considered, 3 different out-of-sample test periods of 2 years each (*i.e.*, 1999-2000, 2001-2002, 2003-2004) follow a 3-year validation and a 3-year training period. In the following, the term market refers to a stock exchange during a specific out-of-sample period. For instance, market Canada-1 (C1 for short) is the TSE 300 during the out-of-sample period 1999-2000. Hypothesis testing is performed with the *Student's t-test* at a 95% confidence level. The samples for statistics are made up of the results of 50 GP runs, 50 runs of equivalent search intensity random search with training and validation (ERS) and 100 runs of lottery trading (LT) with parameter $\alpha = 0.2$ (see §2.2 for the definition of α). The following results were obtained with GP2:

- In 4 out of the 9 markets (*i.e.*, C3, J2, T1, T3), there is evidence that there is something to learn from the training data (case 3 in Table 1 - GP2 and ERS outperform Lottery Trading). This is consistent with [4] where GP1 performs outstandingly in these 4 markets (respective total return: 0.34, 0.17, 0.52, 0.27).
- In markets C1, J3 and T2, pretests 4 and 5 suggest to us that there is nothing to learn (case 1 in Table 1 - neither GP2 nor ERS outperform Lottery Trading). Except for C1, GP1 also performs poorly (-0.18 for J3 and -0.05 for T2). [17]

---

[16] See [4] for a discussion on how non-normalized data affects the performance of GP.

[17] The two markets that are not listed, i.e. C2 and J1, correspond to cases where "there may be something to learn." Precisely, they both belong to case 2 in Table 1, that GP beats LT but random search does not beat LT.

- Finally, in the 3 markets where GP2 is shown to beat ERS ($\mathcal{H}_{1,0}$ is rejected in favor of $\mathcal{H}_{1,1}$ for J1, J2 and T1), the GP results are very good: both GP1 and GP2 produce positive returns and outperform the buy-and-hold strategy.

Although more comprehensive tests are needed, the experiments conducted here on 9 markets show some preliminary evidence that the proposed pretests possess some predictive ability. Indeed, when the outcome is "nothing to learn," the two GP implementations perform very poorly (except in one case). On the contrary, when the pretests suggest that there is something to learn, at least one GP implementation does well.[18]

When pretests suggest to us that a market is efficient, we cannot conclude that there is no way of making consistent profits in this market, because the concept of efficiency is of course relative to the investors considered. What can be concluded is that a group of investors making their investment decisions by running GP2 on the past price time-series will not be able to consistently outperform the market. It is also worth noting that the efficiency of a market is variable over time; for instance, pretests suggest to us that T2 is efficient while T1 and T3 are not. As highlighted in [4], GP not being efficient is often due to the training interval exhibiting a time series pattern which is significantly different from the out-of-sample period (e.g., "bull" versus "bear", "sideways" versus "bull", ...). Thus, a first way of making improvements that can be investigated is to rethink the data division scheme.

In light of the pretests, we should also conclude that our GP implementation (*i.e.* GP2) is more efficient than random search (GP2 outperforms ERS in 3 markets while ERS never beats GP2 with statistical significance). However, in our experiments, searching trading rules at random, with the same set of functions and terminals as used in GP, is usually enough to come up with trading systems that outperform lottery trading when GP does as well. This suggests to us that GP2 may only be able to take advantage of "simple" regularities in the data.

5 Conclusions

The main purpose of this paper is to enrich the earlier research on Genetic Programming (GP) induced market-timing decisions by proposing pretests aiming to shed light on the GP results. In actual fact, in the literature, the results of applying GP for market-timing decisions are typically not very convincing, but the investigators always suggest the possibility of further improvements. If the investigators can first be convinced that there is something to learn and that GP is suitable for that task, then their conclusion would be less vague and uncertain. We propose here a series of

---

[18] In all 4 such cases (C3, J2, T1, T3), GP2 beats LT, but in 2 cases where the market is bullish (C3 and T3) the returns earned by GP2, which are 5% and -4%, respectively, are far less than those of Buy-and-Hold, which are more than 30% during the out-of-sample period. As a result, one cannot say that GP2 is performing superbly. However, in those 2 cases, GP1, which seems in general to be the best implementation, happens to be very efficient (only a few percent less than buy and hold).

pretests, where GP is tested against a random behavior (*lottery trading*) and against strategies created at random (*zero-intelligence strategies*) that aim to answer these two crucial questions. Of course there is the risk of getting a wrong pretest result and the possible reasons why GP may have failed should be thoroughly investigated before drawing a conclusion. But, in the end, analyzing the results in light of the pretests should help us to draw more fine-grained conclusions.

Acknowledgements

This research was conducted when the second author (Nicolas Navet) was a visiting researcher at the AI-ECON Research Center, National Chengchi University (NCCU), Taipei, Taiwan. The financial support from the AI-ECON Research Center, INRIA, as well as NCCU is greatly acknowledged. The authors would also like to acknowledge the grant from the National Science Concil #95-2415-H-004-002-MY3.

A Genetic Programming Settings

Program GP2 implements strongly typed GP with the set of functions and terminals described in Table 1. The parameters here are basically identical to the ones in [4] (program GP1) except when fine-tuning GP2 has highlighted that better results may be obtained with different parameters. Precisely when we make use of more elitism, the size of the tournament selection is set to 5 and numerical mutation is implemented.

References

1. Allen F, Karjalainen R (1999) Using genetic algorithms to find technical trading rules. Journal of Financial Economics 51:245–271
2. Boffetta G, Cencini M, Falcioni M, Vulpiani A (2002) Predictability: A way to characterize complexity. Physics Reports 356:367
3. Chen SH, Kuo TW (2003) Overfitting or poor learning: a critique of current financial applications of GP. In: Ryan C, Soule T, Keijzer M, Tsang E, Poli R, Costa E (eds) Proceedings of the sixth European conference on genetic programming. Springer-Verlag:34–46
4. Chen SH, Kuo TW, Hoi KM (2007) Genetic programming and financial trading: how much about "what we know"? In: Zopounidis C, Doumpos M, Pardalos PM (eds) Handbook of financial engineering. Springer. Forthcoming.
5. Danilov D, Magnus J (2004) Forecast accuracy after pretesting with an application to the stock market. Journal of Forecasting 23:251–274
6. del Arco-Calderón CL, Viñuela PI, Castro JCH (2004) Forecasting time series by means of evolutionary algorithms. In: PPSN:1061–1070
7. Gagné C, Parizeau M (2002) Open beagle: a new versatile c++ framework for evolutionary computations. In: Late breaking papers, genetic and evolutionary computing conference (GECCO):161–168

Population size	500
Number of generations	100
Maximum tree depth	10
Function set	+,-,*,/,norm,average,max,min,lag,and, or, not, >,<,if-then-else,true,false
Terminal set	price, real and integer ephemeral constants
Value range for real constants	[-1,1]
Value range for integer constants	[0,1000]
Offsprings created by:	
crossover	50%
standard mutation	20%
swap mutation	15%
reproduction	10%
ephemeral constant mutation	5%
Initialization	ramp-half-and-half
Evolution scheme	generation-by-generation replacement strategy
Elitism	25 best individuals kept for next generation
Selection scheme	tournament selection of size 5
Fitness function	accumulated return
Transaction costs	0.5%
Validation	
number of best trees saved	1 individual per run is saved for validation

Table 1: Control parameters of GP

Fig. 1. GP control parameters

8. Gagné C, Schoenauer M, Parizeau M, Tomassini M (2006) Genetic programming, validation sets, and parsimony pressure. In: Collet P, Tomassini M, Ebner M, Gustafson S, Ekárt A (eds) Proceedings of the 9th European conference on genetic programming. Springer Verlag:109–120

9. Giles J, Giles D (1993) Pre-test estimation and testing in econometrics: recent developments. Journal of Economic Surveys 7(2):145–197

10. Hong J, Chung Y (2003) Are the directions of stock price changes predictable? Statistical theory and evidence. Technical report, Cornell University

11. Kaboudan MA (1999) A measure of time series' predictability using genetic programming applied to stock returns. Journal of Forecasting 18:345–357

12. Kaboudan MA (2000) Evaluation of forecasts produced by genetically evolved models. In: 6th international conference on computing in economics and finance. Society for Computational Economics

13. Langdon WB, Poli R (2002) Foundations of genetic programming. Springer-Verlag.

14. Li J, Tsang E (2000) Reducing failures in investment recommendations using genetic programming. In: 6th international conference on computing in economics and finance. Society for Computational Economics

15. Neely C, Weller P, Dittmar R (1997) Is technical analysis in the foreign exchange market profitable? A genetic programming approach. Journal of Financial and Quantitative Analysis 32(4):405–427

16. Palus M, Pecen L, Pivka D (1995) Estimating predictability: redundancy and surrogate data method. Working Paper 95-07-060, Santa Fe Institute. available at http://ideas.repec.org/p/wop/safiwp/95-07-060.html

17. Santini M, Tettamanzi A (2001) Genetic programming for financial time series prediction. In: Miller J, Tomassini M, Lanzi PL, Ryan C, Tettamanzi AGB, Langdon WB

(eds) Proceedings of the fourth European conference on genetic programming. Springer Verlag:361–370

18. Schreiber T, Schmitz A (2000) Surrogate time series. Phys. D 142(3-4):346–382
19. Shalizi CR (2006) Methods and techniques of complex systems science: an overview. In: Deisboeck T, Yasha K (eds) Complex systems science in biomedicine. Springer Verlag, New York:33–114
20. Sullivan R, Timmermann A, White H (1999) Data-snooping, technical trading rule performance, and the bootstrap. Journal of Finance 54:1647–1692
21. Zumbach G, Pictet O, Masutti O (2001) Genetic programming with syntactic restrictions applied to financial volatility forecasting. Technical Report GOZ.2000-07-28, Olsen & Associates.

Nonlinear Goal-Directed CPPI Strategy

Jiah-Shing Chen[1] and Benjamin Penyang Liao[2]

[1] Department of Information Management, National Central University, Chungli 320,
   Taiwan jschen@mgt.ncu.edu.tw
[2] Department of Information Management, Overseas Chinese Institute of Technology,
   Taichung 407, Taiwan lpy@ocit.edu.tw

An investor will in general designate a goal in the investment process. The traditional constant proportion portfolio insurance (CPPI) strategy considers only the floor constraint but not the goal aspect. This paper proposes a goal-directed (GD) strategy to express an investor's goal-directed trading behavior and combines it with the portfolio insurance perspective to form a piecewise linear goal-directed CPPI (GDCPPI) strategy. This piecewise linear GDCPPI strategy shows that there is a wealth position M at the intersection of the linear GD strategy and linear CPPI strategy. This M position guides investors to apply the CPPI strategy or GD strategy depending on whether the current wealth is less or greater than M, respectively. In addition, we extend the piecewise linear GDCPPI strategy to a piecewise nonlinear GDCPPI strategy with a minimum function. These piecewise GDCPPI strategies when applying the minimum function can fully maintain the features of the CPPI strategy and the GD strategy without considering the explicit M. This minimum function in fact can obtain the concept of the explicit M, but it operates the M implicitly. Furthermore, we argue that the piecewise nonlinear GDCPPI strategy owns a larger solution space and it can then outperform the piecewise linear GDCPPI strategy in terms of the return rate performance measure. This paper performs some experiments using the Brownian, GA and forest GP techniques to prove with statistical significance that the piecewise nonlinear GDCPPI strategy can outperform the piecewise linear GDCPPI strategy and that there are some data-driven techniques that can find better piecewise linear GDCPPI strategies than strategies based on the Brownian technique.

Key words: Portfolio Insurance Strategy, Goal-directed Strategy, Piecewise Linear GDCPPI Strategy, Piecewise Nonlinear GDCPPI Strategy

1 Introduction

Avoiding losing large amounts of money in the investment process is important when pursuing high investment returns, and always maintaining current wealth above a certain floor level is a type of portfolio insurance used to achieve this objective. The optimal trading for a constant floor turns out to be the popular constant proportion portfolio insurance (CPPI) strategy ([6, 42]) and can be expressed as $x_t = m_1(W_t - F)$, where x_t is the dollar amount invested in the risky asset at time t, W_t is the wealth at time t, m_1 is a constant risk multiplier, and F is the floor. The CPPI strategy is a special case of the portfolio insurance (PI) strategy. This optimal strategy states that one should invest more in the risky asset when the wealth increases. In practice, a mutual fund manager generally sets up a performance objective in terms of wealth or return at the beginning of an investment period. Then the fund manager has to do his best to achieve this objective or goal. Now if a fund manager follows the CPPI strategy and the current wealth is very close to the goal, he will invest a large portion of the capital in the risky asset and will have a greater chance of failing to achieve his almost reached goal. This possibility is not desirable to mutual fund managers. The major reason for this is that the CPPI strategy only considers the floor but does not take the goal's state into account, while fund managers do have the goal's state in mind during the investment process.

The evidence shows that an investor will change his risk-attitude under different wealth levels. The CPPI strategy demonstrates this phenomenon. In addition, some studies show that fund managers change their risk-attitudes based on their perfor- mance compared to the benchmark. However, there are contradictory observations among these studies. Some studies have observed that fund managers engage in risk- seeking behavior when their performance is worse than the benchmark while some other studies have noted that fund managers engage in risk-averse behavior when their performance is worse than the benchmark.

These contradictions in fact can be explained based on the portfolio insurance perspective and the goal-directed perspective, respectively. The goal-directed per- spective proposes that an investor in financial markets will consider certain invest- ment goals. A goal-directed investor will engage in risk-seeking behavior when the distance from his current wealth to the goal is large and will engage in risk-averse behavior when the distance from his current wealth to the goal is small. Obviously, the changing direction of a CPPI investor's risk-attitude is opposite to that of a goal- directed investor.

We therefore construct a *goal-directed (GD)* strategy $x_t = m_2(G - W_t)$ under the constraint $W_t \leq G$, where G is the goal and m_2 is a constant. The concept of the GD strategy can also be supported by Browne's study ([8]). We further combine the portfolio insurance constraint and goal-directed constraint as $F \leq W_t \leq G$ to construct a *piecewise linear goal-directed CPPI (GDCPPI)* strategy, $x_t = m_1(W_t - F)$, $F \leq W_t < M$ and $x_t = m_2(G - W_t)$, $M \leq W_t \leq G$. The $M = \frac{m_1 F + m_2 G}{m_1 + m_2}$ is a wealth position at the intersection of the GD and CPPI strategies. This M position guides investors to apply the CPPI strategy or GD strategy depending on whether the current wealth is less or greater than M, respectively. In addition, if $m_1 \to \infty$, the piecewise linear GDCPPI strategy reduces to the GD strategy, and if $m_2 \to \infty$, the piecewise linear GDCPPI strategy becomes the CPPI strategy. That is, the piecewise linear GDCPPI strategy is a generalization of both the CPPI and GD strategies.

The piecewise linear GDCPPI strategy is based on a linear situation that we can see from the generated piecewise GD strategy and CPPI strategy under the Brownian motion assumption. It naturally can be inferred that some nonlinear strategies might be found in the solution space when the Brownian motion assumption no longer holds. Therefore, we extend the piecewise linear GDCPPI strategy to be the *piecewise nonlinear GDCPPI* strategy with the minimum function: $x_t = min[m_1(W_t - F), m_2(G - W_t)], F \leq W_t \leq G$. Applying the minimum function can solve the difficulties of preassigning an explicit M value from the intersection of the nonlinear CPPI-oriented strategy and nonlinear GD strategy. The minimum function can also hold the features of the CPPI and GD strategies. This minimum function in fact can obtain the concept of an explicit M, but it operates the M implicitly. We then apply the genetic programming technique to generate the piecewise nonlinear GDCPPI strategy.

The optimal m_1 and m_2 strategy parameter values can be theoretically derived based on the Brownian motion assumption for stock prices as in the traditional CPPI strategy ([6, 42]) and Browne's study ([8]). There are some parameters in the optimal formulas of m_1 and m_2 that need to be estimated using historical data. However, the stock prices in the real financial markets might not follow the Brownian motion assumption, especially in short-term periods. We therefore apply genetic algorithms (GAs) to find a set of good parameter values in a piecewise linear GDCPPI strategy based on historical data in order to improve its performance. The statistical test shows that the parameters found by the GA are better than those calculated based on the Brownian motion assumption for the ROI performance measure. In addition, statistical tests show that the strategies found using the forest GP outperform the strategies found by GA which in turn outperform the strategies found by the Brownian technique for the ROI performance measure.

The remainder of this paper is organized as follows. Section 2 reviews the technique of evolutionary algorithms applied in this study, which include genetic algorithms and forest genetic programming adapted from traditional genetic programming. Section 3 formulates the models of our series of goal-directed strategies. Section 4 describes our experiments to show the learning effects of genetic algorithms for the piecewise linear GDCPPI strategy and forest genetic programming for the piecewise nonlinear GDCPPI strategy. Section 5 presents our conclusions and directions for future research.

2 Evolutionary Algorithms

Evolutionary algorithms (EAs) are based on Darwin's theory of evolution: *survival of the fittest*. Genetic algorithms (GAs) and genetic programming (GP) are two typical EAs. Genetic algorithms and genetic programming are frequently used to solve various problems in trading ([22, 29, 32, 34, 48]). Evolutionary algorithms use an evolutionary process resulting in a fittest solution to solve a problem. The evolutionary process consists of several genetic operators: selection, crossover and mutation ([2, 3, 25, 39, 47]). Genetic programming (GP) basically is an extension and generalization of genetic algorithms. Originally GP tried to automatically build computer programs to solve problems, i.e., the solution generated by GP can be directly executed by computers.

Evolutionary algorithms are computationally simple and powerful. Evolutionary algorithms are very good and flexible tools for optimization problems since they make no restrictive assumptions regarding the solution space. Evolutionary algorithms have been applied to effectively search complex, highly nonlinear, and multi-dimensional solution spaces ([36]).

2.1 The Basic Evolutionary Algorithm

To solve a problem using an evolutionary algorithm, an encoding mechanism must first be designed to represent each solution as a chromosome, where a binary string serves as the default for a GA and a tree encoding mechanism is generally applied using GP. In GP, trees generally represent expressions, i.e., expressions are directly executable. An expression consists of functions (or internal nodes) and arguments (or terminal nodes). In the encoding stage for GP, users have to pre-designate the function set and terminal set. Functions in genetic programming can be arithmetical operators, logical operators, and comparative operators, etc. The functional parameters can generally be constants and the decision variables of the problem. After operating the tree structure, new tree offspring generally are of dynamic or variable length, which is quite different from Holland's simple GA with fixed length chromosomes. A fitness function is also required to measure the goodness of a chromosome. Evolutionary algorithms search the solution space using a population which is simply a set of chromosomes. When initializing the population, Koza initially suggested three techniques for GP: grow, full and ramped-half-and-half initialization ([35]). During each generation, the three genetic operators: selection, crossover and mutation, are applied to the population several times to form a new population. Selection picks two chromosomes according to their fitness: a fitter chromosome has a higher probability of being selected. Crossover recombines the two selected chromosomes to form new offspring with a crossover rate. Mutation randomly alters each position in each offspring with a small mutation rate. New population is then generated by replacing some chromosomes of the population with new offspring. This process is repeated until some termination condition, e.g., the given number of generations, is reached. Figure 1 shows the pseudo code of the basic evolutionary algorithm.

When the entire population is replaced by offspring, it is referred to as a generational (or nonoverlapping) evolutionary algorithm. When only some individuals are replaced by offspring, it is called a steady-state (or overlapping) evolutionary algorithm ([44]).

The advantage of evolutionary algorithms lies in their parallelism. Evolutionary algorithms search for a solution space using a population of individuals so that they are less likely to get stuck in local optimums. However, this is achieved at a cost, i.e., the computational time. Evolutionary algorithms can be slower than other methods. Nevertheless, the longer run time of evolutionary algorithms can be shortened by terminating the evolution earlier to obtain a satisfactory solution.

procedure BasicEA
   Initialization: Generate a random population of n chromosomes
   while (termination condition is not satisfied)
      Evaluation: Evaluate the fitness of each chromosome in the population
      loop (do genetic applications k times for each generation)
         Selection: Select two chromosomes according to their fitness
         Crossover: Cross over selected chromosomes to form new offspring
            with a crossover rate
         Mutation: Mutate each position in each new offspring with a mutation rate
      endloop
      Replacement: Replace chromosomes in parent population with new offspring
   endwhile
   Report the best solution (chromosome) found
endprocedure

Fig. 1. The basic evolutionary algorithm

2.2 Forest Genetic Programming

In this study we will develop a framework of piecewise strategies in Sect. 3. A piecewise strategy consists of multiple sub-strategies. Each sub-strategy can have its own objective and application condition. When applying GP to generate a piecewise strategy, each sub-strategy can be encoded as a tree and the whole piecewise strategy is represented as a forest. Adapting a single forest chromosome implies the evolution of multiple trees concurrently. We then generalize the traditional GP into a *forest* GP for dealing with the piecewise characteristics. In what follows, we will describe the contents of the forest GP and show its main differences compared to traditional GP in certain respects, which include encoding and fitness evaluation.

A Forest Genetic Programming

In this study, we accommodate the GPQuick, a GP algorithm developed by Andy Singleton, to process the forest chromosomes. The forest GP algorithm is shown in Fig. 2, which is a specialized evolutionary algorithm as shown in Fig. 1. In forest GP, each chromosome is a forest which consists of multiple trees.

There are five genetic operations in this forest GP: crossover, mutation, anneal crossover, anneal mutation, and copy.

For each generation, one of five genetic operations will be selected using the roulette wheel method. Before executing these genetic operations, a possibly replaced target chromosome is selected using the tournament method or anti-tournament method. The tournament method selects the best chromosome as the target chromosome from a subset of the population and in turn generates the new non-anneal offspring candidates. The anti-tournament method selects the worst chromosome as the target chromosome from a subset of the population and in turn generates the new

procedure ForestGP
   Initialization: Generate a random population of n forest chromosomes
   Evaluation: Evaluate the fitness of each forest chromosome in the population
   while (termination condition is not satisfied)
     do (genetic applications k times for each generation)
       SelectOperation: Select one genetic operation by the roulette wheel method
       Selection: Select a necessary number of chromosomes by the tournament
         or anti-tournament method
       cases (do one of the following genetic operations)
         Crossover: Cross over selected non-anneal chromosomes to form
           a new offspring
         Mutation: Mutate each position in selected non-anneal new offspring
           with a mutation rate
         AnnealCrossover: Cross over selected anneal chromosomes to form
           a new offspring
         AnnealMutation: Mutate each position in selected anneal chromosome
           with a mutation rate
         Copy: Copy the selected non-anneal chromosome directly as the
           new offspring
     endcases
     enddo
     Replacement: Replace chromosomes in parent population with
       new offspring
   endwhile
   Report the best solution (chromosome) found
endprocedure

Fig. 2. A forest GP algorithm

anneal offspring candidates. A necessary number of offspring candidates will be selected starting from the selected target chromosome using the tournament method except the anneal mutation. Therefore, for non-anneal genetic operations, the selected target chromosome will always be replaced by the selected offspring candidates. For anneal genetic operations, the final offspring is the best one among the selected target chromosome and the offspring candidates.

For non-anneal crossover operations, the new offspring is the best non-anneal offspring candidate and will replace the target chromosome. For anneal crossover operations, the new offspring is selected among the target chromosome and the anneal offspring candidates. For non-anneal and anneal mutation operations, each tree node of the new offspring will be mutated with a mutation rate. The constant terminal node will also be possibly mutated. In addition, a subtree might be shrunk (eliminated) or mutated in the mutation operation. The copy operation directly duplicates the selected target chromosome as the new offspring.

Some forest GP parameters have to be preassigned and are described as follows. The population size assigns the number of forest chromosomes being evolved. The termination approach is applied to the generations. The depth assigns the tree levels, where the depth of the root node is 1. The five genetic operations will be selected using the roulette wheel method under their own selected rate: the crossover rate with a default of 0.71, the crossover annealing rate with a default of 0.0, the overall mutation rate with a default of 0.21, the overall mutation annealing rate with a default of 0.0, and the copy rate with a default of 0.08. When the mutation operation is selected, some further parameter values of the sub-mutation operations have to be assigned: mutate the un-constant node rate with a default of 0.45, mutate a constant node rate with a default of 0.45, mutate the shrink rate with a default of 0.05, mutate the subtree rate with a default of 0.05, and for each selected node mutation rate with a default of 0.1.

Features of Forest Genetic Programming

Basically, forest GP is different from traditional GP in some respects, which include encoding and fitness evaluation.

For encoding, each chromosome in forest GP consists of multiple trees. However, each chromosome in traditional GP consists of a single tree.

For fitness evaluation, forest GP has to evaluate each tree's fitness, which introduces the multi-objective fitness evaluation. The framework of forest GP has a similar concept but also different features from the traditional multi-objective GP. The forest GP constitutes multiple objectives, which is the same as the traditional multi-objective GP. However, a chromosome in traditional multi-objective GP only represents a single tree which tries to achieve multiple objectives. On the other hand, a chromosome in forest GP consists of several trees and each tree is allowed to have its own structure and evolving objective.

In this study, each tree will be evaluated by designating a single objective to simply prove the features of our piecewise trading strategies, although there can also be multiple objectives under this framework. Therefore, the framework of forest GP is the extension and generalization of traditional multi-objective GP. The forest GP can also have the capability of presenting the structure of hierarchical objectives.

In sum, in forest GP, each chromosome represents a forest. A forest contains multiple trees. Each tree has its own objective, function set and terminal set, which can be totally independent of the other trees. The framework of forest GP can be designed to solve multi-objective problems. However, in order to show the basic features of a piecewise strategy, we reduce the multiple objectives into the single objective framework by assigning the same objective to each sub-strategy.

2.3 Evolutionary Algorithms in Financial Investment

Financial investment is an important means of capital management both for individuals and organizations. Investment procedures can involve the following steps: policy development, investment analysis, strategy design, strategy execution, performance evaluation, and feedback ([46]). Policy development sets up the investment objectives and constraints. Investment analysis tries to understand the features of investment targets and the investment environment in order to make good investment decisions and control the investment. Generally, the investment analysis includes value evaluation, price (or series) prediction, pattern discovering, trend prediction, etc.

There are many tools that can be applied to execute the investment analysis, which may be classified as *mechanical* tools ([51]) and *intelligent* tools. The mechanical tools include traditional tools such as technical analysis, fundamental analysis, and other expanded tools from these two types of analysis. The intelligent tools are the mechanisms which apply intelligent techniques to solve problems, with soft computing being the major representative. The soft computing includes neural networks, fuzzy logic, fuzzy sets, and evolutionary computation. The evolutionary computation applies the evolutionary algorithms to solve problems, which includes genetic algorithms, learning classifier systems, genetic programming, evolutionary programming, evolutionary strategies, ant algorithms, artificial life, etc.

The strategy design generates investment ways or rules in order to achieve the policy objectives under given constraints. Investment strategies can be divided into three sub-strategies: selection, timing and allocation. Selection strategies select the security to be invested. Timing strategies decide the timing for entering and exiting the market. Allocation strategies decide the proportion of investment capital for each selected security. In general, the mechanical tools applied in the investment analysis accompany their own trading strategy. For example, if the spot price is under the intrinsic value, it implies the market price will be going up and investors should buy the asset to enter the market, which is the timing strategy.

Performance evaluation tries to evaluate the investment results using many measures in order to provide information for further investment control and to show the effectiveness of applied investment strategies. These performance measures can be the rate of return, risk, the Sharpe index ([45]), etc.

Feedback adjusts the investment activities when the goal is deviated from.

The applications of evolutionary algorithms in financial investment should generally consider the whole investment procedure. However, some steps are mechanism-driven and other steps are evolution-driven. The mechanism-driven steps refer to the accompanying activities being predefined and not developed by evolutionary algorithms. The evolution-driven steps refer to the accompanying activities that are developed by evolutionary algorithms. Most applications in the literature only apply the evolutionary algorithms to execute part of the activities in the investment procedures. The application of evolutionary algorithms mainly involves the steps of investment analysis and strategy design.

The investment analysis includes value evaluation, time series forecasting, indicator forecasting, and pattern discovering. Value evaluation tries to find out the true value of securities. Reference [11] first applied genetic programming to develop a valuing strategy. Then they applied the fuzzy technique to determine multiple stock values generated by the developed valuing strategy. For time series forecasting, the security price and market index were two major targets to be forecasted. For indicator forecasting, indicators can be financial (or fundamental) indicators and technical indicators. Such studies can be found in [12]. For pattern or trend discovering, the chart patterns such as head and shoulders, inverse head and shoulders, complex head and shoulders, and so on ([40]) will be discovered. These patterns can facilitate investors engaging in investment activities, such as in the timing of decisions. Such studies can be found in [43].

In the strategy design, selection, timing and allocation strategies should be developed. In addition, there are two types of applications of evolutionary algorithms in the strategy design: parameter optimization and strategy rule generation.

The parameter optimization only tries to optimize the parameter values of the predefined strategy structure. Genetic algorithms are the major evolutionary technique used to optimize the strategy parameters. For example, [10] applied genetic algorithms to optimize four technical indicators using historical data. Reference [37] applied learning classifier systems to optimize a set of strategy parameters in daytrading with instant learning. Financial applications of genetic algorithms are starting to show promising results. Bauer used genetic algorithms to generate trading rules which are Boolean expressions with three of the ten allowed time series ([4]). Reference [21] applied genetic algorithms to find the lengths in the moving average crossover strategy. Reference [23] studied methods of using genetic algorithms to train a neural network trading system. Reference [27] applied genetic algorithms to develop a selection strategy.

For strategy generation, genetic programming is one major applied evolutionary technique. Financial investment applications of GP have been applied and show promising results. Reference [31] applied GP to forecast the daily high and low stock prices to execute a single-day-trading-strategy (SDTS). Reference [20] approximated the relationships between the option prices, its contract terms and underlying stock prices using GP and shows that GP outperforms other methods in the option pricing models. Reference [33] tried to build analytical approximations for implied volatility of option prices by genetic programming and the results show that the formulas are very close to the numerically calculated ones. The other financial applications of GP can be found in [1, 5, 13, 14, 15, 17, 16, 18, 24, 30, 41, 50].

In this paper, strategy design is our study problem. However, our piecewise strategy design is different from traditional strategy designs. We will apply genetic algorithms to optimize the strategy parameter values for m_1 and m_2 in piecewise linear GDCPPI strategies. In addition, we will apply forest genetic programming to generate piecewise nonlinear GDCPPI strategies. Then we will compare the strategy performance between the piecewise linear GDCPPI strategies and the piecewise nonlinear GDCPPI strategies to justify our piecewise strategy propositions.

3 Trading Strategies

3.1 Constant Proportion Portfolio Insurance Strategy

The formulation and solution of the optimal portfolio insurance problem will be described following the work of [26]. Assume there are two assets: a risk-free asset such as a T-bill and a risky asset such as a stock. Let the stock price dynamic be

$\frac{dP_t}{P_t} = \mu dt + \sigma dz_t$, where μ is the mean of the return rates, σ is the standard deviation of the return rates, and z_t is a Brownian motion at time t. The portfolio wealth dynamic is then $dW_t = rW_t dt + x_t(\mu dt + \sigma dz_t)$, where r is the risk-free rate of return and x_t is the dollar amount invested in the risky asset. Suppose an investor tries to maximize the growth rate of expected utility of the final wealth under the portfolio insurance constraint. The problem becomes:

$$\sup_{X} \lim_{T \to \infty} \frac{1}{\gamma T} \ln E[\gamma U(W_T)]$$
$$\text{subject to } W_t \geq F, \, \forall t \leq T, \tag{1}$$

where X denotes the set of admissible trading strategies, $0 \neq \gamma \leq 1$, and $F > 0$ is the floor. If F is fixed, the optimal strategy for the above optimization problem is:

$$x_t = \frac{\mu}{\sigma^2(1 - \gamma)}(W_t - F). \tag{2}$$

Equation (2) can be simplified as:

$$\zeta_t \equiv x_t = m_1(W_t - F), \, W_t \geq F, \tag{3}$$

where $m_1 = \frac{\mu}{\sigma^2(1-\gamma)}$ can be regarded as the investor's risk multiplier, and F is the protecting floor. This ζ_t is the popular constant proportion portfolio insurance (CPPI) strategy, which is a special case of the portfolio insurance (PI) strategy.

3.2 Risk Attitudes

Studies have shown that there are two different types of risk attitudes. Tournament theory studies the behavior of fund managers with respect to the benchmark. Some studies have observed that under-performers become risk-averse and out-performers become risk-seeking ([49, 19, 9]). Reference [49] showed that when both managers are active, the winning manager is more likely to gamble, especially when the midyear performance gap is high. Reference [19] found a positive correlation between past performance in excess of a benchmark during the first three quarters of the year and increases in tracking error volatility in the subsequent quarter. Reference [9] found that funds that are ranked above the median fund in their category increase total risk more than below-median funds.

On the other hand, other studies observed that the under-performers will become more risky than the better-performers in mutual fund markets ([7, 28]). Reference [28] found that an investor's risk behavior changed around the 1987 market crash. Before the crash, the value of the risk-averse function was positive. On the other hand, after the crash, there was evidence of investors' risk-seeking behavior. After the crash, the risk-averse function was partially negative, i.e., implying risk-seeking. This means that, when investors lose a large amount of wealth, they will engage in a riskier behavior.

Therefore, we name these two types of risk attitude changes as low wealth risk aversion and high wealth risk aversion, respectively, and summarize them as follows:

Low wealth risk aversion: An investor will become risk-averse when his current
wealth is low and will become risk-seeking when his current wealth is high.
High wealth risk aversion: An investor will become risk-averse when his current
wealth is high and will become risk-seeking when his current wealth is low.

Although low wealth risk aversion can be explained by the CPPI strategy, high
wealth risk aversion can not. We argue that these contradictions can be explained
from two perspectives: the portfolio insurance perspective and the goal-directed (or
goal-seeking) perspective. That is, low wealth risk aversion can be explained by the
portfolio insurance perspective. High wealth risk aversion can be explained by the
goal-directed perspective which will be examined in the next subsection.

3.3 Goal-directed Strategy

In the study by [8], one of the investment problems is to maximize the survival probability in the danger zone or to maximize the probability of reaching the goal before
reaching the bankruptcy point. The model can be described as follows:

$$\max_{X} P(\tau_a > \tau_b), \text{ s.t. } a < W_t < b < S, \tag{4}$$

where X is the set of admissible strategies, $P(\cdot)$ is the probability function, a is the
bankruptcy point, τ_a is the escape time when $W_t = a$, τ_b is the escape time when
$W_t = b$, and S is the safe point which is generally set up to be c/r, with c being
the minimal consumption, and r being the risk-free rate of return. This model tries
to find an optimal trading strategy which minimizes the probability of reaching the
bankruptcy point a before reaching the goal b. The optimal strategy turns out to be:

$$x_t = \frac{2r}{\mu - r}(S - W_t), \tag{5}$$

where μ is the mean of the return rates for the risky asset. If $b \to S$, S in fact can
be regarded as the goal G that an investor wants to achieve. Then we define a *linear
goal-directed (GD)* strategy as

$$\eta_t \equiv x_t = m_2(G - W_t), \ W_t \le G, \tag{6}$$

where $m_2 = \frac{2r}{\mu - r}$ is a constant.

The GD strategy shows that an investor should engage in a riskier action when
the goal distance (i.e., the distance from current wealth to the goal) is large and
should engage in a less risky activity when the goal distance is small. This behavior
is consistent with the high wealth risk aversion. In other words, the high wealth risk
aversion can be explained by this GD strategy.

3.4 Piecewise Linear Goal-directed CPPI Strategy

As we have noted, investors seem to have two different types of wealth risk aversion:
the low wealth risk aversion and the high wealth risk aversion. Intuitively, investors

will adopt a different strategy when they posit a different risk attitude. That is, if their risk attitude is low wealth risk aversion, they will adopt the CPPI strategy. If their risk attitude is high wealth risk aversion, they will adopt the GD strategy.

Recall that the constraint of the CPPI strategy, $W_t \geq F$, is different from the constraint of the GD strategy, $W_t \leq G$. In addition, the objective of the CPPI strategy, i.e., maximizing the growth rate of certain utility, is different from the objective of the GD strategy, i.e., maximizing the possibility of reaching the goal first. By combining the two constraints $F \leq W_t$ and $W_t \leq G$, a new problem with constraint $F \leq W_t \leq G$ is derived. This new problem can be regarded as containing two objectives which are composed of the objectives of the CPPI and GD strategies. The CPPI and GD strategies are depicted in Fig. 3.

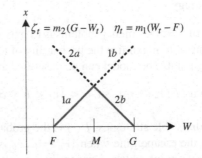

Fig. 3. The piecewise linear GDCPPI strategy.

We can see that the CPPI strategy only considers the floor and the GD strategy only considers the goal. In addition, there is a wealth position M projected from the intersection of these two strategies and the value of M can be calculated by

$$M = \frac{m_1 F + m_2 G}{m_1 + m_2}. \tag{7}$$

M seems to be a natural dividing point for changing strategies. Since the CPPI strategy only considers the floor F but not the goal G, an investor can apply the CPPI strategy when $W_t < M$. On the other hand, since the GD strategy only considers the goal G but not the floor F, an investor can apply the GD strategy when $W_t \geq M$. We therefore build a *piecewise linear goal-directed CPPI (GDCPPI)* strategy as:

$$\theta_t \equiv x_t = \begin{cases} 0, & W_t < F \\ \zeta_t, & F \leq W_t < M \\ \eta_t, & M \leq W_t \leq G \end{cases} \tag{8}$$

It can be seen that the piecewise linear GDCPPI strategy θ_t combines the portfolio insurance perspective and the goal-directed perspective, as the segments $1a$ and $2b$ in Fig. 3. Note that θ_t is a generalization of both the CPPI and GD strategies. In particular, if $m_1 \to \infty$, $M = \frac{m_1 F + m_2 G}{m_1 + m_2} = F$ and the constraint $M \leq W_t \leq G$

for the GD segment will be $F \leq W_t \leq G$. Therefore, the piecewise linear GDCPPI strategy reduces to the GD strategy. If $m_2 \to \infty$, $M = \frac{m_1 F + m_2 G}{m_1 + m_2} = G$ and the constraint $F \leq W_t < M$ for the PI segment will be $F \leq W_t < G$. Therefore, the piecewise linear GDCPPI strategy reduces to the CPPI strategy.

Moreover, when the current wealth is above the goal G, the investor can set a new goal G' and the original goal becomes the new floor. Therefore, (8) can be regarded as the strategy unit block under the $F \leq W_t \leq G$ constraint form, which can generate new piecewise linear GDCPPI strategies consecutively.

The traditional CPPI strategy is based on the assumption of a Brownian motion for stock prices. Browne's study ([8]) on goal seeking objectives also made this assumption. When investors try to apply these above strategies, the parameter values are generally obtained by the long-term expectation method. That is, the mean and variance of the return rates are the long-term expectations from historical data.

However, the historical data might not follow the Brownian motion ([38]). Better parameter values for m_1 and m_2 in the piecewise linear GDCPPI strategy might be directly obtained using other data-driven optimization methods with historical data. The genetic algorithm is the method chosen to search for better parameters values for m_1 and m_2 in this study due to its success in many applications.

3.5 Piecewise Nonlinear Goal-directed CPPI Strategy

The piecewise linear GDCPPI strategy consists of two major piecewise sub-strategies, which are the CPPI sub-strategy for constraint $F < W_t < M$ and the GD sub-strategy for constraint $M \leq W_t \leq G$. The piecewise linear GDCPPI strategy is based on the assumption of linearity. However, the sub-strategies within the framework of the piecewise strategy need not be linear when the Brownian motion assumption does not hold anymore. Therefore, the CPPI strategy can relax its linear feature to form a *nonlinear CPPI-oriented (CPPIO)* strategy, and (3) can be rewritten as:

$$\zeta'_t \equiv x_t = \aleph(W_t, F), \ W_t \geq F, \tag{9}$$

where $\aleph(\cdot)$ is a nonlinear function.

The GD strategy also can relax its linear feature to form a *nonlinear GD* strategy, and (6) can be rewritten as:

$$\eta'_t \equiv x_t = \aleph(W_t, G), \ W_t \leq G, \tag{10}$$

where $\aleph(\cdot)$ is a nonlinear function.

The piecewise linear GDCPPI strategy can then first be extended to a piecewise nonlinear GDCPPI strategy with an explicit M and is defined as:

$$\xi'_t \equiv x_t = \begin{cases} 0, \ W_t \leq F \\ \zeta'_t, \ F < W_t < M \\ \eta'_t, \ M \leq W_t \leq G, \end{cases} \tag{11}$$

where $M = \frac{m_1 F + m_2 G}{m_1 + m_2}$. However, this explicit piecewise nonlinear GDCPPI strategy will face the difficulty of preassigning the explicit M value. That is, we cannot easily preassign the explicit M value when we do not know the real structure of the nonlinear CPPIO strategy and the nonlinear GD strategy.

To solve this problem, we can review the features of the CPPI strategy and the GD strategy. The CPPI strategy generally shows the risk-averse behavior when the current wealth is close to the floor and shows the risk-seeking behavior when the current wealth is far above the floor. Therefore, the CPPI strategy exhibits a monotonic increasing feature with a positive slope. On the other hand, the GD strategy generally shows the risk-averse behavior when the current wealth is close to the goal and shows the risk-seeking behavior when the current wealth is far below the goal. Therefore, the GD strategy exhibits a monotonic decreasing feature with a negative slope.

Now in rechecking the curve of the piecewise linear GDCPPI strategy, we find that this strategy can achieve the same effect by applying the minimum function. Therefore, the piecewise linear GDCPPI strategy can be redefined as an *implicit piecewise linear GDCPPI* strategy:

$$\delta_t \equiv x_t = min(\zeta_t, \eta_t), \tag{12}$$

That is, θ_t is totally equal to δ_t. The obvious advantage of applying the minimum function is of eliminating the assigning of an explicit M value but of maintaining the M concept in an implicit way. We can apply the minimum function to form a *piecewise nonlinear GDCPPI* strategy which is defined as:

$$\xi_t \equiv x_t = min(\zeta_t', \eta_t'), \tag{13}$$

where ζ_t' is the nonlinear CPPIO strategy and η_t' is the nonlinear GD strategy. The features of the piecewise nonlinear GDCPPI strategy when applying the minimum function for some cases can be discussed below and are shown in Fig. 4.

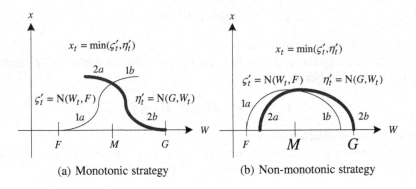

(a) Monotonic strategy   (b) Non-monotonic strategy

Fig. 4. The piecewise nonlinear GDCPPI strategy.

The first case depicts the monotonic piecewise nonlinear GDCPPI strategy, as shown in Fig. 4(a). That is, the nonlinear CIPPO strategy is monotonic increasing and the nonlinear GD strategy is monotonic decreasing. This case shows the full feature of portfolio insurance and goal-seeking. The piecewise nonlinear GDCPPI strategy comprises the connected segments of $1b$ and $2a$.

The second case shows the non-monotonic nonlinear GDCPPI strategy, as shown in Fig. 4(b). After applying the minimum function, the piecewise nonlinear GDCPPI strategy consists of the connected segments of $1b$ and $2a$. When $W_t \leq M$, segment $2a$ will be applied and exhibits a positive slope which matches the behavior of portfolio insurance. When $W_t > M$, segment $1b$ will be applied and exhibits a negative slope which matches the goal-directed behavior. However, this is a special case which can match the requirements of portfolio insurance and goal-seeking. In addition, it seems to provide some interesting research topics on M values, e.g., multiple implicit M values and so on.

In sum, after applying the minimum function, we can extend the piecewise linear GDCPPI strategy to a piecewise nonlinear GDCPPI strategy. Furthermore, these two piecewise strategies can exhibit the features of portfolio insurance and goal-seeking. Since there are drawbacks of a piecewise nonlinear GDCPPI strategy with an explicit M, we will not apply this strategy anymore in this study. In addition, the piecewise linear GDCPPI strategy and piecewise nonlinear GDCPPI strategy are then two special cases of *piecewise GDCPPI* strategies.

3.6 Proposition

In this study, we consider the goal perspective and portfolio insurance perspective to form piecewise goal-directed CPPI strategies. By analyzing these GDCPPI strategies, we make the following propositions:

Proposition 1: The piecewise nonlinear GDCPPI strategies can outperform the piecewise linear GDCPPI strategies.

  Since piecewise nonlinear GDCPPI strategies obtain a larger solution space than piecewise linear GDCPPI strategies, we then infer that we can find better solutions in the nonlinear solution space than in the linear one.

Proposition 2: There are some data-driven techniques that can find better piecewise linear GDCPPI strategies than the solutions found by the Brownian technique.

  Since there are some who assert that the financial markets are not following a random walk, especially in short-term periods, it is reasonable and possible to adopt other data-driven techniques to find better solutions than found by the Brownian technique. The GA and GP techniques are two data-driven techniques applied in this study.

4 Experiments and Analyses

In this study we apply the Brownian (B), genetic algorithm (GA), and forest genetic programming (GP) techniques to generate piecewise GDCPPI strategies. Technique B produces a piecewise linear GDCPPI strategy according to (3) and (6) under the

Brownian motion assumption and does not require a learning process as opposed to the GA and GP methods. Technique GA finds the fittest m_1 and m_2 constants to form a piecewise linear GDCPPI strategy. Technique GP is applied to generate a piecewise nonlinear GDCPPI strategy. The strategies generated by these three techniques are referred to as the B strategy, GA strategy, and GP strategy in this study for simplicity.

4.1 Experimental Purposes

The main experimental purpose of this study is to try to justify our proposition for piecewise GDCPPI strategies: a piecewise nonlinear GDCPPI strategy can outperform a piecewise linear GDCPPI strategy. This purpose can be justified if the GP strategy outperforms both the B and GA strategies. The other experimental purpose tries to show that the GA strategy can outperform the B strategy to provide investors with another feasible piecewise linear GDCPPI strategy rather than the B strategy. These experimental purposes then introduce three basic experiments: the B-GP, GA-GP, and B-GA experiments, respectively. The ROI (rate of return) will be applied as the performance measure in these experiments.

When applying these three techniques to generate piecewise GDCPPI strategies, some parameter values have to be designated before learning. These parameter values are derived by three pretests. The first pretest tries to decide a suitable pair of *year length* and γ for the B technique, where γ is defined in (1). The *year length* is applied to calculate the expected return rate μ and variance σ^2. In turn, the μ, σ^2 and γ will be used to calculate the parameters m_1 and m_2 in the B strategy, where m_1 is defined in (3) and m_2 is defined in (6). The second pretest tries to decide the GA learning length. The third pretest tries to decide the GP learning length.

4.2 Experimental Data Description

We randomly select 5 stocks as the experimental targets from the 30 components of the Dow Jones Industrial Average (DJIA), namely, American International Group (AIG), IBM, Merck (MRK), HP (HPQ), and Exxon Mobil (XOM). We also randomly select 5 starting learning dates, which are 1999/12/13, 2001/6/6, 2002/2/27, 2003/4/28 and 2004/12/03. Three different floors in the experiments for the piecewise linear and nonlinear GDCPPI strategies are pre-assigned and calculated by the ratios of the floors to initial wealth, which are 0.7, 0.8, and 0.9. In addition, 3 different goals in the experiments for piecewise linear and nonlinear GDCPPI strategies are pre-assigned and calculated by the ratios of the goals to initial wealth, which are 1.1, 1.2, and 1.3. The risk-free rate of return is 0.0001 per day. For each sub-experiment, there are ($5 * 5 * 3 * 3=$) 225 cases that then generate 225 samples for the statistical tests. In addition, transaction costs are not considered in this study.

4.3 Pretest for Brownian Strategy Parameters

The first pretest tries to decide a suitable pair of *year length* and γ values for the B technique, where γ is defined in (1). The *year length* is decided in order to calculate the expected return rate μ and variation σ^2. In turn, the μ, σ^2 and γ will be used to calculate the parameters m_1 and m_2 in the B strategy, where m_1 is defined in (3) and m_2 is defined in (6).

The suitable pair of *year length* and γ values implies that the accompanying B strategy performance is better than the other pairs'. We search for a suitable γ value from the set $\{0.1, 0.3, 0.5, 0.7, 0.9\}$. Considering the available data in this study, the *year length* will be decided in the range of 5 years to 16 years. Then, 60 (*year length*, γ) pairs are pretested.

The pretest target is the GM stock randomly selected from the 30 components of DJIA. The pretesting strategy performance for each (*year length*, γ) pair is the average return rates of 45 samples. These 45 samples are produced by 3 floors, 3 goals, and 5 starting learning dates as defined above.

This pretest shows that the better *year length* for calculating the expected values of μ and σ^2 is 8 years. In addition, the better γ value is 0.1.

4.4 Pretest for GA Learning Length

The second pretest tries to find a good learning length for GA learning. A good learning length implies that the GA strategy under this found learning length outperforms other GA strategies under different learning lengths.

The pretest target is the GM stock, the same as in the first pretest. Five training lengths are pretested, which are 20, 40, 60, 80, and 100 days. For each training length, the GA strategy performance comprises the average return rates for 45 samples. These 45 samples are produced by 3 floors, 3 goals, and 5 starting learning dates as defined above.

Finally, the GA pretest shows that the better learning length is 100 days for GA learning.

4.5 Pretest for Forest GP Learning Length

The third pretest tries to find a good learning length for GP learning. A good learning length implies that the GP strategy under this found learning length outperforms other GP strategies under different learning lengths. The pretest settings are the same as in the GA pretest, which will generate 45 samples.

Finally, the GP pretest shows that the better learning length is 100 days for GP learning.

4.6 GA Learning Design

When the Brownian motion assumption does not hold, it is possible that better piecewise linear GDCPPI strategy parameter values m_1 and m_2 can be found by other methods. The purpose of applying the GA technique in this optimization process is to search for satisfactory strategy parameter values m_1 and m_2 to achieve better investment performance. We generate 225 samples produced by 5 stocks, 5 starting learning dates, 3 floors, and 3 goals, as defined in Sect. 4.2 on page 198. The training length is 100 days as derived from the GA pretest.

In addition, each m_1 and m_2 strategy parameter will be encoded as a 7-bit long gene in a GA chromosome. Therefore, the length of each chromosome is 14 bits. If the decimal value of each gene m_1 and m_2 is D, each gene will be decoded as values within $[1.0, 13.7]$ by $(10 + D)/10$. Moreover, better m_1 and m_2 values imply better investment performance in the case of the piecewise linear GDCPPI strategy. The ROI is applied as the fitness function for each experiment.

The other main GA system parameters are set up as follows: the population size is 40; each run executes 20 generations and then there are 800 fitness evaluations in each run; the crossover is two-point; the mutation rate is 0.001 per bit; and the selection method is the integral roulette wheel selection. The searching space will then be $2^{14} = 4096$ points and we in fact search for 800 points which is about 25% of the searching space.

4.7 Forest GP Learning Design

In this study, each forest consists of two trees which represent the CPPI strategy and GD strategy, respectively. In this forest GP learning, better piecewise nonlinear GD-CPPI strategies will be generated. We generate 225 samples produced by 5 stocks, 5 starting learning dates, 3 floors, and 3 goals, as defined in Sect. 4.2 on page 198. The learning length is 100 days as derived from the forest GP pretest. In the forest GP, the terminal set, function set and other system parameters are pre-assigned as follows:

For the PI strategy, the terminal set includes the floor, current wealth, and constant within $[-127, 127]$. The function set includes operators $+, -, *, /$.

For the GD strategy, the terminal set includes the goal, current wealth, and constant within $[-127, 127]$. The function set includes operators $+, -, *, /$.

The ROI is set up as the fitness function for each experiment. The population size is 40. The generation size is 200. The tree depth is limited to 4, for which the depth of the root node is 1.

Note that the feature of the CPPI strategy shows that investors should engage in risk-averse behavior when the current wealth is close to the floor. Furthermore, the feature of the GD strategy is that it also shows that investors should engage in risk-averse behavior when the current wealth is close to the goal. Therefore, our forest GP maintains these features by verifying the curve slope of the generated strategies for sampling some curve points. That is, the slope of the sampling curve points of the CPPI strategy should be positive and the slope of the sampling curve points of the GD strategy should be negative.

Therefore, for each tree, there are 8 terminal nodes possible. Each node can have 3 possible values and then have 3^8 possibilities. For each tree, there are 7 internal nodes, and each can have 4 possible operators and then have 4^7 possibilities. For a complete tree, there are $3^8 * 4^7 = 3^8 * 2^{14}$ searching points. In addition, if we consider the possibilities of possible incomplete trees, the searching space will be larger than the searching space using GA in this study. Therefore, the 8000 evaluations are a very small portion of the searching space compared to the GA's learning design. The other parameter values are assigned default values as defined in Sect. 2.2.

4.8 Statistical Testing Design

Three types of paired-sample t tests are applied to check the advantages among the B, GA, and GP strategies for different piecewise GDCPPI strategies under the ROI measure. The first type of tests tries to show that the GA strategy can outperform the B strategy. The second type of tests tries to show that the GP strategy can outperform the GA strategy. The third type of tests tries to show that the GP strategy can outperform the B strategy. Therefore, these three types of paired-sample t tests can provide support to our two propositions in Sect. 3.6.

To test the piecewise GDCPPI strategies, there are 3 null hypotheses defined as: $H_0 : ROI_B(\theta) \geq ROI_{GA}(\theta)$, $H_0 : ROI_{GA}(\theta) \geq ROI_{GP}(\xi)$, and $H_0 : ROI_B(\theta) \geq ROI_{GP}(\xi)$.

4.9 Test Results for Piecewise GDCPPI Strategy

The results of 3 paired-sample t tests for the in-sample and out-sample data for the piecewise GDCPPI strategy are shown in Table 1 and Table 2, respectively. We can see that the pairs of the B-GA, GA-GP and B-GP tests all achieve statistical significance for the in-sample and out-sample data. That is, the GP strategy can outperform both the GA and B strategies, and the GA strategy can outperform the B strategy. These experimental results can prove that the piecewise nonlinear GDCPPI strategy can outperform the piecewise linear GDCPPI strategy for ROI measures that are statistically significant.

Table 1. Paired-sample t tests for in-sample data for the piecewise GDCPPI strategy.

pair	t-value	df	Sig.
$ROI_B(\theta) - ROI_{GA}(\theta)$	-9.721	224	.0000***
$ROI_{GA}(\theta) - ROI_{GP}(\xi)$	-4.375	224	.0000***
$ROI_B(\theta) - ROI_{GP}(\xi)$	-8.609	224	.0000***

*** : $p < 0.01$

Table 2. Paired-sample t tests for out-sample data for the piecewise GDCPPI strategy.

pair	t-value	df	Sig.
$ROI_B(\theta) - ROI_{GA}(\theta)$	-2.303	224	.0110**
$ROI_{GA}(\theta) - ROI_{GP}(\xi)$	-3.622	224	.0000***
$ROI_B(\theta) - ROI_{GP}(\xi)$	-4.046	224	.0000***

*** : $p < 0.01$, ** : $p < 0.05$

In addition, two special cases will be analyzed to show the features of the B strategy, GA strategy, and GP strategy. Each strategy proposes a dollar amount (strategy value) invested into the risky asset. The relationship between strategy value and wealth will be presented using figures.

The first selected case is the experiment for the AIG stock and its environmental settings are defined as follows: performance measured by the ROI index; initial wealth=100, floor=70; Brownian middle wealth=70.0861 (by parameter values $m_1 = 187.9$ and $m_2 = 0.3$ for the CPPI and GD sub-strategies, respectively); genetic middle wealth=98.4332 (by parameter values $m_1 = 13.7$ and $m_2 = 2.3$ for the CPPI and GD sub-strategies, respectively); goal=130; the starting learning date is 1999/12/13 and includes 100 training days with 30 testing days.

The forest GP strategy expressions will be presented as the operator prefix format, which are generated by the forest GP originally. The expression of the B strategy is θ_t which contains ζ_t and η_t, where $\zeta_t = 187.9 * (W_t - F)$ and $\eta_t = 0.3 * (G - W_t)$.

The expression of the GA strategy is θ_t which contains ζ_t and η_t, where $\zeta_t = 13.7 * (W_t - F)$ and $\eta_t = 2.3 * (G - W_t)$.

The expression of the GP strategy is defined as:

$$\xi_t = \quad min(\zeta', \eta_t'), \text{ where} \tag{14}$$
$$\zeta_t' = (-(+126\ 127)(/W_t(-W_t\ 35)))),$$
$$\eta_t' = \quad (+(+(-G\ W_t)127)97).$$

The GP strategy shows the nonlinear feature, which differs from the B and GA strategies. The relationships between strategy value and wealth for these three strategies are shown in Fig. 5. Hereafter, the vertical bold lines in the figures for these three strategies are referred to as the middle wealth. The vertical bold line for the stock price separates the training from the testing zones.

The experimental ROI values of the out samples for the B, GA, and GP strategies are 0.0034, 0.0159, and 0.0224, respectively. This shows that the GA strategy can outperform the B strategy and the GP strategy can outperform both the GA and B strategies in our piecewise models. We can find the nonlinear features of the GP strategy in (14). We can also see the implicit M effect in Fig. 5(d).

The second selected case is the experiment for the IBM stock and its environmental settings are defined as follows: performance measured by the ROI index; initial wealth=100, floor=70; Brownian middle wealth=70.2567 (by parameter values $m_1 = 37.2$ and $m_2 = 0.2$ for the CPPI and GD sub-strategies, respectively); genetic middle wealth=83.3333 (by parameter values $m_1 = 9.8$ and $m_2 = 4.9$ for the CPPI and GD sub-strategies, respectively); goal=110; the starting learning date is 2001/6/6 and includes 100 training days with 30 testing days.

The forest GP strategy expressions will be presented as the operator prefix format, which are generated by the forest GP originally. The expression of the B strategy is θ_t which contains ζ_t and η_t, where $\zeta_t = 37.2 * (W_t - F)$ and $\eta_t = 0.2 * (G - W_t)$.

The expression of the GA strategy is θ_t which contains ζ_t and η_t, where $\zeta_t = 9.8 * (W_t - F)$ and $\eta_t = 4.9 * (G - W_t)$.

The expression of the GP strategy is defined as:

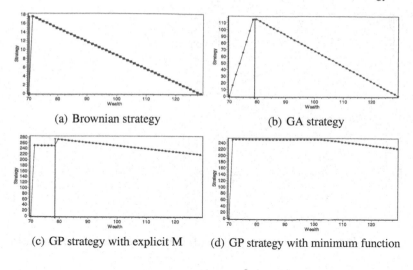

(a) Brownian strategy   (b) GA strategy

(c) GP strategy with explicit M   (d) GP strategy with minimum function

(e) Price

Fig. 5. Relationship between strategy value and wealth under piecewise GDCPPI strategies for the AIG stock.

$$\xi_t = min(\zeta', \eta'_t), \text{ where} \tag{15}$$
$$\zeta'_t = (+126\ W_t),$$
$$\eta'_t = (+G(/98(+ -70\ W_t))).$$

The GP strategy shows the nonlinear feature, which differs from the B and GA strategies. The relationships between strategy value and wealth for these three strategies are shown in Fig. 6.

The experimental ROI values of the out samples for the B, GA, and GP strategies are 0.0053, 0.0459, and 0.1148, respectively. This shows that the GA strategy can outperform the B strategy and the GP strategy can outperform both the GA and B strategies in our piecewise models. We can find the nonlinear features of the GP strategy in (15) and Fig. 6(d). We can also see that the nonlinear GD strategy dominates the piecewise nonlinear GDCPPI strategy in Fig. 6(d).

5 Conclusions

A traditional portfolio insurance strategy such as the CPPI, which is a special case of the portfolio insurance (PI) strategy, does not consider the goal perspective and

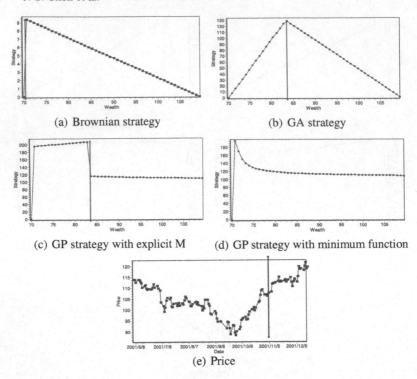

(a) Brownian strategy

(b) GA strategy

(c) GP strategy with explicit M

(d) GP strategy with minimum function

(e) Price

Fig. 6. Relationship between strategy value and wealth under piecewise GDCPPI strategies for the IBM stock.

may almost fail to achieve the goal as a result. Although Browne's study ([8]) considers a similar goal-seeking objective, it still does not consider the objectives of floor protecting and goal seeking. This paper combines the CPPI strategy and the goal-directed strategy derived from Browne's study to form a piecewise linear goal-directed CPPI (GDCPPI) strategy under the constraint $F \leq W_t \leq G$. This new strategy in fact extends the strategy solution space and can satisfy those two objectives. In addition, the piecewise linear GDCPPI strategy reduces to the GD strategy when the parameter $m_1 \to \infty$ and reduces to the CPPI strategy when the parameter $m_2 \to \infty$. Furthermore, we extend the linear feature of the piecewise linear GDCPPI strategy to consider the nonlinear situation. We first build a piecewise nonlinear GDCPPI strategy with an explicit M value, but it shows the difficulty associated with preassigning an explicit M value for an uncertain structure of a nonlinear CIPPO strategy and a nonlinear GD strategy. We then apply the minimum function to build a piecewise nonlinear GDCPPI strategy, which will maintain the features of portfolio insurance and goal-seeking.

The traditional CPPI strategy and Brownes' goal-directed strategy are both based on the Brownian motion assumption for price movements. However, there are still many who assert that such an assumption might not be true, especially in short-term situations. In addition, even if one follows the Brownian motion assumption, there are two strategy parameters, the mean and variance of the return rates, that still need to be calculated from historical data. Therefore, it is reasonable to try finding m_1 and m_2 directly from historical data using other optimization techniques rather than this theoretical method. This paper thus applies the GA technique to optimize the piecewise linear GDCPPI strategy. In addition, in order to prove that the strategies generated by the GP technique can outperform the GA, we perform some experiments to compare the performance of piecewise nonlinear GDCPPI strategies and piecewise linear GDCPPI strategies. Basically, the test results can justify our propositions.

Our current piecewise GDCPPI strategy is based on a constant floor and goal. We plan to extend our piecewise GDCPPI strategy based on the time invariant portfolio protection (TIPP) idea. The TIPP strategy replaces the floor F in CPPI with αK_t, where $K_t = \max_{\tau \le t} W_\tau$ is the maximum wealth up to time t and $\alpha \in (0, 1)$ is a constant. The TIPP version of the GD strategy might be obtained by simply replacing the goal G with βK_t, where $\beta > 1$ is a constant. In addition, the characteristics of forest genetic programming will be exploited further. The piecewise trading strategy is interesting and is worth developing further in the future.

References

1. Andrew M, Prager R (1994) Genetic programming for the acquisition of double auction market strategies. In: Kinnear KE (ed) Advances in genetic programming. The MIT Press, Cambridge, MA:355–368
2. Bäck T, Fogel DB, Michalewicz T (eds) (2000) Evolutionary computation 1: basic algorithms and operators. IOP
3. Bäck T, Fogel DB, Michalewicz T (eds) (2000) Evolutionary computation 2: advanced algorithms and operators. IOP
4. Bauer RJ (1994) Genetic algorithms and investment strategies. John Wiley & Sons, New York
5. Bhattachary S, Pictet O, Zumbach G (1998) Representational semantics for genetic programming based learning in high-frequency financial data. In: Koza J, Banzhaf W, Chellapilla K, Beb K, Dorigo M, Fogel D, Garzon M, Iba H, Riolo R (eds) Genetic programming 1998: proceedings of the third annual conference. Morgan Kaufmann, San Francisco, CA:11–16
6. Black F, Perold AF (1992) Theory of constant proportion portfolio insurance. Journal of Economic Dynamics and Control 16:403–426
7. Brown K, Harlow W, Starks L (1996) Of tournaments and temptations: an analysis of managerial incentives in the mutual fund industry. Journal of Finance 51:85–110
8. Browne S (1997) Survival and growth with a liability: optimal portfolio strategies in continuous time. Mathematics of Operations Research 22(2):468–493
9. Busse JA (2001) Another look at mutual fund tournaments. Journal of Financial and Quantitative Analysis 36(1):53–73
10. Chen JS (2005) Trading strategy generation using genetic algorithms. Asian Journal of Information Technology 4(4):310–322

11. Chen JS, Lin PC (2003) Multi-valued stock valuation based on the fuzzy genetic programming approach. In: Proceedings of the 7th joint conference on information sciences (The third international workshop on computational intelligence in economics and finance):1124–1127

12. Chen JS, Wu PC, Liao PY (2000) Neural network forecasting of TAIMEX index futures. In: Proceedings of the second Asia-Pacific conference on genetic algorithms and applications. Global-Link Publishing Company, Hong Kong:403–408

13. Chen SH (1996) Genetic programming, predictability, and stock market efficiency. In: Vlacic L, Nguyen T, Cecez-Kecmanovic D (eds) Modelling and control of national and regional economies. Pergamon Press, Oxford, Great Britain:283–288

14. Chen SH (1998) Hedging derivative securities with genetic programming. In: Application of machine learning and data mining in finance. Workshop at ECMI-98 Dorint-Parkhotel, Chemnitz, Germany

15. Chen SH, Yeh CH (1995) Predicting stock returns with genetic programming: do the short-term nonlinear regularities exist? In: Fisher D (ed) Proceedings of the fifth international workshop on artificial intelligence and statistics:95–101

16. Chen SH, Yeh CH (1997) Toward a computable approach to the efficient market hypothesis: an application of genetic programming. Journal of Economic Dynamics and Control 21:1043–1063

17. Chen SH, Yeh CH (1997) Using genetic programming to model volatility in financial time series. In: Koza J, Deb J, Dorigo M, Fogel D, Garzon M, Iba H, Riolo R (eds) Genetic programming 1997: proceedings of the second annual conference. Morgan Kaufmann, Stanford University, CA:58–63

18. Chen SH, Yeh CH, Lee WC (1998) Option pricing with genetic programming. In: Koza J, Banzhaf W, Chellapilla K, Beb K, Dorigo M, Fogel D, Garzon M, Iba H, Riolo R (eds) Genetic programming 1998: proceedings of the third annual conference. Morgan Kaufmann, San Francisco, CA:32–37

19. Chevalier J, Ellison G (1997) Risk taking by mutual funds as a response to incentives. Journal of Political Economy 105:1167–1200

20. Chidambaran N, Trigueros J, Lee C (2002) Option pricing via genetic programming. In: Chen SH (ed) Evolutionary computation in economics and finance. Physica-Verlag, Heidelberg, New York:383–397

21. Colin AM (1994) Genetic algorithms for financial modeling. In: Deboeck GJ (ed) Trading on the edge: neural, genetic and fuzzy systems for chaotic financial markets. Wiley:148–173

22. Deboeck GJ (ed) (1994) Trading on the edge: neural, genetic and fuzzy systems for chaotic financial markets. John Wiley & Sons, New York

23. Deboeck GJ (1994) Using GAs to optimize a trading system. In: Deboeck GJ (ed) Trading on the edge: neural, genetic and Fuzzy Systems for chaotic financial markets. Wiley:174–188

24. Eglit JT (1994) Trend prediction in financial time series. In: Koza J (ed) Genetic algorithms at stanford. Stanford Bookstore, Stanford, CA:31–40

25. Goldberg DE (1989) Genetic algorithms in search, optimization and machine learning. Addison-Wesley

26. Grossman SJ, Zhou Z (1993) Optimal investment strategies for controlling drawdowns. Mathematical Finance 3(3):241–276

27. Hall JW (1994) Adaptive selection of U.S. stocks with neural nets. In: Deboeck GJ (ed) Trading on the edge: neural, genetic and fuzzy systems for chaotic financial markets. Wiley:45–65

28. Jackwerth JC (2000) Recovering risk aversion from option prices and realized returns. The Review of Financial Studies 13(2):433–451
29. Jang GS, Lai F (1994) Intelligent trading of an emerging market. In: Deboeck GJ (ed) Trading on the edge: neural, genetic and fuzzy systems for chaotic financial markets. John Wiley & Sons:80–101
30. Kaboudan M (1998) Forecasting stock returns using genetic programming in C++. In: Cook D (ed) FLAIRS proceedings of the eleventh international Florida artificial intelligence research symposium conference. AAAI Press, Menlo Park, CA:73–77
31. Kaboudan M (2002) GP forecasts of stock prices for profitable trading. In: Chen SH (ed) Evolutionary computation in economics and finance. Physica-Verlag, Heidelberg, New York:359–381
32. Kamijo K, Tanigawa T (1990) Stock price pattern recognition: a recurrent neural network approach. In: Proceedings of the 1990 international joint conference on neural networks:215–221
33. Keber C (2002) Evolutionary computation in option pricing: determining implied volatilities based on American put options. In: Chen SH (ed) Evolutionary computation in economics and Finance. Physica-Verlag, Heidelberg, New York:399–415
34. Kimoto T, Asakawa K, Yoda M, Takeoka M (1990) Stock market prediction system with modular neural networks. In: Proceedings of the 1990 international joint conference on neural networks:1–6
35. Koza JR (1992) Genetic Programming: on the programming of computers by means of natural selection. MIT Press, Massachusetts
36. Koza JR (1994) Introduction to genetic programming. In: Kinnear KE (ed) Advances in genetic programming. The MIT Press, Cambridge, MA:21–42
37. Liao PY, Chen JS (2001) Dynamic trading strategy learning model using learning classifier systems. In: Proceedings of the 2001 IEEE congress on evolutionary computation:783–789
38. Lo AW, MacKinlay AC (1999) A non-random walk down Wall Street. Princeton University Press, Princeton, NJ
39. Mitchell M (1996) An introduction to genetic algorithms. MIT Press
40. Murphy JJ (1999) Technical analysis of the futures markets. New York Institute of Finance
41. Oussaidene M, Chopard B, Pictet O, Tomassini M (1996) Parallel genetic programming: an application to trading models evolution. In: Koza J, Goldberg D, Fogel D, Riolo R (ed) Genetic programming 1996: proceedings of the first annual conference. The MIT Press, Cambridge, MA:357–362
42. Perold AF, Sharpe WF (1988) Dynamic strategies for asset allocation. Financial Analyst Journal Jan/Feb:16–27
43. Pratt KB, Fink E (2002) Search for patterns in compressed times series. International Journal of Image and Graphics 2(1):89–102
44. Sarma J, DeJong K (2000) Generation gap methods. In: Bäck T, Fogel DB, Michalewicz T (eds) Evolutionary computation 1: basic algorithms and operators. Institute of Physics Publishing, Bristol:205–227
45. Sharpe WF (1963) A simplified model for portfolio analysis. Management Science 9:277–293
46. Shieh JCP (2003) Fundamentals of investment. BestWise, Taipei
47. Srinivas M, Patnaik LM (1994) Genetic algorithms: a survey. Computer 27(6):17–26
48. Tanigawa T, Kamijo K (1992) Stock price pattern matching system: dynamic programming neural networks approach. In: Proceedings of the 1992 international joint conference on Neural Networks:465–471

49. Tayler J (2003) Risk-taking behavior in mutual fund tournaments. Journal of Economic Behavior & Organization 50:373–383
50. Warren MA (1994) Stock price prediction using genetic programming. In: Koza J (ed) Genetic algorithms at stanford. Stanford Bookstore, Stanford, CA:180–184
51. Yoda M (1994) Predicting the Tokyo stock market. In: Deboeck GJ (ed) Trading on the edge. John Wiley & Sons:66–79

Hybrid-Agent Organization Modeling: A Logical-Heuristic Approach

Ana Marostica[1], Cesar A. Briano[2], and Ernesto Chinkes[3]

[1] Doctorate Department, School of Economics, University of Buenos Aires
Cordoba 2122, Buenos Aires, 1120, Argentina
mmarost@econ.uba.ar

[2] Informatics, School of Economics, University of Buenos Aires
Cordoba 2122, Buenos Aires, 1120, Argentina
cbriano@econ.uba.ar

[3] Informatics, School of Economics, University of Buenos Aires
Cordoba 2122, Buenos Aires, 1120, Argentina
pchinkes@econ.uba.ar

This paper describes a hybrid-agent organization model from a logical-heuristic point of view. The organization model is an ordered set composed of an environment (or domain), the hybrid agents as elements of the environmental structure, as well as some connecting functions. A hybrid-agent in an organization structure is composed of a heuristic-decision support system (HDSS) and the decision-maker (the user) is one of the units. By using this hybrid-agent organization modeling, we can provide instruments that will help with the making of decisions in a financial organization such as a commercial bank.

Key words: Hybrid Agents, Heuristic-Decision Support System, Semiotics, Semiotic Tree

1 Introduction

This paper describes a type of hybrid-agent, namely, a hybrid-agent organization model. We understand a model as a framework for the structure of an organization. Our organization modeling tries to capture, in a flexible way, the main part of an organization used by a team of hybrid-agents to satisfy their goals.

From a logical-heuristic point of view, the organization model M is an ordered set composed of an *environment* or domain, *hybrid agents* as elements of the environmental structure, and *some connecting functions*.

$M = (environment, hybrid agent, function)$.

Organizational decisions often have important consequences. In order to succeed, organizations (such as commercial banks) try to maintain a high level of performance while minimizing the occurrence of mistakes, due to either excessive optimism or pessimism in interpreting the information coming from the environment.

By using a hybrid-agent organization model, where the hybrid-agent is composed of a heuristic-decision support system (HDSS) and the decision-maker is a unit, we can provide instruments to help with the making of decisions in a financial organization such as a commercial bank.

The remainder of this paper is organized as follows. Section 2 describes the different types of environments. Section 3 briefly explains what constitutes a hybrid decision support system (HDSS). Section 4 deals with the structure of the decision-makers mind. Section 5 presents hybrid agents. Section 6 explains the connecting functions. Section 7 presents an example of hybrid agents in a financial organization. Finally, Sect. 8 contains our concluding remarks.

2 Organizational Environment

The environment is the domain where the agents act. We can distinguish two main types of environment, namely, a physical and a semiotic environment. The usual physical things make up the physical domain. The semiotic environment is composed of all the meanings the agent has of physical and mental things. The physical environment can be understood as the things (i.e., physical and human) with which the agent interacts, and comprises everything beyond the agent. For example, the decision-maker in a financial organization, such as a commercial bank, interacts mainly with the financial world.

Even though all of the things beyond the agent make up the environment, it is also true that an environment has some meaning in relation to the task of the user. This is why we can introduce the term *scope of the environment*. It is related to the different domains that the environment could have. We can have a *wide scope* that for us is almost equivalent to the physical environment, and a *narrow scope* that is equivalent to the semiotic environment related to the topic under consideration.

To explain what we mean by a *semiotic environment*, let us use some of the ideas of one of the creators of scientific semiotics, Charles S. Peirce ([13]). Peirce conceived of the whole universe as a framework of signs. These signs have, among other things, meanings. These meanings can be arranged in a semiotic tree ([7]). This new type of arrangement (i.e., these semiotic trees) is based upon Peirce's semiotic trichotomies ([13]), Martys Peircean lattices ([11]), a transformation of a lattice into a tree structure, and a simplification algorithm (i.e., Shapiro & Sterlings "divide and query") [7].

In Peirce's semiotics, a combination of all the ideas previously presented give rise to Peirce's semiotic trichotomies. However, these semiotic trichotomies are, from a mathematical point of view, combinations with repetitions of three elements taken n at a time, where n could be $(4+0)-1$, $(4+3)-1$, $(4+3+4)-1$, etc. In connection with these combinations of elements (i.e., 1, 2, and 3) we find the principle at the base of these combinations. The principle in question is that whatever is a 1 determines only a 1; whatever is a 2, determines a 2 or a 1; and whatever is a 3 determines a 3 or a 2 or a 1.

By changing the order of Peirce's numbering of these trichotomies, we can generalize these combinations and obtain further semiotic trichotomies that will reveal new aspects of the meanings of a sign. By using the theory of lattices and Peircean semiotics, R. Marty, has shown that the semiotic trichotomies for $n=3$, 6, and 10 can be arranged in a natural way as the formal elements of lattice structures ([11]). As in the case of Peirce's trichotomies, Martys lattices have been generalized in order to introduce a new arrangement ([7]).

Since we need to explain some meanings related to inductive arguments, we need to transform the semiotic lattices into a tree structure because we need to use a decision tree in that type of algorithm (e.g., Quinlan's ID3). In order to transform Marty's lattices into a tree structure, we have to duplicate each branch of a tree where there is a node with two ancestors. This is why we twice repeat each branch with two ancestors in the transformation ([7]).

In the economic field, inductive inferences are very important. They are indicative types of processes. In inductive generalizations used in the economics and financial fields, the random sample is an index of what we will find in the population. This is because we must properly classify the elements of that sample. As a consequence, it is very important to detect and analyze the meanings of all the indices involved when making further decisions. We can do that in the tree presented above. Of course, according to the topic at hand, we can use trees that are more complex (i.e., where the corresponding lattices have 10, 28, 64, etc., elements).

In order to classify and simplify the trees, we have to eliminate all the nodes that do not correspond to indexical meanings. To begin this operation, we may use a modification of the heuristic technique *divide and query* that Shapiro and Sterling used in PROLOG ([14]).

By using credit risk assessment in a bank as an example of the classification of meanings in a semiotic environment, the following reduced tree (which indicates the meanings of the signs where there are 28 elements) shows the advantage of this type of taxonomy. In this example, we have the meaning of concepts such as *Income, Salary, Debt* (i.e., the size of the loan requested), and *Credit Risk*, etc. In order to classify these types of indexical meanings, we cannot use the tree structure corresponding to Peirce's three trichotomies (i.e., where $n=3$) because this classification does not involve a process ([7]). However, the concepts involved in business represent processes. Therefore, we need a tree in which the concepts involved represent processes, too. The six-lattice (where $n=6$, and there are 28 elements) and its corresponding tree structure will provide us with an adequate semiotic classification in this semiotic domain. In this structure, the concepts with their meanings are evolved from the past to the present, and also have their future meanings.

Turning back to our concrete example of a semiotic environment related to credit risk analysis, we will use only the branch we need in the tree. For this, see Fig. 1. There, the nodes of the six-tree structure (where $n=6$), that serves to illustrate our claim, are the following: 25, 24, 23, 16, and 11.

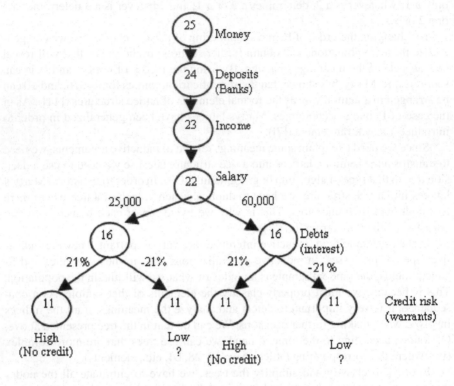

Fig. 1. A semiotic tree

25: This node is a concept of a general state of facts. For example, *money* is a type of social relationship, and is used as a medium of exchange. Nowadays, it is a paper note authorized to be used as a medium of exchange. It is symbolic or conventional. It is an abstract unit of exchange.

24: This is a general state of facts that evolves from conventions or symbols. In effect, symbols, like those of a language, are conventions among people, for example, money *deposited in a bank*, i.e., the money a person has in a bank. It indicates a persons capacity to pay a loan.

23: This is an index of a general state of facts. For example, *Income* is the money a person receives periodically for services or for realized works (like a salary), or for an investment or the renting of properties.

22: This is an index of a particular state of facts. For example, a *Salary* is the monthly (or another certain period of time) payment for realized work. This payment could be from the government, private corporations or other persons.

16: This is an index indicating a singular state of facts. However, in the future there is a fact that will determine the whole state of facts. For example, Debt (the money a person is asking for in the way of a loan) indicates a contract or agreement to do something that is put in writing and is enforceable by law. A person that borrows money has to pay *interest* on it. The repayment instalment is in the future and is an important part of the loan that the person has asked for.

11: This is an index indicating a state of facts that in the present and in the future can be determined by a particular fact. For example, *Credit Risk* is an index of uncertainty that could adversely affect the financial agreement. In order to reduce the uncertainty, banks and financial institutions have to diversify risks. In order to avoid losses, banks have to ask for collateral. This protection reduces the uncertainty and possible losses due to credit risk.

3 Heuristic Decision Support Systems

An agent, according to some authors, is a computational entity such as a software program or a structure that can be viewed as perceiving and acting upon its environment. In addition, it is an autonomous intelligent entity. This is because its behaviour is at least partially dependent on its own experience ([16]). Agents can accomplish individual and broader goals. Within a financial organization, our hybrid agents (i.e., the heuristic system HDSS and the user of the system as a unit) play roles required by their specific goals.

Let us examine the components of these hybrid agents separately. A common decision support system (i.e., a DSS) is generally described as having five parts:

1. The User Interface,
2. The Model-based Management System,
3. The Knowledge Engine,
4. The Data Management System, and
5. The User.

These five parts are the ones recognized by some authors (e.g., [3]). All these parts correspond, more or less, to the parts we find in an information system ([5]) with the exception of the Model-Based Management System. This software includes different types of models, for example, financial, statistical, management, etc., which give the system analytical capability and appropriate administration of the software. For more details of a common DSS go to ([3]) and ([5]).

The heuristic tools, in our system, first set precise definitions of the ambiguous variables and a kind of boundary for the vague or fuzzy variables ([9]). The architecture specified in Fig. 2 shows the two parts of a heuristic-decision support system (HDSS). The left part is the DSS itself mentioned above, and the right part of the figure is a heuristic-data mining mechanism that is a complement of statistical data mining. This heuristic part of the architecture is embedded into the original DSS. See Fig. 2.

We consider a decision as the conclusion of an inference, and its premises are the *alternatives*, namely, *possible consequences* related to the expected utility hypothesis, *weak preferences* related to the principle of rationality or optimality, and the *state of the environment* related to subjective probabilities. For example in a financial context, ambiguity could arise when decisions related to a prescription that the

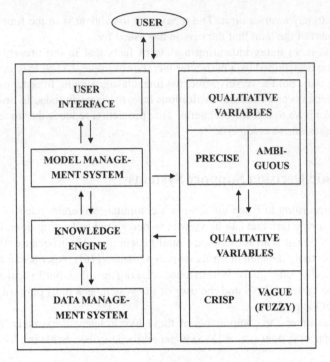

Fig. 2. A heuristic-decision support system

Central Bank should vary reserve requirements in order to allow a "smooth functioning of the banks" could call for either an increase or a decrease in the requirements according to the circumstances.

In the information we find in a HDSS, after giving precise definitions, it is possible to check the status of each variable (i.e., our n-adic predicates) to see if it is ambiguous or not by using the following algorithm:

Algorithm: AMBIGUITY

1. Evaluate the type of variable in the set of alternatives
2. IF the variable is quantitative or precise, GOTO 4
3. For $I = 1, 2, ..., N$ Do
   a) Select M(I)
   b) Evaluate M(I)
   c) If M(I) $\neq$ PM(I)
      END IF
   Next
4. IF there are more variables, GOTO 1
5. END

The symbol PM(I) represents the "precise meaning" of a node I (i.e., the variable I). Calling AMBIGUITY recursively, it performs the algorithm. SELECT is a procedure that chooses an element from a set of nodes, such that this element obeys a set of conditions, for example, in choosing precise qualitative variables instead of ambiguous ones. For more details, see [10].

Since decision-making involves the selection of the best available alternative, according to the rationality principle, sometimes the set of alternatives, which contains a solution to a decision-making problem, cannot always be defined explicitly because it contains *vague* or *fuzzy* variables. Vagueness is a quantitative problem, and has to do with representations of the world through natural languages. Decision-making in finances, for instance, uses natural languages where we have the problem of vagueness. In order to use fuzzy set theory as a tool for vagueness, it is necessary to explain fuzzy membership functions ([14]). In decision inferences, we can say that the fuzzy membership function of a decision or goal in a decision problem is:

$$F(x) = A \rightarrow [0, 1] \tag{1}$$

A, in this formula, represents a set of possible alternatives that contain a solution to a decision-making problem we are considering. A fuzzy decision D is a fuzzy set on A characterized by the above membership function, which represents the degree to which the alternatives satisfy the specified decision goal. In general, a fuzzy decision indicates that the target should be obtained, but also quantifies the degree to which the target is fulfilled ([14]). In the fuzzy sets, "fuzzy categories" are sometimes constructed according to the following algorithm:

Algorithm: VAGUENESS

1. Define the type of variable in the set of alternatives
2. IF the variable is qualitative or crisp, GOTO 4
3. IF the variable, or set, is fuzzy
   a) Create fuzzy subsets or fuzzy categories (given by experts)
   b) Determine the relative membership of elements of the original fuzzy set
   c) Return the relative membership of those elements
      END
4. IF there are more variables, GOTO 1
5. END

The following algorithm performs the relationship between the DSS and the Heuristic-data mining:

Algorithm: HEURISTIC-DSS

1. Define the type of variable by using the AMBIGUITY and VAGUENESS algorithms
2. IF the variable is an n-adic predicate where $n = 4, 5, \ldots$,
   a) Apply the Reduction Principle

3. IF there are more variables, GOTO 1
4. END

Peirce's *Reduction Principle* ([13]) roughly says that any n-adic predicate (i.e., where $n > 3$) can be reduced to some n-adic predicates (i.e., where n $\leq$ 3). Monadic, dyadic and triadic predicates are irreducible.

4 The Structure of the Decision-Makers Mind

We will now analyze the user as a complex architecture. From a logical-heuristic point of view, the architecture of the mind when thinking uses different types of processes to solve problems or to make decisions.

The main types of processes of the mind are the following: *abductive explanation*, which is the most plausible explanation found (according to the circumstances) for an anomalous fact. After the abductive process, we find *deductive predictions* of the consequences related to that previous explanation. Following the deductive process, we have the *quantitative inductive* process, which consists of checking those consequences against real data.

Since the world evolves, the mind must create worldviews (simplified *scientific models*) in order to extract uncertain information from evolving data. This is precisely the job fulfilled by qualitative induction that creates the *models* and *controls* the information received by the mind. With its model generator role, qualitative induction solves the first part of the problem because it allows the scientist to create a framework for the best plausible explanation of an anomalous fact, that is, how to do things properly. Under any circumstances, the possible "correct things" do not apply in the majority of cases, and the "optimum things" are but the "appropriate ones" under given circumstances.

Qualitative induction through its *principles* provides the limits of the mind processes to be controlled. In addition, the activity of qualitative induction can be adapted continuously in order to respond to the process changes through time. In qualitative induction, these changes are heuristic approximations.

The *two principles* involved in qualitative induction can be considered as heuristic principles. For example, the first one performs a heuristic search among the explanatory hypotheses arrived at by abduction.

When the most promising hypothesis has been selected, qualitative induction activates deduction in order to predict observable consequences related to that explanatory hypothesis. After that, it activates quantitative induction for checking the most promising predictions. If the evaluation of the checking of all elements of the sample set is considered to be successful, then qualitative induction allows quantitative induction to generalize for the population. The last part of this work is performed by a *second heuristic principle* that qualitative induction has. This second principle supervises the partial checking of the likely elements of the sample related to the most promising explanatory hypothesis.

To sum up the heuristic work (or "things to do") performed by this controller, we could sketch it in the following algorithm:

Procedure: (Qualitative inductive controller)

1. Begin
2. Analyze anomalous fact
3. Create a model for that fact
4. Activate abduction
5. Select the first plausible explanatory hypothesis
6. Activate deduction
     Allow observable predictions
7. Activate quantitative induction
     Allow generalization and checking with the
     environment
8. If checking is OK
     Successful end
9. Select the next plausible explanation
10. If that is the last hypothesis
     Dead end
   Else
     Goto step 6.

After that, the mind creates the model or appropriate framework where the most plausible explanatory hypothesis must be presented. With abduction, we start with new ideas. It is necessary to create an explanation for the anomalous fact. The following algorithm summarizes the main activity of abduction:

Procedure: (Abductive explanatory hypothesis)

1. Begin
2. Write the anomalous fact in statement form
3. Accept the model given by qualitative induction
4. Search for information in the predicate of the anomalous fact for finding an explanation
     Use the *Reduction Theorem* when needed
5. If it is an adequate explanation for the anomalous fact
     Successful end
6. Else go to step 2.

Once we have settled the best possible explanation for the anomalous fact, the mind process continues with the deductive part, namely, the *prediction* of the most important consequences related to that explanatory hypothesis. In deduction, with formal procedures we can arrive at the conclusion of an inference, which is a logical consequence of the premises.

Even though there is not a full decision procedure for the first-order calculus, we can use a *resolution rule* as a single rule to minimize the search problem in deduction. We can take advantage of the already existing logical method used in AI, the *resolution* method. The following algorithm shows the deductive prediction procedure:

Procedure: (Resolution for deductive prediction)

1. Begin
2. Symbolize the inference in first-order logic
3. Apply the *Reductio ad Absurdum* rule [Take the premises and the negation of the conclusion] to the deductive inference.
4. Eliminate quantifiers of symbolized statements [existential quantifiers are eliminated by *Skolemization*]
5. Transform the expressions into *Horn clauses*
6. Apply the resolution rule to any premises with inconsistent clauses
7. If you arrive at the *null* clause
      Successful end
8. Else go to step 2.

Quantitative induction is the last part of the mind processes. Even though the statistical generalization probability of inferences is applied (e.g., by using an interval estimation), we cannot conclude with certainty that the generalization to the population will be true when the sample set has been true. This is because in induction, where the form is not enough to check the correctness of an inference, there is a need for heuristic criteria to check what type of sampling we should choose for a specific kind of population. Before we check whether a sample is random, large and varied enough, it is important to note that the heuristic checking of the meaning of the quantitative and qualitative variables involved in the population and sample is the most accurate possible. ID3 of Quinlan induces concepts from examples in a top-down way. Quinlans decision tree induction algorithm, which is an intelligent algorithm, begins with the sample of classified elements of the target properties. ID3 relies heavily on its criteria for selecting the test at the root of each subtree. We choose this inductive algorithm to generalize from sample to population. Any other programs that generalize would be useful as well.

Procedure: (ID3 algorithm)
Function induce_tree (sample_set, Properties)
Begin
If all entries in element_set (the properties of the sample set) are in the same class
      Then return a node labeled with that class
      Else if Properties is empty
      Then return node labeled with disjunction of all classes in element_set
      Else begin
            Select a property, P, to test on and make it the root of the current tree;
            Delete P from Properties;
            For each value, V (Yes or No), of P,
                  Begin
Create a branch of the tree labeled with V
Let partitionV be elements of sample_set with V for property P;
Call induce_tree (partitionV , Properties), attach result to branch V
                  End;

   End;
   End.

ID3 applies the induce_tree function recursively to each partition and can eventually reproduce a given tree. If we accept that decision-makers would always behave perfectly rationally based on an immediate and accurate representation of the environment, we may have the *homo economicus*. However, even in financial domains, decision-makers sometimes make decisions based on emotions. In this paper, we are only concerned with a *logical* type of inference related to decisions.

Procedure: (Connection between HDSS and Decision-Maker Architecture)
Begin

1. Select the problem
2. Activate HDSS and decision-maker structures
3. The decision-maker suggests a possible decision
4. Obtain the appropriate information from the HDSS
5. If decision-makers possible decision is NOT guaranteed by HDSS
        Goto 3
    Else
        The decision is confirmed
6. End

The design of a system like this allows producing real interactions between HDSS and its user, the decision-maker.

5 Hybrid Agents

Now let us consider *hybrid agents* as single agents. They are like actors with different abilities. Those capabilities allow agents in an organization to accomplish individual and system-wide goals. Within an organization, agents play roles required by their goals ([12]). We consider *goals* as a consistent set of desires (i.e., the state of affairs toward which the agent has a positive disposition).

For us, an agents *state* is whatever information is available to the agent. We assume that the environment provokes the state in the agent. The agent takes sensory input from the environment and has an internal state, and produces, as output, actions that affect the environment. The state of a hybrid agent is an instance of the set of the agent states at a point in time. The interaction between the agent and the environment is usually an ongoing, non-terminated one. Different agents may have different goals, actions and domain knowledge according to the type of decisions that these agents must take in an organization ([15]). A key pattern of interaction in multiagent systems is goal- and task-oriented coordination. An organization (such as a commercial bank) possesses at least one goal, one role to accomplish the goal and one agent to play the role where the agent that plays the role must possess the capabilities required by the role. We consider a *role* as an entity that performs some functions within the system. It is similar to the roles played by actors in a typical company structure and has specific capabilities and relationships defined in order to meet the general company goal ([12]).

Robert Lucas provided the notion of an *economic agent*. This decision agent can be regarded as a collection of decision rules and a set of preferences used to evaluate the outcomes arising from a particular situation-action combination ([1]). The premises of a decision inference are provided by the heuristic decision support system (HDSS) and the conclusion of that process, the actual decision, by the decision maker (or user of the HDSS). In Chen's paper ([1], p.137), a comparison is made between Lucasian agents and genetic algorithms (e.g., to decision rules there correspond strings of binary ones and zeros, and to the review of decision rules there corresponds a fitness evaluation, etc.). We think that improving decision support systems with heuristic tools and notions such as hybrid agents is useful. This is because the important research in genetic programs and multiagent systems in the field of organizations in general and financial ones, in particular, is nowadays applied with restrictions. The traditional decision support systems, in turn, are applied everywhere without restrictions but they lack intelligent tools. In the near future, research related to this topic where "hybrid agents" take decisions and consider the decision-maker to be part of the agent that exhibits intelligence must be considered. As for the user, we find the mechanisms of natural selection and natural genetics. In this way, the hybrid agent that starts with an initial set of random solutions as a whole can converge to the best solution which hopefully represents the optimal or near-optimal solution for a decision problem ([2]).

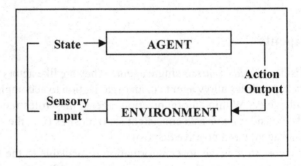

Fig. 3. The agent-environment interaction

6 Connecting Functions

In logic as well as in heuristics, a *function* is a relation that satisfies certain conditions. In the most general sense, a single-value function $F(x)$ of one variable x is a correspondence by which, to each element x of a set X, there corresponds a single element y of a set Y. The set X is called the *domain*. It is a function of a member of X taking a member of Y as the value. Sometimes a function is called an *operation* on a member of X producing a member of Y. The set Y is the *range* of the function F. In our present case, the function F could be the following:

$$F(x) = S_n \rightarrow A_n$$

The stimulus of the environment creates a *state*, S_n, in the agent as input, and generates as output A_n the agents *action*. See Fig. 3.

Another connective function, G, is a transition function among the agents *states*. This function defines the ability of the agent in an organization. If we have one *agents internal state* as input, the function G gives as output a different *internal state*. The function is as follows:

$$G(x) = S_n \rightarrow S_{n+1}.$$

The domain of both functions is the same, i.e., the set of all possible states produced by the stimulus of the environment. However, their range is different, for it is the set of all possible actions in the first case, and the set of all of the agents possible internal states in the second case.

The joint action of these two functions shows that, given the stimulus of the environment and the agents internal state, an action is determinate if it will change the environment. At the same time, the agent will have another internal state. The function F gives the answer of the agent to the stimulus of the environment. The function G gives the agents natural learning (through the decision-maker part of the hybrid agent), which is how to change from one state to another.

7 Hybrid Agents in a Financial Organization

A financial organization contains, in general terms, human and software information sources. The fusion of data from these sources provides the foundation for the information for decision processes. In this paper, we assume that in a financial organization (e.g., a commercial bank), our hybrid-agents are economically rational. Furthermore, although the set of agents may be small, they must have a common language and common problem abstraction, and they must reach a common decision. Agents that follow this protocol create a deal (i.e., a redistribution of tasks). This deal is a joint plan among the agents that would satisfy all their goals. A conflicting deal appears when the agents cannot reach a deal, and the negotiation has to continue ([16]).

If we consider a limited setting, as to whether or not a decision-maker (i.e., a component of a hybrid-agent involved in a decision process) will adopt a particular decision, this will depend on the information given by the correspondent HDSS. For example, in a financial organization such as a commercial bank, a big problem in these types of organizations is the credit-risk problem for physical persons as clients. For example, the main decision-makers must fix the bank policy related to possible loans to clients of that bank. As for the other decision-makers, i.e., the directors of the corresponding departments, when a client applies for a loan, these directors must obtain the appropriate information from the HDSS regarding that client before reaching a decision. Then they will make the decision of whether or not to give the money requested. However, since credit risk is an index of uncertainty that could adversely affect the financial agreement, in order to reduce the uncertainty, commercial banks diversify their risk. In order to avoid losses, banks impose collateral on some loans. This protection reduces the uncertainty and possible losses that would arise as a result of decisions related to credit risk.

8 Concluding Remarks

We have presented a very simple model of a financial organization from a logical-heuristic point of view. This work is part of an effort to build a more fully useful financial organization based on a multi-agent system that contains hybrid agents as elements of that model. This will allow us to improve the decision support systems used in financial organizations (e.g., a commercial bank). Another goal of this type of research is the idea of fully evaluating the effectiveness, for this model, of our organizational reasoning techniques with the hybrid agents involved in it. If a financial organization has become inefficient, then the use of this type of system can help with a reorganization of the banks activities to improve its efficiency. In the near future, we plan to enlarge the application of this approach to other types of organization.

Acknowledgements

We would like to thank Dr. Daniel Heymann for his helpful comments and suggestions, and Dr. Fernando Tohme for his explanation related to the connecting functions.

References

1. Chen SH (2001) On the relevance of genetic programming to evolutionary economics. In: Aruka J (ed) Evolutionary controversies in economics. A new transdisciplinary approach. Springer, Tokyo
2. Han C, Damronwongsiri M (2003) A genetic algorithm based supply chain inventory and distribution cost reduction model. In: Proceedings of the 7th joint conference on information sciences:1049–1052
3. Marakas GM (1999) Decision support systems in the 21st century. Prentice-Hall International Limited, London
4. Marostica A (1992) Ars combinatoria and time: Llull, Leibniz, and Peirce. Studia Lulliana, XXXII. 87:105–135
5. Marostica A (1997a) A nonmonotonic approach to tychist logic. In: Houser N, Roberts DD, van Evra J (eds) Studies in the logic of Charles Sanders Peirce. Indiana University Press, Bloomington:535–559
6. Marostica A (1997b) Semiotic classifications for inductive learning systems. The Journal of Management and Economics 1, www.econ.uba.ar/sevicios/publicaciones/journal/

7. Marostica A (1999) Semiotic trees and classifications for inductive learning systems. In: Deely J, Spinks CW (eds) Semiotics 1998. Peter Lang Publishing, New York:114–127
8. Marostica A (2003) Decision-making processes in organizations: a logical-semiotic perspective. KIMAS 2003, IEEE, Boston:254–259
9. Marostica A, Briano C (2002) Towards the implementation of the heuristic-information system. In: Proceedings of the 6th international conference on complex systems:1131–1134
10. Marostica A, Tohme F (2000) Semiotic tools for economic model building. The Journal of Management and Economics 4:27–34
11. Marty R (1989) LAlgebre des signes. Essai de semiotique scientifique dApres Charles Sanders Peirce. John Benjamin Company, Amsterdam
12. Matson E, DeLoach S (2003) An organization-based adaptive information system for battlefield situation analysis. KIMAS 2003, IEEE, Boston:46–51
13. Robin RS(1967) Annotated Catalogue of the Papers of Charles S. Peirce. University of Massachusetts Press
14. Sterling L, Shapiro E (1994) The art of prolog: advanced programming techniques. MIT Press, Cambridge, MA
15. Sousa JMC, Kaymak U (2002) Fuzzy decision making in modeling and control. World Scientific, London
16. Stone P (2000) Layered learning in multiagent systems. The MIT Press, Cambridge, MA

Index

the language of science

springer.com

Shu-Heng Chen,
National Chengchi University, Taipei, Taiwan;
Paul P. Wang, Duke University, Durham, NC, USA (Eds.)

Computational Intelligence in Economics and Finance

Computational
Intelligence
in Economics
and Finance

XXII, 480 p. Hardcover
ISBN 978-3-540-44098-7

We have recently witnessed a phenomenal growth in the application of computational intelligence methodologies to forecasting problems in economics and finance, because of their ability to handle specific characteristics such as nonlinear relationships, behavioral changes, and knowledge-based domain segmentation.

In this volume, Chen and Wang collected not just works on traditional computational intelligence approaches like fuzzy logic, neural networks, and genetic algorithms, but also examples involving more recent technologies such as rough sets, support vector machines, wavelets, and ant algorithms.

After an introductory chapter with a structural description of each methodology, the subsequent parts describe novel applications of these to typical economics and finance problems like business forecasting, currency crisis discrimination, foreign exchange markets, and stock markets behaviors.

Contents: Part I Introduction. - Part II Fuzzy Logic and Rough Sets. - Part III Artificial Neural Networks and Support Vector Machines.- Part IV Self-Organizing Maps and Wavelets - Part V Sequence Matching and Feature-Based Time Series Models - Part VI - Evolutionary Computation, Swarm Intelligence and Simulated Annealing - Part VII State Space Modeling of Time Series

Svetlozar T. Rachev, University of California, Santa Barbara, CA, USA (Ed.)

Handbook of Computational and Numerical Methods in Finance

VI, 435 p. Hardcover
ISBN 978-0-8176-3219-9

The subject of numerical methods in finance has recently emerged as a new discipline at the intersection of probability theory, finance, and numerical analysis. The methods employed bridge the gap between financial theory and computational practice, and provide solutions for complex problems that are difficult to solve by traditional analytical methods. Although numerical methods in finance have been studied intensively in recent years, many theoretical and practical financial aspects have yet to be explored. This volume presents current research and survey articles focusing on various numerical methods in finance.

Key topics covered include: methodological issues, i.e., genetic algorithms, neural networks, Monte–Carlo methods, finite difference methods, stochastic portfolio optimization, as well as the application of other computational and numerical methods in finance and risk management. The book is designed for the academic community and will also serve professional investors.

Contents: Preface.- Skewness and Kurtosis Trades.- Valuation of a Credit Spread Put Option: The Stable Paretian Model with Copulas.- GARCH-Type Processes in Modeling Energy Prices.- Malliavin Calculus in Finance.- Bootstrap Unit Root Tests for Heavy-Tailed Time Series.- Optimal Portfolio Selection and Risk Management: A Comparison Between the Stable Paretian Approach and the Gaussian One.- Optimal Quantization Methods and Applications to Numerical Problems in Finance.- Numerical Methods for Stable Modeling in Financial Risk Management.- Modern Heuristics for Finance Problems: A Survey of Selected Methods and Applications.- On Relation Between Expected Regret and Conditional Value-at-Risk.- Estimation, Adjustment and Application of Transition Matrices in Credit Risk Models.- Numerical Analysis of Stochastic Differential Systems and its Applications in Finance.- A. List of Contributors

Anthony Brabazon; Michael O'Neill,
University College Dublin, Ireland

Biologically Inspired Algorithms for Financial Modelling

XVI, 275 p. Hardcover
ISBN 978-3-540-26252-7

Predicting the future for financial gain is a difficult, sometimes profitable activity. The focus of this book is the application of biologically inspired algorithms (BIAs) to financial modelling.

In a detailed introduction, the authors explain computer trading on financial markets and the difficulties faced in financial market modelling. Then Part I provides a thorough guide to the various bioinspired methodologies – neural networks, evolutionary computing (particularly genetic algorithms and grammatical evolution), particle swarm and ant colony optimization, and immune systems. Part II brings the reader through the development of market trading systems. Finally, Part III examines real-world case studies where BIA methodologies are employed to construct trading systems in equity and foreign exchange markets, and for the prediction of corporate bond ratings and corporate failures.

The book was written for those in the finance community who want to apply BIAs in financial modelling, and for computer scientists who want an introduction to this growing application domain.

the language of science

springer.com

Rüdiger U. Seydel, Universität zu Köln, Germany

Tools for Computational Finance

XIX, 304 p. Hardcover
ISBN 978-3-540-27923-5

This book is very easy to read and one can gain a quick snapshot of computational issues arising in financial mathematics. Researchers or students of the mathematical sciences with an interest in finance will find this book a very helpful and gentle guide to the world of financial engineering. SIAM review (46, 2004).

The third edition is thoroughly revised and significantly extended. The largest addition is a new section on analytic methods with main focus on interpolation approach and quadratic approximation. New sections and subsections are among others devoted to risk-neutrality, early-exercise curves, multidimensional Black-Scholes models, the integral representation of options and the derivation of the Black-Scholes equation.

New figures, more exercises, more background material make this guide to the world of financial engineering a real must-to-have for everyone working in FE.

Contents: Modelling Tools for Financial Options.- Generating Random Numbers with Specified Distributions.- Simulation with Stochastic Differential Equations.- Standard Methods for Standard Options.- Finite-Element Methods.- Pricing of Exotic Options.- Appendices.